Notes and Tones

Notes and Tones

Musician-to-Musician Interviews

By Arthur Taylor

A Perigee Book

Perigee Books
are published by
G. P. Putnam's Sons
200 Madison Avenue
New York, New York 10016

Library of Congress Cataloging in Publication Data

Taylor, Arthur.
  Notes and tones.

  Includes index.
  1. Jazz musicians—Interviews. 2. Afro-American
musicians—Interviews. I. Title.
ML394.T4   785.42'092'2 [B]   81-7360
ISBN 0-399-50584-9 (pbk.)   AACR2

First Perigee printing, 1982
Printed in the United States of America

☰ Contents ☰

Notes and Tones

☰ Foreword

The purpose of this book is to pay homage to several of the musicians and to the music that has contributed vital knowledge, joy and pleasure to my life. When I first started as a professional drummer more than thirty years ago, my decision was based on the pure joy and pleasure of playing music. It was a passion then and still is now. When, later, I had the opportunity to share musical experiences with people like Bud Powell, Charlie Parker and Thelonious Monk, it was a dream come true. I learned, as I traveled to many cities around the world, just how effectively music serves as a universal language. When you like what you do, to have other people enjoy it plus not having to do a job nine-to-five, is like icing on a cake. Looking back at my association with musicians like Jackie McLean, Kenny Dorham, Paul Chambers, Sonny Rollins, Oscar Pettiford, Red Garland and John Coltrane, I have come to the conclusion that my life has been one of luxury. I will always be grateful for the opportunities they provided.

In 1966 I began tracking down and interviewing the musicians whom I had worked with or known for many years. They gave me encouragement when it seemed I would never get this work published and urged me to publish the book privately, which I did in Europe in 1977. My predominant motivation in publishing Notes and Tones *was that it was inspired by the real voices of musicians as they saw themselves and not as critics or journalists saw them. I wanted an insider's view. These conversations, which were taped between 1968 and 1972, may not always reflect how the artists feel today, but I believe their candid statements represent important insights into a very particular period in history. In order to get a cross section of thoughts and ideas, the topics of music, travel, critics, religion, drugs, racism and the word* jazz *are repeated throughout the book.*

In effect, my questions established a rhythm against which each of the musicians could spin out his or her own tune and counterpoint. I also made it a point to discuss Charlie Parker and Bud Powell extensively with everyone I interviewed, because I was trying to get as much accurate information about them as possible. The true details of their lives seem to have eluded even the best efforts of the journalists who've written about them in the past. What all these musicians told me may shock some people and may move others, but I think their candid words, spoken in a musician-to-musician setting, are revelatory.

Finally I want to give thanks to all the musicians I have interviewed and especially the twenty-seven in this book. Their warmth and individual personalities are ever-present, as are their common love and affection for the music and their fellow musicians. I also owe thanks to the many friends who—directly or indirectly, knowing or not knowing—helped me with this project. I hope Notes and Tones will be worthy of all of them.

—Arthur Taylor
New York, 1981

"I don't have to hold the audience's hand."

Do you have a list of things you want to ask me?

No, I would like to ad-lib.

Hello, hello, hello, hello my ding. Look out, look out, my duke. What do you want to talk about, Arthur?

Why do you go to the gymnasium so often, Miles?

I go to the gym to keep my body in shape, so I can hold notes longer, so my stomach will be flat and so I'll look handsome.

How long have you been doing this?

Let's see . . . ever since I can remember. The reason I started doing it was to make my legs stronger.

Do you think boxing is comparable to music?

I think it is. You have to have rhythm and good time to do both. Timing has to be good on both of them. Doing exercise makes you think clear and your blood circulate. It makes you think stronger, feel stronger, and you can play whatever instrument you play with greater strength, whether it's wrong or right.

What about drums? Do you remember we were talking about drums the other day?

Drums? Drums? Oh, yeah! I think all musicians should have some kind of knowledge of drums and piano; not necessarily the bass, but at least piano and drums. Because drummers scare a lot of musicians. Like Tony [Williams]—a lot of musicians can't play with him because they're used to playing on the first beat and he accents on the second and third beats if you're in 4/4 time. Sometimes he might accent on any beat. And he might play 5/4 time for a while, and you've got to have that. You've got to know about rhythms and the feel of different rhythms in order to play with him, because he might haul off and do anything rhythmically. If you don't have any knowledge of time and different time changes, he'll lose you. You have to have it when you first start out, so it'll be back in your head, so it'll be natural.

How do you go about picking a drummer for your band?

First I look at my ding! When I look at a drummer, it's just like when I look at a fighter. I watch his reactions to different things, his quickness, whether he's on time and whether he can clean up, you know what I mean?

Would you be more explicit about that?

Say a guy makes a phrase and the phrase isn't exactly what he wants it to be; well, the drummer is supposed to be hip enough to sorta add to the finished phrase. If you know your drummer is capable of doing that, then you won't feel funny if you miss a certain phrase you're thinking of. It might be one of those off-beat phrases, or out of time.

The first thing I listen for in a drummer is if he can roll. You know, a lot of drummers can't roll. When you end a song, a roll is the most natural way for it to die off, and you can cut off. I also watch to see how fast his hands move. I look at a drummer's hands to make sure that he does not play with his arms but with his wrists and to see how his wrists are. If they are nice and fast, then he can be cultivated and you just let him go. I listen to check if he has good time and he doesn't play the bass drum too loud. The bass drum has to be played even. And I listen to the top cymbal to hear whether he plays it even or not. He may not play it like I want him to play it, but he can be taught how to play it if he plays even. I changed Joe's [Philly Joe Jones] top cymbal beat. He was kind of reluctant at first, but I changed it so it could sound more ad-lib than just straight dang-di-di-dang-di-di-dang: I changed it to dang-di-di-dang-di-di-di-di-dang, and you can play off that with your snare drum.

But you sometimes get a drummer who plays with his arms or else his foot is too heavy . . . it may be heavier than the group he's playing with or lighter than the group . . . well, it's best to be lighter, because you can always come up. Right? I made Tony play his bass drum, because he didn't play it at all. And he didn't play his sock cymbals, so I started him on the sock cymbals. I made him play the bass drum even, and all the rest he had. I suggested he cut all his phrases off on the fourth beat, so it wouldn't sound like you're starting in a chorus every time. Like 1-2-3-4, you say 1-2-3 . . . 1, accent on the fourth beat. Erroll Garner accents on the fourth beat. A lot of people don't know that. And let's see who else? Baby Laurence. It's like a pickup. Or else you can leave it. It's hipper to leave it. I also told Tony not to stop his roll but just to let it die out and keep the tempo.

Where did you get the idea of using a guitar for the record Miles in the Sky?

I got it from my head. I wanted to hear a bass line a little stronger. If you can hear a bass line, then any note in a sound that you play can be heard, because you have the bottom. We change the bass line quite a bit on all the songs we play. It varies. So I figured if I wrote a bass line, we could vary it so that it would have a sound a little larger than a five-piece group. By using the electric piano and having Herbie [Hancock] play the bass line and the chords with the guitar and Ron [Carter] also playing with him in the same register, I thought that it would sound good. It came out all right. It was a nice sound.

Did you compose all the music?

Well, Herbie, Wayne [Shorter] or Tony will write something, then I'll take it and spread it out or space it, or add some more chords, or change a couple of phrases, or write a bass line to it, or change the tempo of it, and that's the way we record. If it's in ¼ time, I might change it to ¾, ⅝ or ⅝.

Is there anything you want to add?

How about my ding? I want to add my ding.

I know you wanted to get that in. What interests you besides music and boxing?

Nothing other than music and girls. Let's see, what else? Drummers, bass players, money, slaves, white folks.

Do you have any particular hobbies?

Making fun of white folks on television. That's my main hobby. That's about it. Driving my Ferrari. I like driving a Ferrari. I don't like to drive anything else. That's a good, fast car.

You can't drive a car like that too fast in the city.

I drive that fast in this block. Whenever you can, you do it. You try not to hurt anybody. Those are about my only hobbies.

Do you go to sporting events often?

I only go to the fights. I like to see nice slick fighters, or else good entertainers like Sammy Davis, Jr., but the rest of that shit ain't nothing.

Has New York changed much since the early days when you were on Fifty-second Street?

They don't have anyplace to experiment for young guys who start playing and who play their own stuff. It's because of all those records they make nowadays . . . you know, the guys copy off the records, so they don't have anything original. You can't find a musician who plays anything different. They all copy off each other. If I were starting out again, I wouldn't listen to records. I very seldom listen to jazz records, because they all do the same thing. I only listen to guys that are original, like Ahmad Jamal and Duke Ellington, guys like Dizzy Gillespie, Sonny Rollins and Coltrane.

Can we start again, Miles?

What? Sock it to me! Come on out with it!

What kind of music interests you besides jazz?

Yesterday I listened to an album of music from Poland: Penderecki's *Threnody for the Victims of Hiroshima*. I have *Dr. Doolittle* here, which Columbia sent me, and *Camelot*.

Of all the music that's been sent to you through the years, how much have you used?

It's all stacked up there. Most of the songs are so weak that you have to rebuild them, so it's like composing yourself.

Is it better for you to compose your own music?

It's better because you can put what you want in it. Gil [Evans] and I looked over most of this music, and it's kind of weak.

Have you and Gil recorded anything that hasn't been released?

We've been working on something for about three years. I don't know how it's going to turn out, though.

Do you think it will culminate soon?

It has to, because we've been working on it for so long.

When you say working on it, what exactly do you mean?

You see these little sketches here at the piano? [He plays] Little things like this . . . trial and error. We write, and then we take out everything we don't like, and what's left is what we record. We try different combinations of instruments, different voices.

Three years seems like quite a long time to be working on one piece of music.

We do it off and on. Gil has to work, and he doesn't work that much. He has to do albums to get money to live on. So we just work on the side.

What about this piece of music on the piano?

Dr. Doolittle has about three songs in it that are worth something, but the rest have to be rebuilt.

Is Dr. Doolittle *playing on Broadway?*

No, they made a movie out of it.

Do you go to the movies often?

I haven't seen any I liked. Let's see, I saw *The Graduate.* That was pretty good. But I can't stand those white movies about white problems. I'd like to see a movie dealing with Negroes as human beings with emotions, not just a black maid or a doctor. I'd like to see one in everyday life . . . like an executive, or the head of a company. One who falls in love and out of love; one who drives a sports car; and one who acts like me or like you; who has girls, white girls, colored girls, Chinese and Hawaiian and German and

French, you know? They don't have that in the movies, so I don't go. Every time I go I feel like I'm giving my money away. Some money! I'd rather shoot tigers or something. I have a funny feeling all day after I've seen a movie with the same white problems. You know, full of girls with long hair and where everybody's having a lot of fun, and we don't have any fun. You don't see any Negroes. It makes me feel funny. It makes me feel like I just gave my money away. If I'm going to give my money away I can give it to something. It's a form of Jim Crow when you have white people dancing and having a good time, and they don't show any Negroes or what Negro feelings are, or any Chinese people, just white girls dancing, with their hair going and going. It's tiresome to me. I want to see somebody acting and living like I do or like you do. Not just white. I saw a movie last night on television. It was just all white all the way through. I figure if the white people keep on showing us their problems on television like they're doing, then we will be able to tell their problems by their facial expressions pretty soon, 'cause they're running out. I was telling Herbie the other day: "We're not going to play the blues anymore. Let the white folks have the blues. They got 'em, so they can keep 'em. Play something else."

Do you like traveling for your work?

It doesn't bother me as long as the band sounds good.

Do you get enjoyment from touring the world with your band?

No, because I'm bringing the pleasure, and whenever I go someplace, I'm going there to please somebody else. So I don't get any kick out of a foreign country unless I go there not to play but on a vacation.

Do you find traveling a strain?

It doesn't bother me, because I don't drink. I stopped drinking.

Do you feel better?

I feel better; a lot better. I don't tire myself out so quickly. When you do one-nighters, like we did in Europe, and you drink every time you eat, you wind up feeling real tired before a concert. You get up early in the morning . . . you might have a hangover and it carries on, and you won't be able to think right. I don't mind traveling, but it just bothers me when guys like George Wein did what he did in Spain and blamed it on me.

What was that?

He tried to slip two extra concerts in and told me he'd pay my room rent, which made me mad, so I left. At the plane I told him I wasn't going to make it. It's all right. He pays enough money and everything, but if he's going to put another concert in and have television, and get paid for it . . . I went along with it, but when it gets so you feel like you're being taken advantage of, it's best to leave, because he's not treating you like a man. I don't think the fact he married a colored girl changes anything. It doesn't matter to me who he married. He married her, not me. I take him for the way he treats me. But he gets real common after a while. He's all right except when he tries to get like one of the boys; then he gets sickening, because nobody's interested in that. All I want to do is play the concert and get the money. He said I stranded my band. They had already been paid, they had their transportation, you know, the tickets.

He wanted everybody to think he was my manager in Europe. I didn't say anything, but that's kind of disrespectful to a musician. And then he would ask me about how I live. It's none of his business. I told him so. I said: "George, you can't live like me because you don't make that much money." He asked me once, "What do you do with your money?" I told him to shut up and don't say nothing 'cause I'd break his neck. If I play a concert, Arthur, I like to play the concert and leave. You don't have to be nice to me or nothing. Let me play the concert and leave me alone. I'll play the music. Pay me off, and that's it. But don't come around to me trying to be a nice guy or a big shot, with some bitches or something, because it doesn't have any effect on me.

The only thing I asked George was, "Wherever we go, try to find a gymnasium in the town so I'll have something to do." He didn't do it. I figured he'd take care of it himself, but he had those in-between guys, the middlemen, who didn't think it was important. But to me it was important. I guess they thought it was a joke. I had a nice time in Europe, because the band played good. That was the only reason. The band plays pretty good sometimes. Oh yeah, George stopped a check because I didn't play in Spain. I was there for two days. So now I'm suing him for what he said. For always dropping all the weight on me. Well, promoters always do this, anyway.

Do you see any solution to problems like that?

Yeah, get your money first. That's what I do. I mean it was all right . . . I called him and said: "George, if we're doing an extra concert, give me some more money." And guess what he said: "Man, like I don't have no bread." So how you going to talk business like that? He tries to use slang and be hip, and: "I don't have no bread, man." I said: "If you don't have no bread, get somebody else, 'cause I'm leaving." So I left.

Do you think it's easier for someone like myself to interview you?

I think it's much easier, if you have something that you want to ask me about music. Because you think the same way, on the same line I think on. Most guys want to know about . . . well, they say I'm rude, and that I turn my back on the audience, and that I don't like white people. And that I don't like the audience. But the thing is, I never think about an audience. I just think about the band. And if the band is all right, I know the audience is pleased. I don't have to hold the audience's hand. I think audiences are hipper than musicians think they are. They wouldn't be there if they didn't want to hear some music, so you don't have to con them into believing that this music is great. I figure they can judge for themselves, and those who don't like it don't have to like it, and those who like it will have a nice time listening. If I go to a concert, I take it like that.

—New York, January 22, 1968

≡ RANDY WESTON

"African Rhythms."

Drums have always been my favorite instrument, and I've always been very close to drummers. I think my style is quite influenced by drum rhythms. So since I'm going to Africa, I think I'm going to study and learn drums based on the tribal system. It will help me in my composing, because I'll have a greater knowledge of rhythms.

Would you like to make your home in Africa?

Oh, yes! I think that by settling in Africa I'll have an opportunity to learn more about myself, my family and my ancestors. I also think I'll learn a little more about the music I play, which is called jazz.

Do you believe our music originally came from Africa?

There's no doubt about it. I've listened to African music and I've heard everything from old-time blues to avant-garde. Africa is the creative source. It is the whole power of the music in the countries that have been influenced by African culture, such as Brazil, Cuba and the United States. Wherever African people have settled, they have created a new music which is based on African rhythms. There is a great West African influence in Brazil, also very much in Cuba and in Puerto Rico. Gospel music, spirituals—they're all African.

Where were you born, Randy?

I was born in Brooklyn, New York. I'm a real, authentic Brooklynite!

How long have you been playing and composing?

I decided to make music my life in 1955.

That late? I thought I had played with you before then.

You had, but I still wasn't sure I had the talent to do it then. It wasn't until 1955 that I made up my mind that music was going to be my life. I actually started when I was around fourteen or fifteen years old. I took piano lessons to keep off the streets. I didn't want to play the piano. It was like forced labor.

I guess you must have come up with guys like Cecil Payne, Max Roach and Ernie Henry in your early playing. They all lived in Brooklyn. Can you think of anyone else?

There were a number of guys. There was one guy called Harold Cumberbatch, who played baritone saxophone and was a fantastic musician. There was Leonard Hawkins, who I thought was one of the greatest trumpet players I ever heard. He stopped playing his horn. At one time the jazz in Brooklyn was unbelievable. We had Tony's, we had the Baby Grand on Sunday afternoons. Lem Davis and I used to give concerts and we would feature Monk, Bennie Green and J. J. Johnson in the early forties. The Putnam Central was the spot, because everybody was there: Dizzy, Miles, Leo Parker, John Lewis, Milt Jackson. Max had a studio at the Putnam Central Club. The owner was a fellow called Johnny Parish, a real West Indian. Somehow it all got together, and it was sort of like a center.

I had the impression that musicians were promoting the sessions at Putnam Central.

They may have, because at that time musicians were doing a lot of things on their own.

Do you think musicians should produce their concerts and records?

I believe the musician of today and of the future has to own everything. He should own his own nightclub, even if it's no bigger than a small room. He should either have his own record company or be able to record his own material and lease it to record companies. I am convinced that it's the only step for us to take now. Considering our experience and how artists are exploited, particularly black artists, we must forget about working for other people and start working for ourselves.

Do you think the popularity of our music has diminished in recent years?

That seems to be the situation. I think there are many reasons for it. Most of the clubs are owned by people who have no love or respect for musicians or for the music. The closeness is not there anymore. There used to be a time when a musician would get five cents off on a drink, and even that would give him a certain degree of respect. In other words, our tradition called for us to play in clubs. We would work, and we would get basic considerations. Then it stopped. I think one reason was the club owners, but the main reason is that the musicians refuse to organize themselves. People who are unorganized usually get stepped on and walked on. The problem is really our own: Because of our own egos, we have not been able to get together as a force, so that anybody can take advantage of us.

The problem we face today is that there's a great emphasis upon commercial music. I call it nonthinking music, because they don't want people to think too much nowadays. Everything is headed more and more toward the robot stage, when people will have numbers and be robots. And jazz is creative music. In the past few years there's been a great emphasis upon avant-garde music, free music or whatever you want to call it. It's usually writers, not musicians, who create this type of attitude. We don't control anything. We should control our own press. We have to depend upon the white status quo to judge us and gauge us with everything from polls to popularity contests to decide who gets this, who gets five stars, who gets one star. I mean it's a combination of all these factors. And again, the reason behind it all is racism.

Do you think young musicians today have the same opportunities we had?

Not really, because today, with so much emphasis upon rock-and-roll music and with so many white men playing jazz and playing the blues, the average black child doesn't have a chance to be involved with other black musicians. You see, it's like a tribal thing with us, a thing that we have to communicate to each other and learn from each other. When we were coming up, there were rehearsals three, four, five times a week. We would go to rehearsals and listen to the bands. Or I could go by Monk's house and all the guys would be there. We would all sit and listen to him play. We had that tribal thing going. It wasn't planned like that, but it was something that happened. It was our culture. I look upon this music as our folk music, as the folk music of the Afro-American, this music that they call jazz.

Do you think the clubs have outlived their usefulness?

Without a doubt. Music has got to be played now to get to the people, because it is a universal music. We have no limitations with this music, and we can use any other form of music in jazz. It's the only really universal music I know. It's the only new thing that's happened in music for centuries. So I think all we need to do is map a campaign. We've got to get to the young children. We have to play in schools in particular. I've always felt very strongly about taking our music into the schools. We've done a program which covers the history of jazz in a number of schools, from elementary schools to colleges. We must go into the churches, invade territories that are alien to us. In other words, we've got to do a mass campaign to get to the people.

We were talking about Birdland the other night. Do you remember?

Well, the vibrations there just cut me off completely. To me, it was a house of evil. What I mean is that it once symbolized the best. It was supposed to have been considered all over the world as the greatest spot for our music. If it hadn't had that reputation—all right, maybe just another funky club, but that was my greatest objection to Birdland.

What about that record you made that you showed me last night? I had never heard it or seen it or read anything about it. When I saw the back cover, it looked like a Who's Who in music to me. Who was in the trumpet section?

Clark Terry, Richard Williams, Freddie Hubbard, Benny Bailey. We had only two trombones: Jimmy Cleveland and Quinton Jackson. Julius Watkins was on French horn. Cecil Payne, Yusef Lateef, Budd Johnson, Gigi Gryce and Jerome Richardson were in the reed section. Les Spann was on the guitar.

Max Roach, G. T. Hogan, Charli Persip, Armando Peraza, Candido Camero and Olatunji were the drummers. Ron Carter and Georges Duvivier played the bass.

When did you make that record, and for what label?

It was the Roulette label, and we did it around early 1960. This particular record is kind of hard to describe. First of all, the purpose of the record was to show that all the black people of African descent are related to one another. So we deliberately got musicians from Africa, Cuba and the United States. We got people from different fields of music and entertainment. We had Brock Peters and Martha Flowers, who is a concert singer, to show that there was a connection between us. The connection was the African rhythms. Langston Hughes wrote the lyrics for a composition of mine called "African Lady." Melba Liston wrote the arrangements and conducted. We also used Swahili to show the beauty of an African language and how the African language is also part of the African rhythms. It came out during a time when we could see things going down. It was not as bad as it is now, but we could feel it happening. We wanted this to be a symbolic gesture by Afro-Americans, to show our pride that some of the countries in Africa were getting their freedom. So the album was called *Uhuru Africa. Uhuru* means "freedom" in Swahili.

This particular album was packaged and put together in 1961. At the time it was a bit unpopular, especially with white people— even white people who were friendly to me. They would hear it once and they wouldn't want to hear it anymore. Especially the first part, where you have the poem. The other problem was with Roulette Records. They wanted to make some sort of a deal where I would be giving them power over my music. They promised to do a big promotion on me, but I have learned one lesson: Never sell a song. Never give the rights of a song. I don't care how sad you think it is. Never sell a tune! I refused, and therefore the album got buried. There was no publicity put behind it. So because of that and because of the message on the record, it was very hard to find.

To my knowledge, Gigi Gryce and Horace Silver were some of the first musicians to form their own publishing companies. Were you involved in that?

Yeah, also Ray Bryant, Art Farmer and Hank Jones. Benny Golson and Gigi were the key figures.

Can you tell me some more about that?

Well, again it goes back to the fact that what we were doing wasn't too advanced. Let me go back a little further: I've always been interested in history. I've always been interested in the history of myself and my people, wherever they may be. I guess maybe it's because I'm a sort of half-breed in the black community. My father was from Panama and my mother came from Virginia. At that time black people were going through their own bit. Divide and conquer had gotten to them. They put each other down. But I always noticed there was a similarity between them, that there were certain basic things which were very much alike. So I discovered it was Africa.

But to get to the point we were discussing—in the twenties and the thirties, black artists had a lot of power. They had a lot of strength. They had a hotel in the neighborhood of Sixth Avenue around Fiftieth or Fifty-first Street. It was called Clef Club. The Clef Club was worth a million dollars. It was a place for black entertainers. Black entertainers and musicians were organized. If you were hungry, if you were a musician or an artist and you came to New York and you didn't have a place to go and didn't have anything to eat, you could go there.

Our ancestors in this business used to give their own vaudeville shows, because segregation was so rough in those days that they had to do a lot of things on their own. And that's how powerful an organization they had. But when they started to build the Sixth Avenue subway, they tore it down. Harlem started to happen, and everybody got split up. So what happened is this: The old-timers let us down, and the reason is because they didn't keep records. It's very hard to find. I've got a book on the history of our people in show business in this country. It's just unbelievable what was happening in the twenties and the thirties. But the old people let us down by not having enough written data on this material. A lot of us grew up playing this music not knowing its history, not knowing how the old people used to work together, support one another and feature each other. And we got away from it more and more. The white man took over more and more, and now he's also pushing his artists. See, in those days we didn't have to worry about that too much.

Well, Randy, you said yesterday, "Let's go and take a swim." Would you explain that?

I think the more complete we get as musicians and artists, the better we will accept the relationships of certain things. Our music is so powerful, so domineering. It is the whole source of creativity of the greatest country in the world. We don't even realize our own power. We haven't had an opportunity to use it yet. While we're going through the changes, while we're finding ourselves and finding our way and getting more and more together as brothers, we should realize that it's important for us to stay healthy. We must keep our strength and keep our minds clear, because we have so many battles to fight. We have to try to create, we have to study, we have to be men and maintain our dignity. So I think we are going to develop our own code more and more. For example, I'm working on a book of what I have experienced as a musician—the things I didn't like, the things that could improve me, what could get us in tune with each other. So myself and Bill Wood, who is a health addict, attempt to go to the gym at least two or three times a week.

A lot of musicians seem to feel that way. I know many who go for exercise. Miles trains all the time, and Walter Bishop likes to swim. Can you think of anybody else offhand?

I know Freddie Hubbard is a very good basketball player. So is the drummer Roy Brooks. He's a beautiful basketball player. He shoots that ball like it's nothing. We played together. In fact, we had a gym for musicians, but some of us left town and it fell through.

Did you ever want to become an athlete?

Not full-time. I just love to play ball. I play basketball in New York at least once or twice a week. I found out I feel better.

Do you ever think you might hurt your hands, or doesn't it enter your mind?

Yes, it does, but it enters my mind in such a way that I always prepare myself mentally to cope with it, and I don't get careless. It can happen.

I would like to do two things in my life: First, I would like to have a museum of jazz in Africa. Why Africa? Because Africa is the source of our music. Second, I'd like us to have a building somewhere with a gym, a masseur and courses on everything from Arabic to Swahili. Kind of a cultural center for black artists, where we could do everything, keep our bodies healthy and develop our own philosophy. Once we develop a philosophy of togetherness, nothing can stop us, because the power of music is just unbelievable.

When we called our organization the Afro-American Musicians' Society, some of the cats were scared because we were saying Afro-American. Ornette was the only cat of bandleader status who showed.

I consider myself a natural philosopher. I try to look at nature as it is. I try to look at life as I see it. Wherever we go we've got a very serious problem. We've got a serious problem in America and in Europe. We even have problems in Africa, and also in South America. I've read about how our ancestors came here in chains, how they had to work for nothing to build America and other parts of the world. Their culture, their music, their language—everything was taken away from them. And yet they managed to survive and multiply, which is fantastic. So I feel that somehow our destiny as Afro-Americans is to help draw all the other people of African descent together. I think this is our purpose. For me this is a spiritual answer; I didn't get it from anywhere, it's just something that I feel deeply. I believe that the cats who play the music we call jazz can play a great role in this. The question is what do we do about the situation? I'm chiefly concerned about the role I can play to help knock down that wall of bigotry, prejudice and lack of contact among ourselves. I'm convinced that we have to have a homeland. We've got to have a place where there are people who look like us; we've got to have leaders who look like us; we've got to have a president or a king or whatever who looks like us. We have contributed enough to the world to deserve this, and I think that Africa is the place. I don't know which part of the continent, but I feel that this is where we should all start aiming for in many ways. We can live in America or Europe. But invest in Africa. Not everybody has to go and live there, but we must start developing those ties. I'm studying African art. I want to learn more about it, and I want to go and live in Africa. Live with the people and communicate with them as best I can, and perhaps help establish a place that we can call home.

What do you think about freedom music?

Well, the first thing I object to in that music is the fact that it is completely built up by white writers. Ornette Coleman was opposite me at the Five Spot when Leonard Bernstein, who was in the audience, jumped up and said this was the greatest thing that had ever happened in jazz, and that Bird [Charlie Parker] was nothing. That sort of thing. I don't know about analyzing music. It's a pretty wild thing to do. I didn't like Ornette when I first heard him and now I love him.

I think freedom music is doing several things. First of all, it is very descriptive of what's happening today. My objection is that I don't see how this music is more free than another. I've heard Monk take one note and create unbelievable freedom. You don't need a lot of notes to create freedom. One note can be a whole composition. This is my point of view. There have been musicians throughout the years who have protested musically and also protested in other ways than in their music. In other words, this freedom thing is not something new. I heard some Jelly Roll Morton that turned me around. I heard some Fats Waller which is as free as anything the avant-garde can play. Freedom is a natural development. I don't know what's going to come out of it, but I think you're also going to get a stronger African influence in our music. It's happening at the same time, though it may not be getting as much publicity as the avant-garde. A lot of the avant-garde I hear reminds me of early European modern classical music. But I haven't heard enough of it to break down one artist from another, because the music I hear disturbs me.

Do you find that the music is not completely developed? Could that be the reason it disturbs you?

No, because I don't think the blues is completely developed, either. I haven't figured out Bird yet.

What did you think of Bud Powell?

Well, I was in business with my father, and we built up a little jazz gallery at a restaurant which was open twenty-four hours a day. One of the reasons I did that was because I was frustrated. I wanted to play, But I didn't have the confidence to think I could play. Duke Jordan was the top pianist in Brooklyn at that time. Everybody would go and listen to Duke and talk to him. He was working with Bird, and he kept saying: "Wait till you hear Bud Powell." Believe it or not, the first time I heard Bud Powell was at the United Service Organization in Harlem, and it was just him and Cootie Williams, a duet. It was for the soldiers. I think Bud Powell is . . . you know, you try to find new words because there are so many words put in jazz magazines to describe where a cat is. Without a doubt he is one of our leaders.

Do you play for yourself or for the audience?

I think I usually do both if there is a good ambience between the band and the audience. Some places just have atmosphere, and it's almost like the people and music become one. I like to play for myself and for the people at the same time, but it doesn't always happen. Sometimes you play something and the people don't dig it. But tonight, for example, we played and the people were dancing, so we were participating with each other. I thought it was nice.

Have you ever played music you didn't like just to get money?

I made one compromise in music—not really in music but recording. I was with United Artists at the time, and we did the *Little Niles* album with Johnny Griffin, Ray Copeland, Idrees Sulieman, George Joyner and Charli Persip. At that time I had met Melba Liston and we had collaborated on the *Little Niles* album; we started to work on a *Freedom Africa Suite*. It was going to have a big orchestra, voices and lots of percussion, a sort of a high-price recording date. I asked United Artists if they would let me record this album. They said: "We don't know yet, but would you consider recording a Broadway musical?" If I did the musical for them, they would let me record *Uhuru*. The musical turned out to be *Destry Rides Again*. Melba Liston and I did the arrangements with Bennie Green. It had four trombones and a rhythm section. We couldn't get anything from the music itself. It wasn't a challenge for me and I wasn't interested, but I did it because I was hoping to do *Uhuru Africa*.

Do you have any peeves about the word jazz?

I'm often sort of on both sides of the question you're asking. First of all, I'm only going on my instinct, the things I've read and being around musicians. I don't have any factual proof on this issue and I don't know if I really would accept any. When I think about jazz, I think about my own experience with the word, what it's meant to me. When I had no idea of being a musician, jazz for me was the music of the black people and it was free, creative and swinging.

You say was *the music of black people?*

Well, yes, it's true, it was. I somehow get the feeling the word *jazz* describes a certain stage in the development of our music, a period when there was a thing that really was jazz. Where people would go and get lifted spiritually. When I think of jazz, I think of people coming into nightclubs and hearing music that would make you feel very sad, very tender. Like Billie Holiday singing the blues, for example. She could bring tears to your eyes, make you feel very sad, but at the same time you would feel spiritually good. While when you hear somebody like Basie or like Duke, it makes you want to swing. Today the word *jazz* doesn't describe what's going on in music. Music has become more modern, more rhythmic. It's more influenced by modern classical music. I think music now has become more personalized. I have been searching for a title to describe my own music and I thought of African Rhythms. Because I play calypso, I play jazz, I play spirituals, I play Latin and I play African music. So how can anybody just call me a jazz musician? What I do is use the root of all this music, which is Africa and the rhythms of Africa.

Have you modified your material or style in recent years?

In a sense. I believe that our music is one of the greatest phenomena in the world and that it can hold its merits anyplace on earth if given the proper chance and atmosphere, the proper people handling it, whether in nightclubs or at concerts. I have decided to search for the roots of jazz, of gospel music, of calypso and of Latin music—all the different music by different people with dark skins spread out all through the New World, producing everything from Bossa Nova to Aretha Franklin, from Ray

Charles to Charlie Parker. There is a definite link between all those people. They're all black, but there is another something else, too, and I think that other link between them is rhythm, a beat. There's a certain something which identifies you with an African drummer. For example, an African drummer would not have any difficulties playing with you, and vice versa.

I've been listening extensively to African folklore music from the Congo, from Nigeria, from Ghana, from Morocco, and the more I listen to this music, the more I'm influenced by it, the more I realize that it contains the elements of all the musical forms of modern Africa and the New World. My style is very definitely being more and more influenced by African folklore, because I think this is the key to everything we're doing. I've heard singers who sang things that were rhythmically just like Charlie Parker playing his horn. I've heard cats who sound like Coltrane. The music of the tribes is just unbelievable.

Is there any protest in your music?

Any protest? No, there's no protest in my music anymore because I've been in Morocco for two and a half years. Historically, especially in Africa, musicians have been the messengers, the storytellers, the people who influenced their society. I now want to aim my music toward seeking a better way of life, because we're protesting but we don't quite know what's a better way of life. I think this is one of the problems. It's not protest anymore, it's almost like another step, beyond protest. I don't know how to describe it.

Have you ever had any bad writeups?

I've gotten a few, but not very many. I've been lucky with critics. At first I don't like it and then maybe I look at it again and listen to the recording. Sometimes I think the critic is b.s.-ing. Sometimes I think he knew what he was talking about. I've reached the point now where I think these people served a purpose as far as getting jazz known to the public. A good musician will perform as much as any human being can perform, as well as possible most of the time. But there are times when we just don't feel right, when something is wrong spiritually . . . anything can happen to stop us from sounding good in a performance. But if you get together with the musicians, ninety-

fact, I was a very good copier. But as I was always playing with rhythm-and-blues bands, they would never let me take a solo.

One night we were playing in Amarillo, Texas, and the band was playing "Stardust." They let me play a solo. I got up, and for the first time in my life, I played what I felt and heard without thinking about changes or anything. And I got fired. They dumped me. The guy kept hollering: "Give 'em vanilla, give 'em vanilla, give 'em vanilla."

Vanilla, what's that?

It means "please them." That night I just started playing, and I knew for the first time that I was right and that I was being put down for something someone didn't dig, didn't know. I decided to find out what I was doing, because this was the most natural I felt about music. That was about 1949.

In 1950–51 I went to California with Pee Wee Crayton. Later I decided to get married and got out of music. I got a job driving an elevator. I said well, I'm never gonna make it. I started studying, writing and trying to figure out how I could get other people to understand what I was trying to do. I kept working, writing and studying. Finally I went to Hollywood, and somebody liked the tunes I was writing. They never liked the way I was playing. When I played a tune, I wouldn't stick to the tune; I'd go where I wanted to go and use the tune as an opener, and I still do that. What happened was that I wrote tunes on changes like be-bop, which everyone could understand. But when I played, I didn't play that way. I went to jam sessions, and certain guys started liking some of the tunes I wrote. Then I went to see a guy at Contemporary Records. He gave me a recording session and told me he liked my tunes but was not necessarily interested in the playing. So that's how I got my first record date, out in California. I knew all the guys, everybody. I was like in the ghetto image of music, so none of the people in California ever took me seriously.

One time I had a gig for three dollars a night, and I was playing better and with more honesty than I'm playing today, because I hadn't been corrupted by being in the spotlight and by articles in newspapers. I hadn't been corrupted by the establishment. I was still unknown, and I was playing my heart out. One night I had a gig in skid row on Fifth Street in Los Angeles, and a Jewish guy told me he would give me three dollars a night. If I wanted any more I would have to come in and mop the place at five o'clock in the morning. There was a black girl sitting there playing with her breasts, and he said: "See that girl? She belongs to me. Don't ever speak to her." Then he dropped a dime on the floor and said: "If you see any money here, don't pick it up. It belongs to me. It's mine." It was the first time I had any dealings with Jewish people, so he corrupted my image of Jews right off the bat. I needed the three dollars because I didn't have a gig and I had no relatives in Los Angeles. After playing there for two or three weeks, I still had no idea if I was going to stay in music or not.

After I made my first record, I got a call from New York about a gig I could have at the Five Spot if I could get to New York. This was four years later, in 1959. I went to Tanglewood and met Nesuhi Ertegun from Atlantic Records. I made a recording session for him and used the money to take the band to New York. I started at the Five Spot at one hundred dollars a week and stayed there for three months. I went to speak with a booking agent, Shaw Artists, to see if I could get on their booking circuit.

They would send me to places where it was so cold that nobody wanted to go out in the street. Say Chicago in February or March. And I'm unknown, right? But what happened was that Miles had been there one week before they sent me there. It was cold, but the place was packed. I was getting eight hundred dollars for the transportation and everything. The union man told me I was crazy, but I didn't know any better. When I complained about being paid so little, they told me I hadn't been on the circuit long enough. I said: "Well, what's that got to do with the place being full?"

That's what I don't understand about America and its way of control. You know, they tell you that you don't draw. Then I hear there are certain bands they still book whether they draw or not, just for the image of the place. When they want a tax loss, they send an unknown person, take a chance on him and just write it off. For some reason I got a certain kind of journalistic publicity which had nothing to do with music. I have had black people and white people against me. The white people created something that didn't exist in my life. The black people were the ones who were already established. They thought I was going to be a threat to them, so they were against me. To this very day I'm in the same position I was in ten years ago. The only thing that's healthier is that I can make more choices. Someone who was ten years old ten years ago is twenty now. That might cover ten million people. And the people who were twenty then are thirty now, so there's no audience problem. They're running that same philosophy about how people don't understand my music, but I know what the real problem is. It's the people who want to design and control the music consumption the way that they want to dictate it. I have been able to make records, but I have never made any money off records, though it has kept some kind of publicity going.

[At this point Ornette turned on his tape recorder so I could hear some music he had written.]

I have come to love writing music. This is a piece of music I wrote for the Black Composers' Society in America. They are all black composers, but they're classical. They have the same problem as white guys as far as playing something without seeing it on paper. I don't feel healthy about the performing world anymore at all. I think it's an egotistical world; it's about clothes and money, not about music. I'd like to get out of it, but I don't have the financial situation to do so. I have come to enjoy writing music because you don't have to have that performing image. But there are no black composers making a living out of music, which is the only kind of music life I like to live. I don't want to be a puppet and be told what to do and what not to do. I want to do the best I can, because the person who doesn't know me is the one who's going to enjoy it, not the person who's paying me. I know my problem is a man's problem. It's a position problem. When I find some people who are in a position to accept me as a human being on my own terms, then we can work together.

What was your reason for starting to play the violin and trumpet?

I started trying to play the violin and trumpet because I didn't want to be known as the best saxophone player, or the best this or that, just to have a gig. I don't like that. Nobody knows how good you are.

It's very bad for black people in America. They learn what's right, but they can't play the game because the decisions are not theirs. Most black people in America know the saying, God bless the child that has his own. Everybody knows how that melody goes. But it's another story when it comes to doing something without someone else's approval. You know people are always asking, Why don't black people have their own record companies? I answer, You know what? They tell me there are twenty-two million black people in America. I know that over one million people in my age bracket alone have one of my records. But I've never got any statement from white people saying that black people bought my records. They say: Black people don't buy your records! For instance, I come from Texas, and they are always telling me it's hard for people in Texas to get my records. There are lots of black people in Texas and in the South, period. So maybe the reason black people don't buy my records is that they don't make it possible for black people to get them. They make it possible for black people to get the blues, so they can be depressed all the time. I would rather have a record company selling only to black people. I'd be richer doing that! But white people won't let you get in a position to communicate with your own people!

They don't even want to see you with a fine black woman. Have you noticed that?

Yeah, I noticed. But you know when it comes to women, that's my failing.

What do you mean by that?

Yeah, but women got another thing going that's very strange. I don't think any women would be impressed by something someone has done unless they understood what they wanted from it. I don't ever have any women to really go to bat for me. I can tell a woman about a bad thing someone has done to me, and she will try to convince me that it's my fault. That's strange, isn't it? I mean if they love you, why try to convince you, when somebody is doing something wrong to you, that you caused it yourself? Like, they'll tell you you can't know something so well. You can't be so different from everybody. Who do you think you are? Nobody is that interested in you to be doing that crap to you. It's all in your mind. But then when they see it go down, that's another story.

What was your reason for adding a tenor saxophone to your group, when in recent years you only had a trio?

I just love the way Dewey [Redman] plays. I have been trying to find a first trumpet player, but they don't exist in jazz.

What do you mean?

I mean trumpet players who can hit as many high Fs and Gs as you want every night without ever going down.

There must be some.

If there are they are all leaders, not sidemen. I love Don Cherry, but I can play first trumpet myself. I haven't found the mouthpiece that will allow me to be consistent more than a few hours. After a couple of hours I pick up the saxophone and I start thinking I have the trumpet in my hands. It's like being three different people. But back to the tenor saxophone: The tenor is a B-flat instrument like the trumpet, so sometimes I write that way. I almost get the same effect with B-flat, E-flat instruments, but not the brilliancy of the brass. I love the way Dewey plays. I have heard him play much better than me sometimes, which is really nice. He can play like everybody.

I'm interested in music, not in my image. If someone plays something fantastic, that I could never have thought of, it makes me happy to know it exists. Only America makes you feel that everybody wants to be like you. That's what success is: Everybody wants to be like you.

I hear your son plays the drums on a recording with you.

You know, man, if it weren't for Ed Blackwell, my drummer, I would rather have him with me all the time. There's one thing I have learned about young kids: If they have talent and you allow it to grow, they'll come up with something that's very useful. Denardo is something else! I can write a tune with seven bars and he will play the right thing every time. I can't get him to practice or anything. He can read drum music, but he's rebelling. Like, I don't want to be a musician because my father is. He doesn't dig that. Every time I wanted him to play for me, I had to damn near beg him. He has something about playing that's really nice, especially in the last year or so.

I made a record with him in 1966, when he was ten. I read a review by Shelly Manne saying it was horrible, just because I had a son, that didn't mean he could play. In fact, for what my son was playing, it was very strong! But Shelly Manne was talking about him like I should send him to a lumber school, that he would make a better janitor or something. So Denardo said: "Daddy, how do they let people talk about other people like that?" In other words, he was asking: Why do I have to be an adult to do something good? Why do I have to be a man when I'm not a man? I like what I'm doing.

So now he doesn't want to play because people think he is too young. He's very sensitive, so I don't try to force him to play. I told him: "If you don't want to play, don't play." People enjoy what you do, but if you get upset, then maybe you can't do it as well as you'd like.

I didn't have any idea he could play the drums. He was living in California, and I was in New York. I called him up one day and asked him what he wanted for his birthday. He told me he wanted a shotgun. I said: "I don't know where to get a gun, but what about a set of drums?" He said: "Okay, forget about the gun and send the drums." He was six, and four years later he was making a record. I can't say I taught him, because that's not true. He did everything himself.

I tell you, man, the music world is a cold world. Very cold! The way Denardo is playing now on the record, *Ornette at 12,* would be a novelty for any other race of people. Someone would have gotten in and said, We can make lots of money with this father and son, the whole trip. Instead they put it down. I just have to stay with it, man, until I can better it. The main point about the music world is that it's invisible when it comes to a straight reason why a person wants to hear a certain performer rather than another. In fact, instead of the person wanting to hear that performer because of what they get from the music, it's usually dictated: This is what's best, everything else is bull.

I find the homosexual problem in music is unequal all the way. If you're a white homosexual there are no closed doors. If you're a black homosexual not only are the doors closed, but they take you and use you against the straight black people. I don't understand that at all. If I was a white homosexual where I am now, I would probably be very wealthy. It's still a big problem for any heterosexual person in the music world. Most people who control the music business become bisexual, homosexual or whatever because their nature is so tense from all the wrong they're doing. When you try to be straight, they take it all out on you.

I've suffered from that myself. Right now I've got three records on the market made from my own tapes which were deliberately taken from me, and I haven't received a penny. All from faggots and homosexual-type people. They scare me to death, man. I don't want to be that tense about controlling someone. I'm not a coward, but I couldn't change that person. The only thing I could do is kill him. And if I kill him I've got a murder on my hands. That doesn't make sense, so I said okay, I'll sleep in a three-dollar-a-day room, and you can sleep in a hundred-dollar-a-day room off my own music. I have three records on the market, and white guys are selling them and making money. Then they tell me, when I ask about it: Do you think Atlantic Records are straight? Do you think BYG Records are straight? They're telling me: I have a license to do this because we're all doing the same thing. So don't come to me and tell me about what I do to you; we all are right! There is an establishment that says if you do this here, we'll give you four dollars, and the government gets some of that. But there's another establishment that says you do this here and I can get it from you without giving you anything. That exists, too. I have been on both trips. I'd like to try to change all that, and not just because of my own condition.

You can't do it by yourself.

No, you can't do nothin' by yourself.

We live in a world where someone can ask who the richest man in the world is and be given a name. But you can't name the poorest man in the world. They come in the millions. If you can do something by yourself, you are automatically above the others. What you must try to do is bring the ones who are down up to the level of what you believe it could be for everybody. Not that you're there yourself, but you just know what the level could be. If more people supported that level, you would have others to work with. Unfortunately, people think, What's in it for me? They can all calculate that very quickly.

What's very strange about music is that there isn't any

measuring point. You can't know how good someone is unless you have something to check what you have already accepted. Like myself—I have never in my life seen anyone explain how and what I'm doing in music. But everybody knows that it's something that hasn't happened before, and that it's not important enough to back. It's strange; they don't do that with material values. If something is rare, then it's more important than anything common; but that isn't the way it goes in human affairs. That's funny, huh?

Yes, it is.

It's backward.

It's primitive.

Yeah, that's what it is. I think if people know you're doing something well and they know that you're not trying to destroy them, they will support you. I grew up in a white society with white rules and a white philosophy, but I grew up with a black conscience. My consciousness of myself as a black man makes me realize that unless I can be integrated into white society and its values, I can't achieve the wealth they have created. They have created a society where any unknown white person can put something on the market and become successful. I don't see why a black person can't do that. They have to control what you do first, then give it to you like welfare.

Maybe it's in the nature of a white person to be against anybody who is not white. But in that case they shouldn't have schools and rules. They should say that no black person is allowed to read and write. They should let you know what your limitations are. They shouldn't say you can succeed if you can learn, because you can't.

I haven't had a booking agent or a manager in ten years. Every gig I've had I got myself. I haven't made any money, but I haven't been without too many meals. People see me with new clothes on and think I have lots of money and that I'm successful. I was born in the black community, where the best thing to do is be clean and not let anybody know what your problems are. I have walked the streets wearing silk suits when I was hungry. I know that if you're clean, at least the dignity of being human is still there. I would rather think human first than think of being defeated because I'm black. I met a white guy the other day who accused me of being an agent for some secret black society. I said: "Man, you got to be crazy." They can't put their finger on me, because I don't belong to any organization. People don't realize you needn't belong to an organization for the betterment of this or that just to do something you believe in. You can do it without joining anything.

One more thing—do you think it's easier to talk with me than with some critic?

I'd rather talk to you than to someone who would use it against me.

Ornette, you understand I want to publish this interview?

You can publish it. I have never been scared of saying anything, because when someone analyzes it, if he's human, he'll understand.

—Paris, October 9, 1969

≡ PHILLY JOE JONES ≡

"Music isn't noise."

Who did you study drums with?

Cozy Cole.

Before Cozy?

I studied with a cat named Philly Joe Jones. Well, I'm a little ahead of myself. Kenny Dennis and I used to go to New York from Philadelphia to visit Max [Roach] every weekend, when he was living on Monroe Street in Brooklyn. We would go through different things with Max, and he would be helping us with licks. Art [Blakey] and Max were coming in and out of Philadelphia and would see me a lot. They would say: "You should be in New York, playing." So I packed up and moved to New York. After I got there I started getting so much action and wanted to get myself together musically, so as not to be embarrassed. I went back home with the intention of studying with Ellis Tollon and enrolled in his school.

Before I left New York I had gone to see Cozy. Max Roach was studying with Cozy at the time. Even Jo Jones was there sometimes, so I knew Cozy was a heavy teacher. He was a beautiful person, and I always liked him. This was when he had the school on Forty-eighth Street.

I took one lesson with Tollon in Philadelphia, and what he was teaching I didn't want to learn. I didn't like the system he had for me to hold the sticks. I think he really messed up several drummers in Philadelphia. They sounded like boy scouts after studying with him. I went back to New York to study with Cozy. Cozy brought me through like I wanted, got me to read like I wanted. He's a top-notch teacher, one of the best in the world.

I've had some lessons with Charles Wilcoxon in Cleveland. He's a beautiful teacher and has some beautiful books out, too. You have some of them. I like Cozy's method of teaching. He gets it to you easy, brings it to you so simple, you don't have any trouble learning. Not only that—he works with you very hard. You go to him for an hour's lesson, you pay for an hour and always get an hour and twenty minutes or an hour and a half. He's not a clock watcher, he's a student watcher.

I see you're wearing the black-power fist around your neck. What are your feelings about it?

What are my feelings about it! What are you asking me! I've got it around my neck! I'm in full accord with it!

Do you see any relation between that and your music?

Yeah. In every way you can possibly think of. That's where all that kind of music comes from—from black weakness. You get black power from black weakness. That's where it all came from! Black torture, poverty, black slavery. That music is born out of all that stuff my grandfather went through. Can you imagine, dig, my father saw his father in slavery.

What effect does that have on you?

I have an inborn thing. I don't harbor hatred. I take people as they are, but I have a dislike for certain people who come from certain areas, because they've been in that. It's like the time I lived in California. I lived there for three years. All the policemen are Southerners, and all of them mess with you. Every last one of them. Not one of them acts like he's supposed to act. A policeman is a public servant and supposed to be protecting citizens. In California it's just the opposite. That's the SS troops out there, man. They're storm troopers. They'll shoot you down as quick as they look at you, especially if you're black.

Can you relate the situation you speak of to your music?

Sure. I think all musicians have those things in their minds . . . like that article about protesting through music in that magazine in your house.

Oh, you mean the Ebony *[August 1969* Ebony, *special issue on the Black Revolution].*

I have a strong feeling that's the best way to protest. Protesting through the music. All that screaming and hollering you hear in the music. All that stuff Trane [John Coltrane] was doing. It's another way to protest, other than the violent way. All your anger comes out there. All the beauty and everything else come out there. It would be hard to provoke a musician to violence unless it was perpetrated on him, you dig it? Then it would come out. You find guys in the street fighting, because that's their thing. They're in the street all the time. Musicians are working people. We travel and meet all kinds of people. I meet beautiful people all over the world, and when I'm talking to them, I don't think of color. It doesn't even come into it. I get drug about certain things. I get drug about a lot of things I see here in France.

So it's all the same thing. Have you been anyplace where you have not run into racial prejudice?

Yes, I have. I've been to one place where I didn't run into a bit of prejudice: Cuba.

I must go there sometime.

You should go there. I went to Cuba the day the revolution was settled. The day they ran Batista out of there. I had my group there to play a concert the day Fidel took over Havana. They took me to the biggest hotel in Havana, the Hotel National. Castro said, "You're the darkest man that ever slept in this hotel." He was showing me what Batista had been doing. He wouldn't ever allow dark Cubans in a hotel in Cuba. A man born in Cuba, he is dark, so he's not allowed in this hotel. He never swam in that pool. I was in that pool, everybody was cool. All the ladies, everybody in the pool . . . dark Cubans, light Cubans, it didn't matter. They were having a ball. Like everybody had gone to heaven. Everything was open for everybody, the whole city.

You spent a lot of time in London. How did you find it there?

London is a different thing to me. I don't know, it's something about the English. They've been barbarians as long as I've read anything about them. But they're humanitarians, too. They've got a good feeling for people. I lived there for fourteen months, although they're selfish with the music end of it and they won't allow any American musician living there to work. I sweated. I stayed there all that time without working. I applied for my card, you understand. They said, you come and stay here for a year, but you can't take any jobs. If you do this, at the end of the year you go before the board and they will give you your card. But you must comply with the rules. Just like they do at home with 802 [Local 802, American Federation of Musicians]. If you do so, you get your card. This happens in New York.

I stayed all that time and refused jobs. I had several calls for jobs, at astronomical figures. I said, I can't make that one. And believe me, I would have loved to have made it, but I didn't know where it was coming from, underneath or what. I got permission to make a couple of record dates. That was all right. They were my own dates. At the end of the time, when I applied for the card, they gave me the runaround for a couple of weeks. I informed them I was going to France and would be coming back to England shortly. I went to France and went back to England and asked them what the decision was at the board meeting. They said, "We have the right to reject or to take anyone in the union that we want to." And they rejected me. I said, "On what grounds?" They would give no answer other than they have the right to decide who they want to come in their union or not. They could have told me that the first day.

I think the English musicians should be stopped from working in the States. If their federation isn't linked with ours, then they shouldn't be allowed to come and take money out of the States. These English pop groups make more money in the States than anywhere in the world. And half of them, you know what they're playing? Nothing. I just got through listening to fifteen or twenty groups in this last festival, day before yesterday. Nothing. One or two of them sounded good. It was a hippie festival that was supposed to be pop and jazz, but the pop just overwhelmed the jazz. They didn't have enough jazz or freedom artists there. In other words, the entire afternoon and evening, all the way up until six in the morning, was devoted to pop music. They've got group on top of group, and they're all working with electronics. They've got the electronics up so high on the guitars, basses and pianos that instead of playing music, they're making sounds. Like you turn your radio on too loud. One guy was playing an instrument and making it sound like an airplane crashing, and one was screaming. It was ridiculous. I enjoyed some parts of the festival because I love music and there were a couple of groups that really had something going.

What do you think of freedom music?

Freedom music doesn't mean anything to me, because I've

been playing free all my life. I don't think you can really play freedom music unless you know your instrument. That was just a door opener. John Coltrane opened the door for a whole bunch of . . . I call them bag carriers. The bags they carry their instruments in. They've been carrying their horn around for maybe a year. Soon as they get an opportunity, if somebody will allow them to get on the bandstand, they jump on and don't know anything about the horn and just make a bunch of noises.

John Coltrane went into a different thing. John Coltrane was a miraculous musician, an accomplished musician. John was very well studied, well read. He was a topnotch musician, and he knew his instrument from top to bottom. When I say top to bottom, I mean above the top and below the bottom. He could go further. The things he was doing with his instrument were not only beautiful but well constructed. In every move he would make, you could hear that he knew his horn backwards.

Same thing with Eric Dolphy. These men were geniuses. They knew exactly what they were going to do. You know yourself, you don't learn an instrument in two years. I've been playing for twenty-seven years and I still haven't learned the drums to my satisfaction. Trane wasn't satisfied with his horn playing, and he surpassed many a saxophone player. I'm still not satisfied with my drumming; so I can't see how one of the bag carriers can be satisfied after two years of an instrument. If you stop and ask one of those guys how many years he's been playing, it won't go past four. My fourth year of playing, I was really scuffling. I didn't have the nerve to get on the bandstand. My fourth year of playing, I was listening to John Coltrane and he was playing beautiful. In those days Eddie Lockjaw Davis was on the bandstand. Benny Golson was playing beautiful then, but we still wouldn't do that. We were listening to the older musicians playing in Philadelphia.

Some great musicians have come out of Philadelphia.

Quite a few. Most of them were born and raised there, but you had a lot of musicians such as John Coltrane and Dizzy Gillespie that came from other parts of the country. They migrated to Philadelphia and made Philadelphia like their home. John considered Philadelphia his home. He was brought from North Carolina when he was ten years old, I think. Of course, Dizzy came when he was a man, but he stayed in Philadelphia for a long time before he went to New York. John left Philadelphia with different bands, but Philadelphia was his home base until we joined Miles's band. He decided he had to live in New York because that was where Miles lived.

In fact, all of us were in New York. I had been in New York, but Red [Garland], Paul [Chambers] and John all came to New York to live so we would be closer to Miles. Music changes around and changes around. It takes all kinds of turns, but it always comes back to the pure swing. Nothing seems to outlast jazz. The real true traditional jazz . . . you can't get away from it. People like to pat their feet and clap their hands.

The freedom musicians have a large following, but the people who are following them have no concept of music or they wouldn't be following them. In some cases people like Pharoah Sanders or Sun Ra give them the whole constellation. Yeah, they're playing that sort of music correctly. Sun Ra is a topnotch musician. I can appreciate it when it comes from a guy who has studied, because I know he's not going to stray too far. He'll go way out, but he won't go so far out that it becomes nothing. Sun Ra has been doing it for years back in Chicago, playing beautiful. He decided to play his cosmic music. He gets his music from the cosmos. That's his feeling. That band sounds beautiful. I watched them groom in New York every Monday night. Every man in that band can play. Pat Patrick and John Gilmore and all those guys. John Gilmore worked with me for two years, playing straight life music, so I know what his concept is. I used to hear him in Chicago, long before he went to work with me. I find him in Sun Ra's band, still playing pretty.

I think freedom music should be limited to those that can play it. It's nothing to open up and play freedom. I like it sometimes, just chaos on your instrument. At least I have a ball with it, because whenever I do something like that, I do it without any unity. I just run through everything that my hands will let me do. And my hands will let me do most anything I want to do. I don't feel limited. You find some guys, especially drummers, that are going to get into playing so-called freedom, they get hung up because they haven't learned the foundation of the instrument first and can do nothing but make noise. I don't think freedom means just making noise, either. Like I said, everybody's been playing free. Every time you play a solo you're free to play what you want to play. That's freedom right there. I don't dig it the other way.

Music hasn't changed that much, because people still like good music. Music isn't noise. Noise is something that no one wants to hear. If there's an unusual sound in the house that's annoying, someone will say, "What is that noise?" Well, that's what some of that freedom does. I've watched people right here in Paris at the American Center pay their admission, come in and sit down for five minutes and get up and walk out. And they don't ask for their money back. They're too glad to get past the door and to keep going. They don't want to hear it. They don't want to stay in there long enough to ask for their money back. Some musicians call it their music. I've heard Charles Lloyd call it his music. That's all a takeoff on what John [Coltrane] was trying to discover. You listen to all the tenor saxophone players, they're trying to play John and embellish on what he was doing. But when you listen to them, you hear all the different licks that John played. They get his records and listen to them and practice with them. I know how they do. I've got a couple of saxophones myself. They're trying to play those licks, then get on the bandstand and play them. They're not playing themselves. I've got a couple of records by Charles Lloyd, and you would be surprised by the things that he plays that come from John Coltrane, note for note.

Everybody's trying to copy, not to be original and go ahead like John did. John was moving further and further. He hadn't even finished what he was doing. It seems funny that most musicians say we wish Clifford Brown had lived a little longer so we could hear him now, we wish Bird had lived a little longer, so we could hear what he would be playing now.

We will never know.

No, you never know what he would be playing now, but I know what Miles is playing now, and he certainly belongs in that class. And Dizzy belongs in that class. Everybody's trying to stay ahead, so to speak, rather than grow stagnant or go backward. There are many young musicians coming through that are playing beautiful today: people like McCoy Tyner, Tony Williams and Herbie Hancock, the young element. They're coming through beautifully, man. They're beginning to talk, beginning to play. I'm very happy that I've been around so much longer than them so I can watch them grow, because it helps me grow. I refuse to become stagnant. I learn something from every musician I listen to.

Tell me some more about the BYG festival.

I was there for two days, but I was subjected to listening to a lot of music that I ordinarily wouldn't pay any attention to. I had to be there because I didn't know when we were going onstage. There were some groups that sounded very good. In fact, the group that went on before we did left the bandstand kinda warm, and Archie Shepp knew it was left warm and he went out there and smoked. Ray Draper was there, playing tuba beautifully. Ray's such an asset to any group. He has perfect pitch. There you are. Right there you've got seasoned men. Ray's seasoned. He's been in quite a few groups, including Max Roach's group, and he is one of the best arrangers around.

All of them stretched out into something we hadn't been playing. We had a few spots that didn't jell because some other performers joined in who really didn't belong in Archie's band. And as soon as they joined in with their noise, it threw everything off. We had set a rhythm pattern. Cliff Thornton, the trumpet player, was playing conga drum, and there was an African drummer, but as soon as we would get the rhythm thing together and the horns would come in, somebody with a guitar from one of the pop groups would do something funny and would throw the whole meter off. We had to change the meter around and get another groove. So it made it kind of hard.

When we started to play, they stayed out of it because they didn't want to make Archie angry. After they saw we were stretching out into freedom, although everybody doing it was professional, they thought it was a cue for them to join in. So when they joined in, it became noise. They would come in with a loud guitar and turn the meter completely around. We had a pulse going, the same way we did on the record date. Remember how we started that record date with Archie? We set the time, set a pulse and had it swinging. This guy came in with a loud guitar and tore the whole structure down. Made noise out of it. So the African drummer and myself got together and overpowered that rhythm. We set another rhythm, but that was still there, and they were recording and televising.

I understand the great one is home: Gene Ammons. Thank

God. We'll have some more beautiful music. That brother can really play. I can't see how they could have kept him incarcerated for so long. After the warden heard all that beauty, he should have said, Let this man out. It's not just the people here who want to hear him: Let the world hear him.

How can a man in charge of keeping men locked up know anything about beauty? Even a policeman seems funny to me.

Of course.

It's another kind of thing. Or is it just a job? Like he's doing his job to get some money.

Well, it actually is just a job.

Is that the way you think most of them look at it?

Well, I've been a policeman myself. Not a civilian—an army policeman. It's the same thing. It's a job, and you do a lot of things you really don't want to do, but you have to do them. I was a military policeman for over four years. It becomes nerve racking after a while, but it's a job that you've chosen, and you have to go along with it.

You were talking about California before. All the cops out there are rednecks.

That's right. They come to California with hatred in them, anyway. I don't know how they pass the examination to get those jobs. I think the only examination they have to pass is to be a redneck. You have to be a redneck to be a trooper in California. That's right. "Let's see how red your neck is—turn around—ah, your neck is red, you got the big freckles on it, you like to whip a nigger, okay get to work."

He's in?

Sure. "Why sure. I've whipped many. Look at the notches in my stick!" I've seen some very mean tricks done out there. . . . Getting back to the music: I don't think the freedom is gonna take it anywhere. In fact, it's dying now. But you don't say that about jazz. Every once in a while jazz gets put in the background a little bit, but all of a sudden everybody runs back and says, where is the jazz, will it come back? Let me pat my feet. Where is the beat at? Can't feel the beat! Ain't no beat there; it's noise!

There was a time when musicians had to go through different bands before they could get a name.

That's right. That's because of the club owners. If they're gonna make some money out of the ignorant public coming in there, then they'll hire the musicians. Some of the club owners who really love good music don't care what the guys are playing as long as they're making money. Like the people who run the Chat Qui Pêche, they don't care whether you're playing well or not. It's how much money they earn. They'll accept all the money and be smiling because they're making money, but deep down inside they say: They aren't musicians, it's just a bunch of noise. But as soon as all that is over, they'll put on some good records and listen to some good music. And walk around and hum the tunes, hum all the breaks in the tunes. But they can't hum those breaks downstairs. They don't know where those breaks are going.

You know where it's at, A.T., you've been doing it for years. There were times in New York when I had an opportunity to go on the bandstand and play but didn't, not because I didn't have the confidence—I had the confidence—but because giants were on the bandstand making such beautiful music, I felt I would rather listen. I'd get plenty of chances to play. It was so beautiful, I didn't think I could have added anything to it. This day and age I feel as though I can add to music when I hear guys playing. I think I have something else that I can say to help make it prettier. In those days when I was trying to forge ahead and play and be a pace setter, at least I wouldn't jump on the bandstand unless I thought I could add something to what was going on. I'd much rather listen to some of that beauty: Charlie Parker, Lester Young, Lucky Thompson, all those beautiful saxophonists. How could you go on the bandstand unless you could really add something beautiful to it?

Joe, you're still bashing on the drums.

I hope Allah gives me strength to continue.

You believe in Allah?

Definitely. All of my life. It's been beautiful. Allah has been beautiful.

—*Paris, October 13, 1969*

≡ DON BYAS

"No such thing as a wrong note."

Who influenced you?

In the beginning, Hawk [Coleman Hawkins]. That sound always stayed with me and never got away. In fact, I think I have a bigger sound now than he had. Apart from that, I dug what he was playing. Art Tatum really turned me on. That's where my style came from . . . style . . . I haven't got any style. I just blow, like Art. He didn't have any style, he just played the piano, and that's the way I play. We were real close, and he loved me. He used to sit down and talk to me and one day he said, "Don, don't ever worry about what you're going to play or where the ideas are going to come from. Just remember there is no such thing as a wrong note." He said, "What makes a note wrong is when you don't know where to go after that one. As long as you know how to get to the next note, there's no such thing as a wrong note. You hit any note you want and it fits in any chord." And that's right! There is no such thing as hitting a wrong note. It's just that when you hit that wrong note, you've got to know how to make it right.

That's when the doors started opening for me musicwise. From that time I started practicing and remembering that and all of a sudden I said, "That's where it is." There's no way you can hit a wrong note, as long as you know where to go after. You just keep weaving and there's no way in the world you can get lost. You hit one. If it's not right, you hit another. If that's not right you hit another one, so you just keep hitting. Now who's going to say you're wrong? You show me anybody who can prove you're wrong. As long as you keep going you're all right, but don't stop, because if you stop you're in trouble. Don't ever stop unless you know you're at a station. If you're at a station then you stop, take a breath and make it to the next station. Tatum turned me onto that. He was a genius. I had been with Tatum for two years on the West Coast. I came to New York in 1935, and we hung out together every night. It was during that time he taught me all those things. I came to New York with Eddie Mallory's band. Mallory's wife, Ethel Waters, opened up in the Cotton Club, Duke Ellington was playing with his band and so was Eddie Mallory, two big bands.

There was nobody playing what I was playing because I played all that stuff from Tatum. That F-sharp, B-natural, E, A, D, G, C, F, like in rhythm, instead of playing rhythm chords. Everybody was saying what is that? Where did this cat come from? Who is he? There weren't any horn players following piano players at that time, so I was ahead of everybody.

Bird [Charlie Parker] got a lot of things from me. I met Bird when he was about fourteen in Kansas City, so I've been knowing him for a long time. Even after Bird got to New York with Jay McShann, we were still real tight, and he used to always come and get me when he wanted to go and jam, which was damn near every night. He would say: "Come on, Don, we're going to play 'Cherokee.'" That was his favorite tune. What people don't know is that Bird got a lot of stuff from me, although he was influenced more by Pres [Lester Young]. Pres was really his boy.

There was another cat, Buster Smith, and somebody else, I forget his name, but those are the cats who influenced Bird. They were all around Kansas City at that time. That was in the early thirties. Bird was a little cat, fourteen years old and blowing! He hadn't developed then. He didn't really start blowing till he got to New York; then he stretched out. That man could blow! You listen to the music now and you ask yourself what people are talking about when they compare somebody with him. Who the hell are you going to compare with Bird? Even Trane [John Coltrane] was influenced by him, although he went much further, but Bird was his idol.

Trane and I were tight. Every time he came to Europe, the first place he would go to, he would ask: "Where is Don Byas?" Always went where I was playing, never said hello. He'd just come in, sneak in. I don't know how this cat did it. He would sit in the club all night long and never move. I wouldn't know he was there. I'd say to myself, that looks like Trane sitting back there. So when the set was over, I would go and ask, "How long have you been here?" He'd say, "I just came in." Trane was something else. You would never know he was in the joint.

Have you ever felt any kind of protest in your music?

I'm protesting now. If you listen you will notice I'm always trying to make my sound stronger and more brutal than ever. I shake the walls in the joints I play in. I'm always trying to sound brutal without losing the beauty, in order to impress people and wake them up. That's protest, of course it is. I've always felt like that. The point is how long will people keep me waiting before they come in. I'm wondering if things will finally come my way before I pop off. Actually right now there aren't that many cats left that are blowing—me and Griff [Johnny Griffin], who else is there? There are a lot of young cats, but I don't even know them. I'm talking about the ones on the top. My form of protest is to play as hard and strong as I can. In other words, you did this and you did that, so now take this!

Do you feel unrewarded for the contribution you made to our music?

Yes, in a way, but I can't say I'm angry, because I split at the top of my success, so actually a lot of it is my fault. I can't get mad at anybody but I can get mad in my music. When I play, I can allow myself to get mad. I split twenty-five years ago. This cat [Calvin Massey, present at the time of the interview] asked me the night before I left, "When are you coming back?" I said, "When they build a bridge!"

You were one of the first musicians to settle in Europe?

I was the first. I came with Don Redman, after the war. I had a beautiful success and made a lot of money. I've just stopped making money during the last three or four years. Things got low. So many cats have come over and are still coming that things have dropped down. There isn't the demand there was before, so that makes it a little rough. I'm not squawkin'. It's just that I'm going to try some different things and see if I can't put a little firecracker under. [Don Byas was expecting to go to Africa with Archie Shepp.] I think it would be nice to change things around a little bit for a while.

I've been going in a straight line for so long, it's not going to hurt me to do that. That tape recorder was on! Yeah, you've got to be a cross-eyed motherfucker to make it in this life.

—Paris, November 11, 1969

≡ RON CARTER ≡

"I think in terms of natural energy."

What do you think is the reason we musicians do not have our own record companies?

One reason, I think, is that musicians have not taken the time to sit down and figure out why they are not making money. None of them seems to know why. I'll give you an example. When I first got involved in publishing-company rights, I was told to go to a lawyer. The lawyer told me that he could get my company set up for fifty dollars. The interview during which we would discuss the setting up of the company would cost me thirty-five dollars an hour. So for eighty-five dollars he would give me a publishing company.

Fortunately, someone I knew told me about another lawyer who did not charge me for the brief ten minute talk we had. I went to a local stationery store, got the same forms a lawyer would have gotten and did everything myself for $7.50. I found out only by refusing to do things the normal way. Until musicians really sit down and figure out why they are not making money, they will never make any and never know why they are not making it.

Well, musicians are always studying and practicing.

They have to learn. You may practice your instrument to a high point of musical proficiency, but there is no point in playing good if someone else always gets the money. That's like a farmer who spends a lifetime learning how to grow wheat, plant it, then lets the farmer next door take all the grain. Or a horticulturist who spends a lifetime figuring out new strains, studying what temperature and what fertilizer is best for this plant, what kind of glass it should have so that the sun comes in just enough; and should he get the ultraviolet glass or should he put a little shade on or should he have water in the room, so the moisture keeps the plant nice. He spends a lifetime figuring out that stuff, man! When he gets to be a real expert, he's not going to let his neighbor, who is not a horticulturist, come in and take all his beautiful plants away and sell them on the market.

It's the same kind of scene, and we musicians have to learn that practicing on our instruments is very important for our performance, but so is being able to afford to play only when we feel like it. It means we can be more creative. If we are forced to create every night, the results can't always be good. I don't care who the artist is. As you know, I've played with most of the big names on the scene. I've seen them forced to create every night whether they felt like it or not. I found out that when they are not under pressure, if they can play when they damn well feel like it, their level of creativity is up by forty percent.

To reach the top level of creativity, you have to be able to control the business end. If you control the press, booking agencies, record dates, publishing companies, music, record royalties, television and radio royalties, you know when you can afford not to work. Until you get this kind of slavery out of your music, it's always going to be a scuffle. There are guys who are forced to play every night because they have only let themselves get involved in playing and have allowed someone else who is not a musician to handle their business. And if you don't play, all you care about is your ten percent. A lot of musicians are victims of their own self-imposed ignorance.

What would be the solution?

I think the younger musician is, in general, better educated. He is going to some kind of music school, he has been allowed to get involved in the classical scene, to check that. BMI and ASCAP have opened up to let him check out what they're into. Whether he gets in or not, it's available for him. He can get his own publishing company now when he feels like it. Before, the companies would never let a guy know that he could start his own publishing company. They would say, We record you, but we must have your music in our company. The cats had no choice. Today, cats have a choice. Younger musicians have all these additional options; they can take on the responsibility of opening up record companies, booking agencies and even nightclubs.

It is up to the younger player to not just be involved in playing.

What happens when his horn is in the case, between sets? Another goal hinges upon the awareness that black colleges must have of our music. I played at some black colleges, and we only got booked because the students raised such a clamor to get some jazz. The people who are in charge, the dean of the school, the dean of music, all the bigwigs were making a point of not encouraging jazz on the campus. This is a tragedy. If you go and play at any nightclub in the world, you'll find that eighty percent of the clientele is nonblack, even in Harlem. Now that this nonblack clientele has other musical interests, such as rock and all the current rock bands, it is no longer so interested in jazz. The clientele has dropped off; therefore the owners' income has dropped, too, so they can only book one or two bands and have to cut their price in order to make it. It's not that jazz musicians have raised their price but that owners are not making the money now they were making ten years ago.

On the other hand, a lot of jazz musicians are playing rock, too, so it encourages that, doesn't it?

It's the only way they can compete against that market.

But doesn't that consolidate the rock market?

Not necessarily. The critics may call it rock, and I guess the public can most easily identify it as rock. I am now teaching a jazz history course at the Manhattan School of Music. In my research I have found that most of the current rock beats are nothing but very poorly executed New Orleans jazz drumming. I think the jazz drummers in particular should be made aware of the original drumbeats. Billy Higgins is a fine example of a New Orleans–beat drummer. He's just playing funeral street beats. But if you listen to the record he made, *The Sidewinder,* with Lee Morgan, it sounds like a rock beat. It is not rock. It is only classified as rock for the commercial value of the term. The guitar players who make jazz records or the jazz bands who hire guitar players to get a rock flavor are playing all rhythm-and-blues licks, which is not rock. Rock today, as the public knows, is nothing but watered down, original B. B. King and Blind Lemon Jefferson. The original field hollers that were stolen by Alan Lomax and released on Vanguard Records in the fifties, jail cries that they played, the seven-bar blues and thirteen-bar blues, Leadbelly [Huddie Ledbetter] and all those cats, are being transferred into white rock bands. All they do is play it louder and much poorer for commercial reasons. I feel that jazz players are not playing rock as the market understands it, but that's what they are going into due to the commercial potential of the term *rock*. They can get work, they may not make much more money, but they improve their chances of greater exposure.

What about your fingers? Do you do any special exercises?

I'm really opposed to specific exercises. You see piano players who sit and tap their fingertips individually on tabletops all day. You see bass players who take a rubber ball or a hand grip. It may give you strength, but it does not give you control; I may not have the strongest physical hand, but I have the ultimate control of all my fingers independent of each other. For me the key word is *finger control* rather than *strength*. Today bass players have been caught up in raising their strings a little higher than normal to get a bigger sound and make their hands stronger. All it does is make their sound less attractive. It makes the sound much harder, but it tires them quickly.

Besides, when a string is that taut, it cannot vibrate to its normal length, because the note is physically shorter. The decay period for this note is shorter than if they were to lower the bridge, say, an eighth of an inch. When the string is not so tight, it vibrates much more freely and is much longer. This makes the body of the bass, which is nothing but a big sound chamber, vibrate at much more frequent vibrations, so you get a much warmer sound. This is my thing. I try to get as warm a sound as I can and use as little physical effort as possible to produce it.

It must take some strength.

Not necessarily. I think it boils down to knowing how much energy it takes to hold the string to the fingerboard without rattling. I call it energy. Energy means a force. If you just drop your arms down and let them relax, you'll feel the gravity pulling your hands down. That's force. That doesn't mean you're strong; it's a natural energy. When you say strength, everybody does this: They clench a fist and get real tense. All you do is get tired.

I think in terms of the natural energy which is already there, and applying this natural energy to the bass to get the most natural sound I can. Bass players are into the thing of pressing down as hard as they can. Let me give you a little scientific example. Take a twenty-ton TNT explosion: You get X-Y-Z decibels in sound. Now if you take a forty-ton TNT explosion, you only get ten. The bigger the explosion, the more the atoms cancel one another out, so you get a smaller sound effect. Bass players who play so hard with both right and left hands are generally feeding more vibrations into the bass than the bass can tolerate. So they just cancel one another out; the sound comes out smaller. The trick is to find at what level of physical energy you can expand to get the maximum sound without overfeeding the bass with these physical vibrations.

Pound for pound, I'm probably not the strongest physical player, but I'll go out on the limb and say that I doubt there is another player who has more independence and coordination than I have. I dare say that if you could measure my sound vibration against the strongest player, his sound would not match mine in color, in length or in strength. A strong, penetrating sound. Miles is not a very strong player—not like some trumpet players we could think of—but his sound is so intense that it seems stronger than it is. It's incredible, man! That's my approach to the instrument, getting the most out of it by exerting the minimum physical effort.

Bass players are required to play all night. You are back there chomping. The piano player lays out and the horn player goes to the bar and has a drink, so the bass player and the drummer got it. There must be some way of performing to your maximum level without having to fall out between sets. I've seen cats do it, and you have, too. They are physically exhausted. I may not work a gig for a month, but because I think in relaxed terms, I can play as long as a bass player who has worked every night for the same period. What I hear I try to match not by overplaying, but by finding how much underplaying I can do and still get the big sound I have been identified with. That's gotten to be my trademark—a big, fat sound. When they start paying bass players by the pound, I start getting worried. Right now it's by the sound, so I have a little while to go.

What do you think about electronics being used in the music?

When you were coming up and when I first got to New York, the thing was to swing. Because it was loud, it didn't mean it was swinging. Now we have got caught up in the back-to-rock syndrome, all the rock bands play as loud as they can. They get amplifiers as big as this room. But it is slowly going out of fashion for three reasons: Number one, they have found out that just because it's loud doesn't mean it's good; number two, it's hard to play loud all night and create some of the moods that they're used to creating when they play at different volume levels; number three, I hate to blame anybody, but the responsibility for the increase in volume levels should be laid to the drummers. Elvin [Jones] and Tony [Williams], who play beautifully, along with other guys who have followed in their footsteps, found it necessary to play louder to get their thing across. The point the other drummers miss is that Tony and Elvin don't always play loud.

Music is in a circle; it's going back to swing. Right now bands are meandering, trying to check out the rock path. I came to New York about a year before freedom really got hot. If you check which bands are functioning now, playing the same music, you'll be surprised to see how few are left. One of them is Archie Shepp, another is Ornette, but he works so infrequently I can't really count him. He is not really into the six-nights-a-week gig style anymore. Those are the only two I can think of who were in freedom when it first started and who are still around. There must be a thousand records in New York made by freedom bands which are still on the shelf because that style is gone. What you have now is a conglomeration of 1953–55 be-bop, 1963–65 Miles Davis and 1969 rock Beatle-style tunes, along with the Ornette Coleman avant-garde.

But the avant-garde is slowly fading away. It will leave its mark, and it's a very valid mark, but the number of musicians who were playing avant-garde when it first came out has diminished incredibly. The players who still play really free find less and less work, because the audiences have tolerated it as long as they can. They want to be able to go home and say, I can remember this phrase. Unless you are an acute listener and unless it is played very well, freedom is hard to relate to when you are not in that environment. If you hear some guy play freedom who does not know be-bop and is not hip to swing, he is just playing off the top of his head. He's not really as free as someone with a musical background.

I'm not opposed to playing free. I do it myself. But I make the freedom more logical because of my previous musical background, which I can build upon. It's gotten to the point now when people say they like to hear children of ten or twelve play because they hear complete freedom. But how can they be free while being so limited? It's like saying you can paint this room any color you want, but you must stay in this room. That limits your freedom to one room. You can play as free as you want, only you should have some kind of musical background to relate to this freedom. Otherwise you're putting yourself into a corner.

If I have the choice, I like to swing any day. Freedom has its place in music and it is as valid as black power, gefilte fish, pizza or a coat and hat in the wintertime. It depends on your attitude to music at that point. If you can adjust your attitude at that moment, it's beautiful. A lot of drummers can't swing, and a lot of freedom bass players can't play changes. If you give them an F-seventh chord, most of them cannot play it. If you give them a string of changes, like a tune that has nothing but chords, most of them cannot play the tune according to those chords. So in order to work, in order to express what they call their musical creativity, they're forced to play free in some form. Freedom for them is valid, but it still is a way out. This is all they can do musically.

The Miles Davis quintet was free in terms of 1955 be-bop. There was a time when we made a one-bar chord into a two-bar chord. We would set it up and, while you felt the change, you would feel it in a happy way. You wouldn't say damn, what is that? You wouldn't turn it off.

All of a sudden black-studies programs have been getting hot. Everybody is a black-music authority. A lot of them aren't, as you know. Two things disturb me. Number one, in the black-studies programs they're interested in art, drama, playwriting, poetry and dance. No one mentions music, though music is the black man's only contribution to the United States besides slave labor. Right? The other thing is that when a college is besieged by so-called militant black students and liberal white students to get a black-studies program going, they grab the first black cat they see, hoping he can do the job. Personally I would like to go out and lecture two days a week at various colleges. I feel that I've done enough research into black music to give lectures and defy someone to question my authenticity or my sources of information. I can give them book, chapter and verse off the top of my head and be right to the nearest paragraph. It's one thing to go out there and be flamboyant and hope they don't call your hand. It's another matter to go out there with your text under your wig and defy them to check you out. I'd like to get involved in that someday and give lectures on jazz.

I call it jazz though I know where the word comes from: It means "intercourse." Down South they believe it was short for a guy named Charles: Chas. Then it went to Chicago in 1919, and they called it the Original New Orleans Dixieland Chas Band. I know all that stuff, so I'm not uptight about the word *jazz*. To me it's just a title, but if you know what the title represents to you as a black person, as a musician and as a contributor to the world's cultural scene, that's what's important. To get bogged down over four letters means you're missing the point. People get involved with the term because this is as far as they can go with the topic.

It's just like a drummer talking to you while you're trying to get him to play a few licks so you can check him out. I've had this experience with bass players, too, so if I say drummer it's all the same. I've had bass players come to me interested in learning some of my hip licks. So I'll tell them, well, if I show them to you, you can't play them because you lack facility. It isn't so much the notes I play as where I decide to play them. They'll get so involved in my hip licks that they will miss the point of how I got to play these hip licks by spending eight hours a day studying. Right? Now, I'm relating that to people who get involved in saying don't call our music jazz, call it something else. They are either unwilling or unable to look beyond the term *jazz* and get really involved in what the music itself has contributed to them as a people, what it has given their country and the world in terms of culture. It's superficial; it's a blindfold.

White universities are so uptight about black students, and they're feeling such guilt—as well they might for the four hundred years of deprivation that the black man has undergone. The black man may go through another four hundred years of it, no matter how liberal whites are becoming, because they're getting so uptight. They go out and grab any black person and let him fill the role. A lot of black cats are not qualified to fill that role. I only hope that they don't become so unqualified that they blow everything for everybody else. Also, I recently found out that for some strange reason—and maybe this applies to painting, sculpture and architecture—whenever there has been a major change in jazz, there's been a major change in everything else afterward. It's incredible how it happens. Freedom music to me represents the younger musicians getting tired of the establishment. The establishment to me is chord progressions and a thirty-two bar form. The student radicals are like the freedom jazz players who want to bypass most of the present standards for playing a tune. They want to play a nine-bar phrase and feel comfortable. A student feels that if he doesn't want to go to school for a week, he can and not get put out, as long as he can pass the course when the test comes. But the establishment says you must go to school X days or hours a week and you're only allowed a certain number of cuts per semester.

In 1959, when Ornette Coleman hit New York, he predicted this social change musically. You can relate the Charlie Parker era to this, also. And you can relate the Dixieland–Louis Armstrong style to the emergence of the black man trying to get free from the slavery he was under.

Do you think kids have a greater awareness today than we did?

I think so, for several reasons. Communications are a lot quicker than they were when the first TV came out. Now you can shoot a bullet in Japan and it can be heard in New York within half an hour. News is instantaneous. Kids always keep abreast of whatever is happening as soon as it happens. For centuries the black male was always suppressed by white society. He couldn't get a job. When he was qualified, they wouldn't let him get a job. The head of the family was often the woman, who could go out and do days. They kept the black male emasculated for over four hundred years. The black male has not yet reached but is reaching some form of manhood; the first place he asserts it is at home. The first people to feel this assertion are his children.

When I was coming up, if I went to a department store, I was always told, "Don't touch anything, keep your hands in your pockets." And I would, too. "Don't touch a thing. It's not for you to touch; just leave it alone." Or we would be afraid to go to a certain movie house if we weren't with a bunch of other black cats. We might have got beaten up. Or we weren't allowed to go into many clubs in black Harlem, because they were owned and patronized by white people. All those clubs up and down Seventh and Lenox avenues were patronized by people from outside the community. Now when my son goes into a department store, I say to him: "Look, whatever you see, you can touch it. And if someone talks to you about touching it, you come and tell me. If you break something, I'll pay for it even if I have to teach school tomorrow." I don't let white society get him uptight.

They used to say, If you're white you're right, if you're brown step around, if you're black get back. I told my son that was out. I said, "If you feel like you want to go to a movie and you have the money to go, go, because I'm backing your play." I symbolize the black male breaking his chains after four hundred years. I let my son know that there are several things in the world which have been created by black people alone. He must learn black history. A good example is TV, which has a lot of influence all over the world. When you see a cowboy show, they show you all-white cowboys. So I said, "If you must watch TV, I have to go and buy you books." I went to Michaux, a very well known bookstore in Harlem, where they sell all the African literature. I got him two books on black cowboys.

You can check it out if you want to, but this is what really happened. There was a guy called Bill Picket who was so bad that when he would get into a town, the sheriff would tell everybody, don't mess with this man because he is notorious. He made Jesse James look like a faggot, according to an account I read. Jesse James is like a big hero now. This guy was a bitch. He was like the Miles Davis of the cowboys. So I let my son know we have a history, too.

They always tell you about Columbus discovering America, Edison inventing electric light and Bell inventing the telephone. But did you know that the first open-heart surgery was done by a black man in Chicago? Did you know that traffic lights were invented by a black man? Did you know the first shoe-lasting machine was made by a black man? Or that a black man called Du Sable founded Chicago? The architect who laid out Washington, D.C., was black. Blood plasma was done by Charles Drew.

I let my son know he has a history behind him so he can go out with his chest stuck out and his head held up high. All we knew was Jack Armstrong, the all-American boy, and Washington throwing the dollar across the Delaware river, which he couldn't have done. There's enough stuff in our history to be proud of. It used to be Sears and Roebuck, and Sears forced Roebuck out of business. Roebuck was a black man. Another black man invented a hip refrigerator that would make General Electric and Kelvinator obsolete, but they wouldn't let him in. This happens to white Americans as well; you occasionally hear about that, like the guy Tucker in Detroit they froze out. But you don't hear about this guy with the refrigerator. So I let my son know he has a heritage, too. As a matter of fact, the other day one of the students brought a bagpipe to school. I said to Ron Jr., "The bagpipe they tell you is from Scotland. It comes from northern Africa, in fact. It was made from a goat's udder and some reeds. When the Portuguese and Scottish traders invaded Africa, they took a lot of things with them—slaves, land rights, government, as well as the music, which included the bagpipe. It was originally an African instrument. The vibes, that's an African instrument too."

—Paris, December 4, 1969

☰ JOHNNY GRIFFIN ☰

"I'm not really from this planet."

What is your reason for living in Europe all these years?

I'm trying to save my life, 'cause it's a cinch that if I had stayed in America, I would be dead by now. I was a stoned zombie when I left.

Can you be more explicit?

I don't have to be more explicit about saving my life. The events that were happening to me were too much. It was too negative.

What's so positive about European society?

I'm not involved in it, that's what so positive about it. I'm a tourist. Just look at my passport.

Come on now, Griff.

You're a tourist, too. We're both tourists. Right now we're on the Channel Islands working, but we're tourists.

That's the truth. When I came to Europe on that first gig in December 1962, I was actually coming here to make some bread for my family for Christmas. Instead of staying six or seven weeks like I was supposed to, I stayed three months. I went back for my kid's birthday instead of going to Copenhagen for the next gig. I went from London back to New York, and as soon as I got off the plane, I felt like I was doomed. I said: "What am I doing back here?" I just realized how negative everything was.

I didn't know it before, but I had been away those three months, not that I had such crazy experiences in Europe. I got a chance to play with Bud [Powell] and Kenny Drew in Paris. I went to some other places and I played with some European musicians. It wasn't too kosher, but I had gotten away from that

American pressure for a minute. The same pressures are in Europe, but the American pressure is just too much.

When I went back to work with the cats, everybody was back to the same thing I grew up with, but I didn't know any better. Everybody is the Great I Am, I am this and you ain't that. It's all me, *M-E,* and nobody else is anything. It was too much for me. I wanted to get away from it all. That was black, white and indifferent!

They've got all the black musicians on the run. Black musicians all over Europe, running away from America. But that's part of the white power structure that's killing us and our music. Just like they killed it with all that so-called cool school, West Coast jive. They sold us down the line. Took the music out of Harlem and put it in Carnegie Hall and downtown in those joints where you've got to be quiet. The black people split and went back to Harlem, back to the rhythm and blues, so they could have a good time. Then the white power structure just kicked the rest of us out and propagated what they call avant-garde. Those poor boys can't blow their way out of a paper bag musically. But the white power structure said they're geniuses, So-and-so is the natural extension of Charlie Parker. That's what they waited for. As soon as Bird died, everybody turned left, Bird had given them the message. They were so glad to see Bird gone, because he was the truth. I don't mean they all turned left, I mean the critics had a breathing spell so they could finish killing us. If it wasn't for the revolution that's taking place, they would probably be writing in fifty years that jazz was all white.

You were telling me you liked Charles Tolliver's playing.

But look where I met Charles Tolliver. Why didn't I meet him in America? He's talking about staying over there six months and over here six months. After a while those six months will be nine months over here and three months over there. Look at Art Farmer and Benny Bailey, Idrees Sulieman and Shihab, they've been over here all these years. Look at all those great musicians. Look how long Kenny Clarke has been over here and the late Sydney Bechet. There are a few cats back there like Freddie Hubbard and Joe Henderson—they're fantastic. But it seems like there has been a cutoff. They've killed it. When I think of my kids and other kids growing up today and they're going to listen to avant-garde, what are they going to study for avant-garde? Antimusic, how not to play?

What about critics? Do they affect you by what they say or write about you?

Of course they affect me, if I read them. I have emotions like anybody else. I don't read them very much. I get an article sometimes, if it's nice, I send it to my mother. I think the critics messed Trane [John Coltrane] up. Messed Newk [Sonny Rollins] up, too. What are they criticizing, anyway? They don't know anything about jazz. They're not jazz musicians. And besides, they're all white. So what are they going to know about black music? White-controlled press, *Downbeat* and before that *Metronome*. Remember how badly they used to write about Bird? Twenty years later they said Bird was a genius, after he was dead. They aren't doing anything but confusing the issue. They're just part of that structure.

Bud Powell seems to have gotten lost in the shuffle. They don't mention him much anymore.

They don't want to mention Bud, because Bud was the truth, just like Bird. Bud was a part of Bird. We're talking about our music, which is called jazz. Already that is a bastard word. The ofay called it jazz. Which has a negative connotation. I'm speaking about Afro-American music. They want to destroy the whole thing. Bud Powell was great; he was a genius. I came to Europe, and in the first interview I had in Paris, when I was asked who influenced me or who were great jazz musicians in my life, I said, Art Tatum, and the man told me Art Tatum wasn't a jazz musician. Now this is a Frenchman telling me this. What the hell does he know about it? So it's not only America; everywhere it's just like that. They want to kill it. I don't know who he's going to say is a jazz musician if Art Tatum was not. That's ridiculous, 'cause Bud comes out of Art Tatum. All those cats can play the piano come out of Art Tatum. Even the horns, 'cause I use Tatum's things like Don Byas. I used to say Don was the Tatum of the saxophone. Until I spoke to Don recently, I didn't know how close he had been with Tatum. As a kid coming up, I could hear something in it. Now twenty years later I find out that Don was around Tatum and he was using his harmonic solutions.

What do you think about me trying to write this book?

I think it's fantastic if they let you put it out, if you live long enough to put it out. I think it's a good thing. You'll get a chance to get to the musicians, 'cause the musicians will talk in front of you. They will say things to you they really mean. Otherwise they won't get a chance to be heard.

Musicians know what's happening to them. Nobody can follow them around and see what's going on. What successful black musicians have really stood up for their people that the white power structure has allowed to come through? Can you name me one who is successful who has been militant or said anything worth recording or writing down that's supposed to be so hip? I can't think of one. They're all part of that same bourgeoisie. White middle class, black middle class, trying to copy the white middle class cancer of the fall of the Roman Empire. Misconceptions of the teachings of the prophet Jesus Christ. That's what's wrong with the whole Western world I've been in, the Western Hemisphere civilization, so to speak. All this mess has got to go. It's all a mess. I'm here in Europe because it's a little lighter on me than it is in America. But it's the same thing. You don't have thirty-five or forty million black have-nots over here like you have in America. But you have them here, because I see them sweeping the streets of Paris and Holland. It's the black man's ass up in the air. He's stooping down picking up the dirt everywhere. The main thing is I'm here because I did something wrong on my planet. I'm not really from this planet. I did something wrong on my planet and they sent me here to pay my dues. I figure pretty soon my dues should be paid, and they're going to call me back home so I can rest in peace.

You're not serious about that, are you?

I can't be from this place, Arthur. There is no love here, and I love people. All I see is hate around me, except for a few of my friends. That's what's wrong with the earth today. Black and white on this planet, there is no love, there is only hate. I was thinking about reading some books on anarchy, because all this government stuff is b.s. anyway. These governments drawing lines between men, tribes between tribes. Yellow people against brown people against black against Muslims against Christians against Hindus. What is all of that? I know I'm not from this planet; I can't be. I must be from someplace else in the universe because I'm a total misfit. I can't get with none of this.

What do you think about protest in music?

I learned how to play music for the beauty that I could derive from compositions and for the catharsis that it gives me when I am able to express myself. That's why I study my instrument—so I can play it better and I am better able to express myself. For me to take my saxophone and make squawks like chickens or elephant sounds is the worst thing I could do. I would stop playing. I'm always talking about using my horn like a machine gun, but not to kill anybody. I want to shoot them with notes of love. I want them to laugh. I want to give them something positive. I'm not playing music for a negative purpose, 'cause that's like a cancer. I'm not studying music to give myself cancer. I'm playing my horn to bring out the positive things in people so they can enjoy what I'm doing. Actually, if I'm too negative I can't even play. I can play, actually, because as soon as I start playing, music takes me away from all this b.s. around me. In fact, music is the thing that saves me. It's my relief. It takes me away from all this black, white, yellow and brown and you're lighter than me; and I've got more money than you; and my car is longer than yours; my old lady is finer than yours; I'm a better pimp than you; my cocaine is more pure than yours.

What do you do to relax when you are away from music?

I read a lot. I read everything I can get my hands on for self-betterment. Recently I've been reading the Koran. I'm very interested in Islam. It's a very beautiful religion. Before that I was reading Hindu philosophy, and I've read about Zen Buddhism, too. I was brought up as a Baptist and a Methodist in Chicago. I read all kinds of self-help books such as *Positive Thinking*. All this stuff is psyche. When I was feeling very bad in New York, I put a sign on my wall in the hotel room, And this too shall change, letting me know that bad as I was feeling, it was going to change—for the better or for the worse. When I was feeling my worst, I'd look in the mirror at myself and say, "Griffin, tomorrow you are going to feel better, boy," and I would go to bed; and through the years I psyched myself and I feel much better. I think I feel pretty groovy.

Who was your first influence on the saxophone?

I have to say two musicians, because they are so much alike, except that they play two different saxophones: Johnny Hodges and Ben Webster. I was playing alto and with a little tempo I'd try to get that big sound like Ben had and play rough. If we played a ballad, I'd try to emulate Johnny Hodges's sweetness. It's the same thing, that Ellington sound. I think it all comes from Sidney Bechet. I found out later on that Johnny Hodges was kind of a Bechet protégé. Bechet had played with Duke first.

When I must have been about fourteen years old, they had a house party at my cousin's. They put this record on by Jay McShann, with Walter Brown singing the blues. I think it was the "Hootie Blues." Bird played a solo, and that stopped me dead in my tracks. I went to the same school Gene Ammons had gone to, and he influenced me, along with Dexter Gordon.

Of course, all that influence actually came from the father of the swing tree: Pres [Lester Young], who influenced Bird. He was actually one of the greatest. I mean other than Coleman Hawkins, who rescued the saxophone from the oblivion of the circus. Pres, my man, who is the trunk of the swing tree from whence came Bird, Dexter and Ammons.

Then Don Byas also had a definite influence on me. I liked the way he mastered his instrument. Like I said before, I thought of him as being the Art Tatum of the saxophone. The strongest influence on me would be Charlie Parker. Bird was the greatest messenger. I wanted to be original, so I was afraid to hang out with saxophone players. I spent my time hanging out with pianists. I learned my lessons from Bud Powell, Elmo Hope and Thelonious Monk. I walked the streets with them in the forties.

Most of my musical knowledge came from them and from Fats Navarro. I used to hang out with Fats, my man. Fats, Brownie [Clifford Brown] and Dizzy Gillespie with his big bands, cats with power. Hot jazz. Hot, fun-loving jazz. Hot, colored jazz. Hot Afro-jazz.

But talking about horn players, they aren't playing with rhythm, at least not the ones I know. Maybe there are some avant-garde musicians who can play, but I have yet to hear them. As for pure musicianship, they sound like children. I've been listening to these cats for years and I say what's happening, am I getting old and can't I hear music, am I getting left behind? I've been listening to this for years and years, and it still repulses me just like the first day I heard it. I ask them, and they say they're playing because of what society has done to them and they want to express it. But I can't understand why they want to express it in music. Why don't they take some pistols and shoot the society? Go to war. But how are you going to go to war with a saxophone?

What about money?

Money is the god. That's the white power structure's god—money. They worship money, and they will suffer for it, because Allah will see to that. When they die, it's not over. Some of them pay during this lifetime. You've seen them get cancer just when they think they're going to spend all that money they've gotten from black slave labor. They think they're going to spend it but get cancer and die. You've seen it in New York and you've seen it in Europe. You see some of the ones with money live to an old age and die. But they've got to face the Maker. In this universe there's always balance one way or the other. When you die, it's not over. You got to pay. We all must pay for our individual doings. I'm a firm believer in individualism. I believe an individual must pay for what he does in life, good, bad or indifferent. What's that saying? What goes around comes around.

You just came back from Scandinavia. Do you still have as good a time as when we used to go up there together?

You know what we were doing up there. There is but so much of that you can do. It's all the same. I had a nice time up there seeing the people again, but it wasn't like when we used to go up there. In the first place, I have my old lady down here, and I'm not chasing after those broads up there. Which is one reason we were having such a ball, 'cause there were so many broads up there. We thought we could have them all. All those polar bears up there. We thought we could have them all and kill ourselves. When we would leave Scandinavia, we would be ready for the hospital, pour us on the plane.

Do you think people's early training reflects in their later life?

Of course it does. Don't you think their training as children has anything to do with what they do when they become adults? During their formative years you don't think it means anything?

When Hitler brought up all those children as Hitler Youths and made soldiers out of them so that they marched all over killing everybody, don't you think that had anything to do with their training as Hitler Youths? They have societies like that in America: the Minutemen, the Ku Klux Klan—how do you think they're bringing their children up? The only thing that can save them is some of the young people in these Western societies. I don't know what's going to save those sad communists behind the Iron Curtain. When I look in those people's eyes, they have no spirit. I could have no part of communism. It is the saddest thing I've ever seen. They're dead to start with.

The young people that are revolting against these Western societies, the students on the campuses, they're going against this middle-class stuff their parents have been trying to instill in them. That's why they're having all these riots on the campuses. These kids don't want to know about it. All that Vietnam for the military-industrial complex. They don't want to be going to Asia killing brown people or to the Dominican Republic and the Congo. They want to live a life of love. But their parents have been living a life where everything is money.

It goes right back to that money. Keep the machine running. When the American economy dips, they go to war. It's easy for them to manufacture a war, start a war anywhere. Look at the American economy through the years and after World War II. I was in the Korean thing. I lived through it, but all the black cats that left from Chicago with me got burned. The only thing that saved me was they put me in the band in Hawaii. Just before that you could see the economy was dipping around 1950. You dig it?

I was in New York with no gigs. Musicians are the first ones to know when there is no money. Then as soon as that war got to cookin', there was money; 1951–53, you were working with Bud, right? Before that I was around Bud, and he wasn't working at all. When I came out of the service, everything went along for a few years. They ran the French out of Indochina. The Americans took up the slack. The economy dipped around 1960, so they went back to war in Vietnam. Money—money—money! Lives mean nothing. 'Specially when it's Asians or Africans. Or when it gets right down to the fact, white people kill each other, too. They don't care. Money is money! Money is god. All conspiracies. Look at the Middle East. Look at the Jews and the Arabs fighting each other. These people belong to the same race. They're all Semites. It's money that has Israel and all those countries divided up. The British and the French divided it up when they took it away from the Turks.

Look how they divided Africa. They just sat down and said well, King Leopold, you can have the Congo, all that is yours. The British: well, we can have Sudan, we can have Egypt, we can have Saudi Arabia and all the oil over there. And the French: you can have Algeria and Tunisia, and the Italians, you can have Libya and the Germans can have southwest Africa and the Portuguese can have Mozambique and Angola, and the Dutch were cool 'cause they had Indonesia and the British had India and they were all kicking China in the ass.

Dig that? I'm telling you I'm from another planet. I'm paying my dues, and they're going to call me home soon, I hope. The only thing I'm sorry about is that I miss my family; I haven't seen my kids. I tell you, I'm frightened to go back to America. For some reason they might keep me there or I might get stuck. I'll go back, but I don't know when that's going to be. Things will have to change for me to go back. I miss my friends and my family. But after that, actually, for me you could erase America off the map. I'm just a passport carrier. I'm an American because I was born there. I'm a man without a country. I'm a tourist over here, but I can't go home. Now what is that? It's a sorry plight. That's the truth.

Like when I saw Nixon honoring Duke Ellington, I thought Duke is a great musician, after all these years he needs to have his honors and things. But Nixon, of all people! That's politics. They're all slaves. I'm telling you we're on the run, just like Dizzy Reece said. They'll have us out on the desert hunting us down.

You know we've been trying to find someplace to go and live. Everybody's looking: Where can we go? I don't know where to go. It's just that black people have this inherent feeling to laugh. They couldn't beat it out of us in slavery. That's why we can laugh. That's why we're so strong. But they're killing us. Anybody who says a word of truth or does anything truthful is on the run. They're either in jail or they get killed or they're in exile.

I'm over here because I'm trying to save my life. I had drunk so much, had used up everything, was all messed up with my woman and everything was so fouled up, I could see nothing clearly. I said, I've got to get out of here. God bless Babs Gonzales. He

I have to, because that's the given name for the music.

Some people think it should be canceled.

Yeah, what it should be and what it isn't is a matter of who controls what. If you control the media you can change the dictionary and put in, "Our form of music is a black experience. It was originated by black people and it should be called Afro-American music"; something like that would be cool. But how the hell are we going to print dictionaries to change the word *jazz?* You know what the definition of jazz is in Webster's dictionary. It's a matter of control. They made a lot of money off the music. That's what they wanted to call it, and that's what it is. Jazz is a derivative of music which was played in the brothels of New Orleans.

Do you like to travel and play in different countries?

Yeah, I like to travel. I like to bring the music to different people. The purest form of it I can bring. 'Cause our music has been clouded so much, dirtied, washed out and dried by the people who are in control of it. Until we gain control over our music, it's always going to be like that. A few players become household names and make a lot of money: Louis Armstrong, Lionel Hampton, Bird, Miles, Dizzy. Yet they don't own any of it—they don't own the record companies which put out their records. They don't own the publishing companies which publish their music. They don't own the magazines which criticize their music.

Do people in other fields of music own these things?

They certainly do. Take Herb Alpert, for instance. He took a form of our music, put it together, promoted it, directed it and made millions off it, formed a record company, publishing company and anything else you want to name. If he wanted to he could start his own magazine to say that his music is the best music in the world.

The way I look at things, if you do something, you do it, that's all.

We know that if you do something, you do it. Musicians know it, but the public is gullible, and if they're reading about such and such a musician in magazines, they're influenced by it. They were influenced by what they read when they went out and bought Bird's records.

The people in control know because they study, and that's their thing—technical evaluation. They know true art form when they hear it, individuals who are playing pure and true. Their thing is also manipulation. When it suits their fancy to turn something into another way of gaining more money, they do that because they're in control. Bird would have got through 'cause he was playing pure and true, and that would have been recognized, no matter what. But he still didn't own a damn thing when he died.

Can you think of any one thing a musician might do which you would dislike?

Not listen. If you have gone through the period of apprentice-ship, trial and error, of learning the right thing to do, and you then get on the bandstand and don't listen, it's detrimental to what's going on, it's self-defeating. Everybody has got to listen. The worst thing a musician can do is not listen.

You have referred to control many times.

The reason we went immediately into that is because what we have now, what we are witnessing, what we are part of and what we are affected by is the result of lackadaisical attitudes in the twenties, the thirties and the forties, when this music became prominent, when people started listening to it and coming out to hear the musicians they had been reading about. Many of the artists were lackadaisical about that. They were just interested in playing. I don't want to leave only a musical legacy but something material, a foundation for the youth to draw from. This is done in all other art forms except ours.

What do you think about drug addiction and alcoholism among musicians?

It's a by-product that's skimming off this particular art form. You just have to be strong enough to let it skim past you and try not to let it affect you. 'Cause it's always gonna be there. Some cats say the establishment put it out there to help break us down, but I can't say that. It's just something that's tangent to our particular art form. You find doctors, lawyers, people in all sorts of professions who are drug addicts but who can afford it. Our particular art form is so low in its financial thing, that the artists affected by it can't afford it; therefore you have a state.

How do you like the new music?

Some of it is good rhythmically, melodically and harmonically. It has to grow on you. All true art forms assimilate the good elements of anything new, retain them and throw out the rest. Most of it is trash and has been thrown out, as far as I'm concerned.

Do you listen to a lot of music?

Yeah, all sorts of music.

How much do you think you're influenced by what you listen to?

I think I'm influenced by all of it. How much I couldn't say. But I retain the good things that come out of anything I listen to.

Do you think musicians copy each other?

Naturally; copying exists in any art form. What counts is the way you copy. If you listen to certain musicians as a youngster, you'll be influenced by them, and naturally you're going to come out sounding like them when you start to play music. Then it's up to you to innovate out of that. Bird did the same.

Do you prefer to play in clubs or concerts?

Well, I much prefer concerts today, because the people come knowing that they've got to pay attention. They're going to a concert, they're going to be seated and they are there to listen to what's going on. At clubs you have to win people's attention a lot of times. Still, I like all of it. All of it gives me an opportunity to stretch out and see where the people are at.

Do you believe in integration?

We're already integrated, so why should I believe in it? It's a fact. We have always been integrated. That word *integration* is used by people in control to separate the poor from the rich, you know, blacks and whites. There's some sort of coalition going on now to get the poor people of all races together. I think a few people who control the world with their money are uptight about that.

Do you dig the Beatles?

It's funny, I've never given the Beatles any thought. Not from the moment they came out until now, when they have all those millions. Because it was something planned and executed long before the Beatles came to America, which is where they really made their big thing. They were promoted, promoted and promoted. Anything that's promoted will sell to the masses.

Their music hasn't affected me at all. Thousands of Afro-American themes and music would have succeeded if given the proper direction. The only credit I can give the Beatles is that they were well directed and produced. I don't have to listen to their music.

What effect did John Coltrane's music have on you?

Tremendous, rhythmically, harmonically and melodically. Any musician knows exactly what I'm talking about. If they are not musicians, I'm sorry.

Who influenced your style on the trumpet?

It's hard to say. There were three people who my particular style sorta came out of: Kenny Dorham, Clifford Brown and Freddie Hubbard. I would also say I was influenced by Louis Armstrong's tone just as much as I was by those three people. Louis is one of the truly great musicians whose talent was adequately directed and produced. He started long ago. He's been a millionaire many times over. So there has been plenty of time for him to get rich. The Beatles, who were in their twenties, got rich overnight. That's the difference.

Where did you study music?

I never studied music. I went to college for three years to become a pharmacist and I canceled on that.

You taught yourself?

Right.

Does what's written about you affect you?

Not at all. I would prefer it if those so-called critics of our music didn't write one damn word about me. The first chance I get, I'll tell them so, and also tell them that we're going to have our own publications one day to pass the word on truthfully about what's going on. There are no critics except musicians. We have critics who are musicians, and they try and play our music. I'm not going to get into a racial thing, but they're all white. They try to play our music, and they wind up criticizing it. They feed off each other. A lot of the biographical information in the books they write is true and a lot of it is not.

Do you have a booking agent?

Yes, me!

You never had a booking agent?

No. I can't afford to give them ten or fifteen percent for something I can do myself, 'specially when you have a band where you're talking about collectivism.

Do you think boxing is comparable to music?

It is to our music, to Afro-American music. Boxing is a ballet, it's *batterie,* it's like the drums and it has continuity like a musical piece.

Do you do any kind of exercise?

Once in a while I try to do a little yoga. I stand on my head and let the blood go the other way. That's about it. I used to be very athletic in high school, as most of us did. Music takes you in another direction unless you really discipline yourself.

Would you say that our form of music stems from black experience in a racist society?

Well, it stemmed from that. We certainly are the innovators of this particular type of music. The only thing for us to do now is to gain control over it—by doing what we've been doing for the last few years; by becoming more aware of ourselves socially, culturally, politically; by being aware of the fact that ownership carries a lot of weight in today's world. You have to own something. We own the musical value, but we don't own the music itself or the direction of the music.

We're playing, and everybody knows who can play. We needn't fight about that. But we should fight together to control it. One of the tricks of the people in control is to keep us uptight against each other—about who's the best on this instrument, who's the best on that instrument, and this or that opinion poll. The result is that we don't have time to think about ownership.

How do you like the way musicians are integrating rock music into our music?

It's good. It has its place in what we're doing, commercially speaking. If you really want to make a lot of money with the proper direction, you can do that and still play your ass off. Cannonball [Adderley] proved that.

Do you find that some musicians overplay?

I don't call it overplaying so much as overenthusiasm. I think of a musician who overplays as being a little more enthusiastic about what he's doing than somebody else would be when playing the same thing. I don't know if it can be detrimental; it's a matter of how you take it.

Did you think you would be successful when you started playing the trumpet?

Yes, when I picked up the trumpet, I knew I would be able to play it. So that gave me satisfaction.

Is everything you play your own music?

Practically. Or else music by other great Afro-American musicians. Our predecessors, only our music.

What's your reason for that?

We are now getting to a point where we own our music, so if we record our own songs or each other's songs, the money will come back financially speaking. Personally and musically, it's the best music to play. We're writing it, so why not play it? I like some of the standard songs outside our music which have been used through the years. Bird played the hell out of them.

Do you think the method used during the Charlie Parker era will be used much longer?

That's the only method to use to play anything advanced. If you don't go through Bird and the cats before him, you're not gonna play, period. And I mean really play it! Play me some be-bop, play it! Anything else is bullshit. End of subject!

—Paris, March 7, 1970

≡ EDDIE LOCKJAW DAVIS ≡

"Music has always been a universal language."

Is that story true about you hanging your horn over the bar in your house and retiring?

Yes, it is. The music business had got sluggish, and I was beginning to work in places with people who I felt weren't contributing anything to music. I decided I would do better in the administrative part, and I did that for two and a half years. I went into the booking business. It was fascinating, because I was booking some of the places where I had worked with a group and booking a lot of people I had worked with. It became a challenge, because some of the people in the office thought I would tend to be partial to and book jazz artists only.

In the booking scheme of things, it's not who you book. You have a territory to book. What counted was for me to familiarize myself with the talent we had to book. They had quite a few rock artists, which was very painful. I did it, though, because I wanted to be impartial, and the end result was that I booked more rock artists than jazz artists. We had more rooms that were going rock, and they were not as difficult to please as jazz artists. Jazz artists are very particular; they have a right to be. A lot of people take jazz artists for granted. They don't take into consideration the fact that they're working on the road, that they need adequate facilities, comforts and job conditions. Whereas in rock they pull up and take out their thing, it's no problem.

The only reason I got out of the booking business is because Basie kept calling and offering me a job as road manager. I considered his offer, because it was still along the lines of administrative work, which is basically what I'm interested in. If you look behind the music scene, there are not too many suedes in the administrative part. I agreed to go out with Basie for a couple of weeks and took a leave of absence. I acquainted myself with the procedure of his business and found it wasn't difficult. I took another leave of three months from the booking agency, and it was during this period that Basie offered me a second job. He said, "Why don't you send for your horn? You're going to travel with the band in the role of road manager, so you might as well play. If you play, that's two jobs. It will mean two salaries." The financial part made sense, so I consented. After the third month I found I could do both jobs and I stopped working for the booking agency. I'm not sorry I made the move.

In an interview I did with Philly Joe Jones, he spoke about musicians getting on the bandstand to sit in before they were ready. He said, "Eddie Lockjaw was on the bandstand." Can you tell me about that?

I think Philly was referring to Minton's Playhouse. In those days musicians would think twice before they got on the bandstand. They felt if they weren't qualified they would be embarrassed. That particular policeman's job, as I call it, was handed to me by Teddy Hill, who was the manager at the time. One night he announced that he couldn't manage the club and the bandstand at the same time, and that he felt whoever was the leader should be responsible for who played and who didn't. That became a sticky job, because I felt that if you're playing and some qualified musician wants to sit in, it enhances the bandstand and the music, true. But with a guy who thinks he's qualified and who isn't, it becomes very embarrassing to have to ask him off the stand because he is not only giving a poor performance, but he's also in the way of the other musicians.

I had to make this decision, and I agreed to do it. You're trying to play, but you're also trying to police the bandstand so that nobody is in the way. There were times when it almost became violent. One or two individuals felt I had no right to make the decision. How did I qualify to be the judge of who could play and who couldn't? In some instances I was labeled as a tyrant, but on the whole the guys appreciated it. The word spread. If you can't play, don't go on Lockjaw's thing, because he'll ask you off. In doing that we got the best musicians. It was most relaxed. You had a chance to hear different stylists, different musicians. It was a big schoolroom and it was pleasant. It was a place to experiment with what you knew.

Now you know this freedom element—I think Europe is responsible for it; I really do. The only way some musicians could acquire any kind of recognition had to be in Europe. People like Albert Ayler and Shepp, there's no way in the world they would have been allowed on the bandstand in the States. So they came over here maybe as adventurers, experimenting. European musicians are not that familiar with the working of jazz, how it comes about or how it takes on different shapes, and they accepted it as part of a new form of music. The critics wrote that this was a new art form, and they liked it.

It reached the trade magazines, and it came back to the States. In the States we read about Albert Ayler and a couple of others. We knew nothing about them, yet they were American musicians. They hadn't performed in America, but they were getting writeups in trade magazines, describing how they were playing in jazz festivals or were caught in the act in one of the nightclubs. And the next thing we knew was that they were coming to the States on concert tours with other artists, giving forth with this freedom bit. I think this is where it reached a point where a lot of young musicians who were studying heard these guys and thought, If they can be up there playing in a jazz festival, what's the sense of me studying and learning? I can do that. Therefore freedom became a trend. Everybody plays whatever he wants. In the interim, they close all the joints. It turned out not to be healthy for the business.

There's one thing about a lot of the new faces in so-called jazz: What is jazz? It's a debatable subject. Everything that is considered pop is not jazz. They call it a culture, and their attitude is that the listener is privileged to hear them perform. But they overlook one thing. The listener is the one picking up the tab, and he's the one who must be satisfied. If you're going to play for someone in a club, you expect to get your wages. The only way you can get your wages is from the people who support the club. The people are going to support the club only if they enjoy what they hear. If a person comes to the club and does not understand or enjoy what the musicians are playing, he's not coming back. Therefore there's no business, you don't get your wages, there's no more entertainment. This is why there are no clubs to speak of today. There's one here and there, and I assure you there are no freedom musicians working in them. It started with the avant-garde, which was supposed to be like the first step, and then it went all out. Freedom has done more harm to the industry than any other form of music. It's a fact.

For every jazz room you get seven rock rooms, not because the rock music is that good but because people understand what they're playing, they understand the rhythm, they can participate and dance and it's not expensive. Every club owner who buys a costly act passes that cost on to the consumer. The rock group doesn't cost that much, your drinks and facilities don't cost that much and you enjoy yourself, so you go back. You got to pay an arm and a leg for a jazz group; you don't understand it; you don't enjoy it; so you won't come back. Of the few groups which are working, one or two of them are getting out of hand financially. They're asking for too much money, and the club owner passes it on to the customer. The customer can only go out once a month at those prices. When you start with a door charge and then you pay for drinks and the price of the drinks is excessive, you can't afford to go out often. This is not enough to keep a club in business. It's a matter of economics.

There was a different atmosphere about jazz years ago. The players themselves projected lighthearted feelings. There was a margin of humor in playing; there was a happier atmosphere. Today the jazz musician comes to the bandstand with a grim outlook; he's too serious. This is infectious. The people who come to the club are afraid to talk loud, afraid to laugh among themselves because the musicians are looking grim. So the whole joint looks like a graveyard. It looks more like a sermon going on in a church than like a nightclub atmosphere. I think this has hurt. The entertainer has always been a person who can be infectious to his audience. If he laughs, the audience laughs; if he smiles, the audience smiles; if he looks grim, the people in the audience are going to look grim.

Jazz was never meant to be that way. To me jazz has always meant an outlet, a form of expression, a relief, a relaxation and a listening pleasure. It ought to be a pleasant experience, not grim. You're not supposed to go with a pencil and pad and figure out what they're playing, where are they now, where is the melody.

One tune takes forty minutes. In a forty-minute period we play five compositions, which gives the listener variety. Today some groups play one tune a set.

Do you think the music business is controlled?

It's always been that way. You have good critics, and you have so-called artists. A critic can take a liking to an artist because of the way he presents himself in terms of his wardrobe, or he likes his particular style. His writing will then lead the reader to believe that an artist is monumental or that a newcomer has tremendous talent. Unbelievably, a lot of future musicians are guided by critics. If they read a favorable writeup about an artist, they might change their thinking and their style of learning to copy this artist. They may feel that this artist is making it or on the brink of making it, that this is the route to go. Just giving an opinion about an artist shouldn't entitle one to the name of critic, yet that's what happens. There is no set standard for differentiating a good artist from a poor one. If you ask five critics how to equate a good artist, I guarantee that there will be no similarity in their answers. For example, one critic will say, I look to see if the artist has a good tone on his instrument. Another might say, I look to see if he can take a good solo. Again another might say, I like to see if an artist can play more than one instrument. There is no set of guidelines to determine who is a good artist and who is not. You get an assortment of opinions. If one or two critics get together and agree that an artist is good for the business or feel that this artist has something to offer, there's collusion, and it's control.

There's no question about it. You can tell by the so-called polls. You could check every list on each instrument: The first two names you recognize, the next twelve you never heard of. All the artists who you knew were active in the business in terms of performance were at the bottom of the list; you didn't know any of the ones in between. This is all control. Here you are in the business and you don't know the artist, so how in the world do you expect the public to know these people? For instance, I'm a saxophone player. I've played with every band and every small group. Okay, I don't expect to win polls, I couldn't care less, but the point is that when I'm reading a jazz poll on tenor saxophones, the first three or four I recognize, Coleman Hawkins and so forth; the next twelve I never heard of. I did a little research. One plays fourth tenor for Lee Castle. Another plays for maybe Jan Garbor. Now I know these are not jazz players. The guys I know who are active, say, Gene Ammons, he's eighteenth; Stanley Turrentine, twenty-second; Ike Quebeck, twenty-fourth. These are guys who have been playing jazz, making jazz records, working at jazz clubs. The polls are definitely rigged or controlled or any other term you want to use. I can assess this, but the guy who just likes jazz, the layman, he doesn't know. It makes him feel, let me go with this guy. This other guy can't be so good because he's twenty-second. That's your answer to the question. Sure it's controlled.

Do you think militancy among blacks has affected our music?

It has affected the music not only listeningwise but also places that present it. The young black militant's attitude is not going to help. When you are dissatisfied, the best approach is to produce even more. Find ways of reaching the public, not violently but with talent and production.

Music has always been a universal language. When people, races, had their differences, it was one area they could agree on. Music has always been the common denominator. The young black militant has overlooked this. He feels that we're not getting credit. Well, we never got credit for a lot of things because of our color, unless we excelled. You couldn't just be good, you had to excel. This is something that we're hung with and that we have to overcome.

Violence has not been the answer; it has hurt. There used to be a ratio of fifty or sixty percent white clientele in a colored club. The militant attitude has caused this attendance to drop off considerably, placing the clubs in jeopardy. The general attitude of the young black militants has hurt the business even more. When an individual has to fear for his life to go and hear a jazz artist, he won't go. Or if he comes out of the club and finds his car gone. I cannot go along with what the young militant hoped to gain by that, because there's nothing to gain. He's only putting himself out of work, and there won't be anyplace left to play. He's showing his contempt and anger in his music, which is not pleasant to the ear. You can tell by his lyrics, in tunes which have lyrics, that he's attacking the very fiber of what we've been striving for, to keep music neutral. Keep it out of politics, keep it out of the church.

You don't think musicians should be involved in politics?

I think they should be neutral in terms of their profession. If I go to hear you play, I want to hear music to give me comfort, relaxation. I don't want to hear your views; I don't want to hear how many bills you owe; I don't want to hear that you're running for political office. Outside of your craft, your other activities are your own. If you're interested in politics or anything else, fine. But I think your purpose is to entertain.

The whole thing wrong with jazz is that it was created by blacks in the States. Our music was created because the black man had nothing else. When he worked or had sad moments, he sang, he found something to play to make a sound, anything to give vent to his feelings. The word *jazz* came from the red-light district, but the actual music was created by black people, as you say, 'cause I still use the word *colored;* somehow *black* doesn't get to me.

The idea was that blacks were messing up music, messing up good instruments. They were "jazzing up" the instruments, or they were "jazzing up" their music. The word *jazz* meant you were going to the red-light district to get a prostitute—"I'm going down to get me some jazz tonight"—that's all it was. When a guy would pass the corner, there would be a black man with a washtub, a board and a harmonica. They would refer to them as those niggers out there, jazzing up the music again.

But that same "jazzing up" was drawing crowds, and they were throwing coins. Then it got a little more refined: They got a cigar box to use as a kitty, and they started receiving requests. The various proprietors were concerned because there were more people on the street corners than in the clubs. So a brilliant idea was born: We'll get these guys off the corner, we'll scrub them down, dress them up and put them in the joint, as long as they don't mingle with the guests. Some musicians will tell you how they worked at many nightclubs where there was a back room for them to congregate and rest. They were not allowed at the bar; they were not allowed to talk to the guests and mingle with them. As this music spread, it became popular and clubs started trying to find musicians—they started calling them musicians later. Then they found they were drawing too many whites and not enough colored people, and they started mixing.

This has been the chief problem in jazz becoming America's number-one culture, because it has always led to the mixing of the races. It happened long before the integration of sports, long before the integration of the services. There's always been a mixture of the races around jazz, so that its greatest adversary was the journalist. No critic or reporter ever wrote favorably about jazz, because one day his daughter might take to it and end up with a colored guy. It was simple as that. Jazz was always put in the context of something bad, something evil. You can look at old movies—anytime there was a scene where girl meets boy, college type, clean-cut, there were violins in the background or an accordion. If the film showed a wayward daughter or a delinquent son, a hot jazz trumpet was used as background music. The only jazz that came through the movies was in foreign films. Whether the films were good or bad, you heard jazz.

Have you modified your style in recent years?

No. I don't try to prove anything. I've been fortunate enough to acquire a few people who like the way I play, and I'm satisfied with those few.

What is your greatest achievement in music?

Managing to survive. I think it is a major accomplishment for a colored musician, regardless of the amount of talent he has, to be able to sit with you after twenty-eight years, with all the obstacles that are deliberately put in front of him.

Do you think the black man will ever have the same rights as the white man in America?

Not a chance; he doesn't deserve them.

Why do you say that?

Many of us are so busy pointing out how we're oppressed that we never point out our faults. The first time I hear one black militant leader point this out, I'll go along with some of his philosophy. It's always a matter of showing our attributes, our assets, our potential, how we're denied, but we never have any faults. And we've got a lot of them.

Let us be fair—there are good and bad in every race. There are some blacks to whom you cannot give authority. If they're followers, fine, but as soon as you give them a little authority, they'll run over the whole building. There's no such thing to me as a born leader. You've got to earn it; you've got to develop it; and just to sit around and beef about what you don't have and what you're denied is not reason enough to give you the authority which you must work to earn. That's the trouble with young militants today. You check them out. You're interviewing me, so why not interview one of them and find out how many jobs he's ever had. He hasn't had any. He's talking about his rights, but ask him how many jobs he ever went looking for.

We musicians have a legitimate beef because we're trying to work and earn our livelihood. The obstacles that have been put in front of us have been economic. For instance, a white artist can be offered a job, and if that same job is offered to a colored artist, it's a different figure entirely. 'Specially in your hotel circuit, your resort areas. The young militant sitting around talking about wanting this and that hasn't worked. I can't go along with his argument, because he's not supporting it with any kind of living proof, work. Get him a job.

Did you ever have any doubts that you would become a successful musician?

I didn't have any thought on the matter. It was just a question of trying to learn the instrument and go from there. As far as having a goal, I didn't ask myself whether I'd be a failure or a success. I just took a chance, because my beginning was a little strange. I didn't buy an instrument for the sake of the music. It's different if someone says he likes music and wants to get an instrument to try to be a musician. In my case I wanted the instrument for what it represented.

By watching musicians I saw that they drank, they smoked, they got all the broads and they didn't get up early in the morning. That attracted me. My next move was to see who got the most attention, so it was between the tenor saxophonist and the drummer. The drums looked like too much work, so I said I'll get one of those tenor saxophones. That's the truth.

That's it. You want to hear the tape?

I'm no egotist.

—*Paris, April 15, 1970*

≡ ERROLL GARNER ≡

"I wrote 'Misty' from a beautiful rainbow."

I never had an influence, for the simple reason that I loved big bands. I think this is where part of my style came from, because I love fullness in the piano. I want to make it sound like a big band if I can. I wasn't influenced by any pianist, because when I came up, I didn't hear too many. We used to have places like the Apollo Theater where you could go and hear big bands. They used to come to Pittsburgh and play at the Stanley Theater. I saw all the great bands. I knew Mary Lou Williams when I was a kid. When Fats Waller came, the piano was so sad that he played organ. I'll never forget how he took that organ, blended in with the band and made it sound like forty-four pieces. That sound was the most fantastic thing! I thought, oh my goodness, how can he do that? That's something new to me. I love Jimmy Lunceford, and I love Duke. Jimmy Lunceford and Count Basie taught me how to keep time. Those two bands really laid that on me, and it was a thrill. I think Freddie Green is one of the greatest timekeepers in the world.

Did you have any doubts when you started as a musician that you would be successful, musically and financially?

When I started out as a musician, I was happy just to get to Fifty-second Street; I didn't think about money. It was an honor for me to be able to join Slam Stewart. I had heard of Slam for years as Slim [Gaillard] and Slam. I looked up to both of them because of how they could play. I would say that Slam and Oscar Pettiford are two geniuses of the bass. At that time, when Fifty-second Street was going, everybody had a job. You could walk from one place to the other, all the musicians were working. Miles [Davis], Max [Roach], everybody was there. We all knew we needed enough money to pay our bills and get a few things out of life, but it wasn't based on how much you're going to pay me this week and I have a hot record now and if I play back at this club again I want this amount, not what he paid me before. I know I make a little money, but I do put it to good use as far as my family is concerned. When I'm playing the piano, the amount I'm getting paid is not what's on my mind. That's a fact. I don't believe you can play thinking about how you're going to get the money and run like a thief, like a lot of artists say. It's all right to say that if you don't like your boss. But the public out there doesn't know you don't like your boss. All they know is that they paid five or six dollars for an album they have at home, and that's what they've come to hear. They don't want you to jive around, pretend, not be the real you and talk about how you don't like your boss. They don't even know him. Sixty percent of the audience wouldn't know who the boss of the club was or who the promoter of the concert was, because that doesn't interest them. All they want to know is if you're there and if you're going to play what they have at home on a record. Audiences are never supposed to be played cheap.

Have you changed any of your material in recent years?

I wouldn't say I've changed it so much as I tried to improve on it. I play a little bit of rock and a little Dixieland for kicks. I might do that in a club, but not in a concert. Whether I get it from someone else or create it myself, I'm always looking for something new. As I can't read music, I don't have to say to myself, this is an arrangement I wrote six months ago and I have to play it note for note. I get as close as I can. Each time I play "Misty"— and I play "Misty" I would say a thousand times a year—I add a little something. I feel that if you liked it last night and you come back to hear me tonight, maybe I can do it better. At the same time I'm creating, and it's not becoming a bore because of sticking to one certain pattern.

How did you come to write "Misty"?

I wrote "Misty" from a beautiful rainbow I saw when I was flying from San Francisco to Chicago. At that time they didn't have jets, and we had to stop off in Denver. When we were coming down, there was a beautiful rainbow. This rainbow was fascinating, because it wasn't long but very wide and in every color you can imagine. With the dewdrops and the windows being misty, that fine rain, that's how I named it "Misty." I was playing on my knees like I had a piano, with my eyes shut. There was a little old lady sitting next to me and she thought I was sick because I was humming. She called the hostess, who came over, to find out I was writing "Misty" in my head. By the time I got off the plane, I had it. We were going to make a record date, so I put it right on that date. I always say that wherever she is today, that old lady was the first one in on "Misty."

What does who chi coo *mean, and how do you spell it?*

Just the way it sounds. *Who chi coo* is an expression that Sarah Vaughan and I used all the time years ago, because we were very good friends. We used to hang out together in Atlantic City. It means "magnificent obsession." If I dig what you do, what you're playing, you're a magnificent obsession; if I don't, I say nothing. So when I say "Who chi who chi coo," that means you really are a magnificent obsession. They decided to name me that. They always say: "Hey, Who chi coo." People who don't really know me call me Erroll. But Sarah Vaughan, Peggy Lee and Carmen McRae all know me as Who chi coo, and that means they love me as much as I love them.

I hear you once said that one of your finest musical experiences was some recordings you did with Charlie Parker. Is that true?

Definitely! I took care of Bird in California when he was sick. We used to play together on Fifty-second Street. Bird was with my group when I got to California. We had Bird, Red Callender and Harold West, who was a great drummer. Playing with Bird was an experience. Every night he would put something new in the tunes we played, like changing chords, playing different progressions. You never felt that you had to play the same thing you had played the night before. We used to wail! That's what I dig. It was one of my greatest experiences; his mind was so fast. Other than playing the saxophone, Charlie was a very brilliant man. He had knowledge and believed in a lot of things people don't believe in today, like education.

What was your impression of Bud Powell?

To me, Bud was the second greatest thing to Art Tatum. Tatum was way out there. He was a genius, ahead of his time. Bud came along later to add on what Tatum had. Let's face it—Bud was a genius on the piano. I knew Bud when he was with Cootie Williams. He was another Tatum, only much more modern, adding to what Tatum had already laid down for the classical pianists and for everybody. I always say Tatum was the master and that Bud developed what the master left. Fantastic! That's what Bud was to me.

Do you play for yourself, for your audience or for the musicians?

I always play for my audience. I can't play to empty tables and chairs. Let's face it—if there are empty tables and chairs, you're not going to get too much money. Therefore you've got to have somebody to play to. If you come to my house in the afternoon and say, "Erroll, sit down and play the piano just for kicks," and you want to play the drums, we jam. You are a public, I am a public, we're playing for each other. Now, you say I'm going to wail this afternoon all by myself and kill who? Say a guy's going to pay me a million dollars if I play for two hours by myself. I may take the million, but I haven't proved anything, I haven't felt anything technically. You need a public. They are buying your records and putting you where you are. The day you say you don't need your public, you should give up your instrument and quit, I don't care who you are.

Do you like traveling?

I love to travel; nowadays it's the only way. We used to say people will come to you, but now you have to go to the people. I'm trying to prove that you can come anywhere I'm playing and forget about your work or your troubles. Relax your mind, say boom, and think about it the next day. If I can do that, I feel I've accomplished something.

Do you think the music business is controlled?

I would say the rock business is, because there are a thousand groups. The kids have been brainwashed to a certain extent. You've got a bunch of young children who are recording today. They're doing their thing, and it's their freedom. They have to be controlled, because they write a song every hour on the hour. They're controlled mostly through record companies. I think as far as jazz is concerned, Dixieland and classical music, it's up to the public. They are the ones who buy what they like and what they really want to hear.

How do you like freedom music?

I dig some of it. It takes some time for the ordinary layman to understand it, because he doesn't know the meaning of *freedom* in a musical sense. He only knows the meaning of it as far as life is concerned. Nonmusicians don't get a chance to go to a club like the one we were in last night, because they've got to get up and go to work in the morning. These are the same people who buy our records. As for the music we heard last night, it's good, but I think it's much better when it's done by an organized group. I can understand that when guys go and sit in, they want to express themselves, but you have a clash because you have too many playing. Unless you've got arrangements, ten guys playing freedom aren't going to sound as good as a group which has rehearsed and has its thing going. When four or five guys drop in off the street and say they're going to sit in tonight, I understand them because I like to sit in myself, but it becomes a clash.

It's like in Dixieland. There's nothing more free than Dixieland, with each cat playing something else. When it gets over nine pieces, they have to make arrangements. Although it's in a Dixieland flavor, it becomes an arrangement. You're not going to hear ten or twenty cats jamming playing Dixieland without somebody saying, "Look, we're going this way, or we are going in his pattern." We all have to know when we're going out, when we say going out we mean when we are going to end it. We have to stop together!

As I don't read music, it takes me a little longer to hear the freedom, because I have to start thinking about what each guy feels and what he's trying to express. Even though he's playing freedom, the freedom has got to come together. That's what's going to make the world in the future—freedom and coming together. People can't be free and going off in opposite directions or else there won't be any foundation.

Some freedom music I like and some I don't care for because I get a feeling that they are trying to copy. That's one thing I don't like in life—when you become a copyist and you try to make a living copying others. I'd just as soon hear the real thing than the imitator. If you take up an instrument, I don't care how much you love somebody, how much you would like to pattern yourself after them, you should still give yourself a chance to find out what you've got and let that out.

How do you like the Beatles' music?

Some of the Beatles stuff I like. I don't say all of it. The Beatles are friends of mine. Ringo [Starr] and I have been friends for quite a while. In the latter years they came up with some good things. Just before they broke up they began to put more melody into what they were writing, and this is what made the grown-up public take notice. They wrote better lyrics, so you could understand the meaning better. That was when the tide turned for them, when the grown-up public began appreciating what they did.

Miles told me you accent on the fourth beat. Would you explain that?

I know what Miles means. It's true. It's almost like playing a waltz. I would do a lot of things on the fourth beat when Miles and I were playing together. I'm the type of piano player that tries to feed the guy, and I knew Miles liked that. Sometimes I'm liable to pronounce the fifth beat. When you pronounce the fifth beat, you're already in it, you've played your fill-in.

What do you think about all the strife going on in America?

They better take time and listen to those kids. I don't care what it is—give them what they want! If they want to see chicks walking around the university naked, let them have it; they're going to have it anyway. It could be in Central Park, he could put her in the back of his car, he's going to see it. If they don't get the studies they want, they're going to go to libraries and read up on it anyway, so if they want a particular study, let them have it and let them be free. If they goof off, let them suffer the consequences. Take it like you give it, an adult man or woman.

What do you do for relaxation in your free time?

I like to play golf, and I stink at it. I just go out and get some fresh air. I play a little tennis. Other than that, I do a lot of walking. I just go around and watch people; that feeds me and gives me ideas. I see what other people are doing during the day. I'm not the type to sleep the day away, to lie in bed and say I've got to work tonight so I'm not going to go out until it's time to work. I like to get out in the daytime and see what others are doing, because they're the same people who come to hear you play the concerts. I like being with people. It feeds me and helps to make my day complete. Nobody can walk around being a loner, that's for sure.

Do you think musicians should be involved in politics or bring it into their music?

No! I don't think there's any way in the world you're going to express politics through music, for the simple reason that you could wake up tomorrow to a completely different story. You don't want to get on the bandstand and play morbid, and I think that's what you would be doing. The best thing a musician can do is vote for what he feels, and he will have the compensation of saying he voted for what he thought was right. That's as far as it should go. Politics is a full-time job. You cannot play and get involved in that.

Are you religious?

I believe in my own way. I admit I don't go to church that much. I'll probably have to throw my hat in the next time I go. I do say my prayers. Things I have prayed for have come true.

Do you like sporting events?

I have been listening to the basketball games on this trip. I heard the Lakers and Knicks. My Knicks came and got them.

Ted Williams is a very close friend of mine. He heard one of my records, *Up in Erroll's Room,* took it to the ball park and put it on the loudspeaker. He told a newspaperman that three of his men started power hitting, started getting the swing of the bat. He said, "Listen to that tempo," and they ended up hitting way above their average, and it worked for them. It was a pleasure to read that. I didn't know anything about it until a guy walked up to me and said, "I just read your name in the sports section." I said: "In the sports section?" He said: "Yeah, Ted Williams was talking about what he did." That's true.

I like boxing but I don't think there are any fighters around.

The best fights I've seen were put together by managers and people who wanted to make a big gate. There are no boxers around right now. Muhammad Ali is a great fighter, but he didn't have anyone to fight in his prime coming up. The fighters he fought were over the hill. He never had a chance to prove whether he was a boxer or a fighter.

Have you ever gotten any bad writeups?

I wouldn't say I haven't. I've seen one or two, but I wouldn't say they were bad, just that the party who wrote me up didn't quite understand what I was doing. Maybe he had records of mine and expected to hear more that type of thing than what I played. As far as my gift is concerned, I cannot play note for note, and I might not have played like one of my records he liked. I've had guys saying that maybe the drums were too loud or the bass was too loud, but there's always a critic, and it doesn't bug me for the simple reason that if he criticizes me I'll check up on myself and find out. I figure I'll bring him in next time and I usually do; I can prove it.

What do you see for yourself in the future?

Music, number one. I hope to write some more movie music. Just keep playing and try to learn something new every day, move with the times, try to make people happy. Create and write more tunes.

—Paris, May 11, 1970

≡ LEON THOMAS ≡

"I'm a song."

Leon, would you tell me what you were saying earlier about your entrance at Newport with Count Basie?

Well, it's just that I never got a chance to sing there, even though I went twice. On the first occasion Joe Williams sang with the band. He was recalled. It was like a big thing, a reunion. On the next occasion Frank Sinatra landed there in a helicopter.

So this year will be your first time to perform at Newport?

Yeah, I'm waiting to see how it's going to be. I'll know when it's over. I don't anticipate anything.

You've changed your style quite a bit in recent years.

It's more development, I guess. When you keep on doing it, you keep on learning about it day by day.

How do you like Europe?

Europe is people-to-people relationships. I haven't had time to go to any of the spots of interest, even though I've seen a lot of interesting spots! I'm slowly coming around to understanding some parts of Europe. The first place I went to was Montreux, in Switzerland, which was very strange. I had a lovely view from a hotel. They had this mountain outside. I had the best view in Montreux I would imagine, though I guess Montreux has a mountain for everybody.

A mountain for everybody?

Yeah, everybody's got a mountain in Montreux, there are so many mountains there. One day I went out on my balcony to look at this mountain, and the clouds were down so deep, there was so much fog, that it looked like an island. I'll tell you what—that mountain disappeared, and everything was strange that day. I couldn't get into the festival because I forgot my badge. Gerry Mulligan and Tony Scott had a bohemian argument on the stage. I think Gerry Mulligan claimed it was his jam session. They really showed themselves to have very poor decorum. Their demeanor was demeaning, demanding discipline.

Anyway, Europe is interesting, but one has to have time, and I may have time at some future date. But twelve days have really offered very few opportunities, unless you consider the clientele of a very intimate jazz nightclub to be a cross section of the people. I have to rest all day in order to handle the tension and the wear on my nerves at night.

Do you sing for yourself, for the audience, for money or for what?

Forever! That's the only thing I sing for: forever. I don't know anything else; that's it. I'm a song, so I've got to sing, you dig.

Do you ever get any bad writeups?

I imagine so, though I haven't read any. I don't read much because I can't find any black magazines that have any opinions about these situations. Somebody's going to have to start really producing some better situations.

The government would subsidize any other art form all the way through.

Oh, yeah. They subsidize anything which is a way of life to them, or they try to pretend that they subsidize it. But the most vital things that really should be subsidized somehow have a way of getting forgotten.

Would you tell me about the record you did with Pharoah Sanders?

Jewels of Thought, which has a song called "Sun in Aquarius" on one side and "Hum Allah Hum Allah Hum Allah" on the other. "Hum Allah" is supposed to be a universal prayer for peace.

Can you elaborate on the reasons you changed your material in recent years?

Because things got worse. I came along at a time when it was impossible to see anything else. I saw what they were doing to all images of black people. There must be some kind of awakening. In order to survive an art must be a stethoscope of the community in which it evolves. It must be a vital part of that community, because as long as the people live, the art lives; the art is the people. As long as the culture survives, the people survive. If they keep on blocking your culture and preventing it from expressing itself, they'll soon move you into a position where you no longer wish to express yourself in your own particular way. The means available to you become so rare that you seek other outlets and alternatives.

Do you think the black man will ever have the same rights as the white man in America?

Yes! Oh yes!

In our lifetime?

Well, in one man's lifetime it will be. Nature has a way of always straightening things out whenever things are too unbalanced.

They've been unbalanced all the time I've been out here.

Yeah, but that's a short time; the black man has suffered a long time.

It seems like fifty lifetimes to me.

Yeah, it is, because you embody the pain of your ancestors, their hopes and their dreams. That's why you're keeping on; you're carrying on the battle. Actually it's time for a change now. But it's happening subtly.

The way you speak makes me wonder how you get involved in playing with European musicians.

That's the only way you can work in Europe to begin with, until you can demand other ways, and the money you make for them is more important than the shit they put on you. It's initiation, so to speak. But the point is that as soon as I present an opportunity for them to make more money by satisfying me, they'll let me do all I want. But only when it satisfies them just as much. I don't mean much to them financially; I do artistically; but they only look at the way they can make money out of it. They're checking me out now to see how they can package me and sell me to the European market. If they figure they have no alternative but to package me the way I want to be packaged, you know, in a brown wrapper, they'll do it that way. By then, with the way things are happening, it will be time for them to present me out there, and they can't stop it. So they'll go ahead and make the money they should have made a little while ago, and I'll start seeming to enjoy myself. I might even be thinking I'm enjoying myself at the time if I'm making money, but it won't be nothing compared to the shit that's going on underneath.

How did you develop your style?

Day to day, man! Singing with different people; it just comes. The more I sing, the more it comes. I can never whistle in public like I can whistle at other times. It's got something to do with total intimacy. I'll have to get some whistling down on wax and not even let myself know I'm doing it. If I can do that and get that embouchure like I know I can, it will be a funny thing. Normally I'm a spontaneous type of person. I don't ever plan anything as such; it never gets down into that.

Are you religious in any way?

I'm religious in any way—anything that works!

What did you think of John Coltrane's music?

I saw Trane when everybody was expecting Sonny Rollins in St. Louis, Missouri. East St. Louis had turned out for Miles's gig at the Peacock Alley. Paul Chambers, Philly Joe, Red Garland, Miles and Trane showed up. The people were drug because they didn't know who Trane was. They had never heard of him, and he was a last-minute substitute for Sonny. They knew they wouldn't dig the way he was playing. I was sitting right up front, and he just blew me out of the place. Wasn't nobody else after that, nobody!

What do you think about the Beatles' music?

I try not to. They wanted me to record one of their tunes on my last album, with Johnny Hodges of all people, and I refused.

Why don't you like that music?

Because I don't like it. Same reason I don't like vaccinations, same reason I don't like nose drops or have sweet oil put in my ear, you dig? It ain't necessary.

Do you go in for any physical exercise?

I do a little yoga. I do some stretches. I do some isometric tummy tighteners, which stretch you like a cat. A cat is hip 'cause he always stretches. Every time a cat moves, he stretches. He does a finger stretch which is just like that roll you do; he does that and tenses his whole body. Quivering. He gets it together and steps on off and leaps three feet in the air if he wants to, like a violin string or piano wire.

Do you spend much time alone?

A lot. I have to. I've never known why, but I just know I have to be alone a long time.

What do you do when you're alone?

Just being alone, that's something. You ever been alone?

Yeah, I've been alone all my life.

That's it. That's when you get with yourself, you dig? Getting with yourself is always a motherfucker. You can't get with yourself if you're not by yourself. When you're left with nobody but yourself, you find that you're two people or more. That's the meanest thing there is, to get with yourself.

I wonder how many people succeed in a lifetime?

I can't really judge that, but I imagine it's got to be a very low ratio, because it takes so much honesty. Few have tried, and even fewer have succeeded.

Do you prefer to play in clubs or concerts?

I prefer to play in community centers, because they have children and old folks and everybody. You can get to the families, not just to a part of the family but to all of them, so they can talk about it together and discuss it. I like to balance audiences. I have to balance everything in life. I figure they can all dig it, and that's what I'm shooting for. The performance which appeals to all of them simultaneously is the only true success, you dig? Yeah, the swinging crowd! You're out there working, but they're out there swinging. They can't be listening to you, but when they do find themselves listening to you, they really get turned around.

What is your highest ambition?

That everybody should go to bed with a full stomach.

—Paris, June 15, 1970

≣ MAX ROACH ≣

"It always comes out."

Are you your own boss as a man?

No, God is my boss, I'm next.

You're religious?

Yes, I am. I believe I am an instrument and being used, and all things are good. It's just how you use them.

I am definitely a Muslim. To me it's a natural concept, and I fall into it easily. However, I am not as prolific and I don't practice as much as I could, but I do my best at it.

How important do you think a musician's concept of life is in the development of his playing?

It's very important. I think the way the individual goes about life in general affects everything he does. I don't believe in genius. If a man or woman doesn't have any handicaps and can do something with an instrument, if they put in an hour, they will get more out of it than if they put in a half-hour. And by the same token if they practice ten hours a day, they should be able to get even more out of it. The sun shines on all of us and rain falls on all of us and we are all touched by it.

Do you do any physical exercise?

I like to walk and swim. I like to play chess, and I enjoy good conversation. I relate to museums. The kind of things I like to read are usually of an imaginative nature, and I use this to stimulate my imagination.

Do you have any hobbies?

I like to do everything seriously. Even when I relax, I do it seriously. *Hobby* is a strange word to me. It's a word like you do something to fool around. I don't like to fool around with anything. If I'm playing chess or if I'm swimming or in conversation, I like to be as honest with it as possible. What I am, I am. God made it, and I'm grateful. That's the way it is.

Would you tell me about your relationship with Bud Powell and Charlie Parker?

Charlie Parker and Bud Powell played a major part in my development. Also Thelonious Monk and Miles Davis. I have been very fortunate to have been associated with men who were not only very fine musicians and artists in the black musical idiom but also very kind people who gave willingly and generously of their knowledge.

Were you influenced by Big Sid Catlett?

I hope everybody I ever came into contact with in music influenced me. I have been around some very fine people, including yourself. I feel with good people. Of course, I didn't hear that much of Big Sid, except on records, apart from the little I heard on Fifty-second Street; but I was influenced by his kindness, his generosity and his wonderfulness. This is what I look for in a person. Kenny Clarke is the same, so are Jo Jones and Philly Joe Jones. People who have helped me are just too numerous to mention, and I mean that. Some of the ones that stick out on my particular instrument have been Jo Jones, Philly Joe Jones, you and Tony Williams. What else can I say? God gave them life, so it's got to be good.

Tell me something about your musical relationship with Clifford Brown.

Brownie was a human being who put in a lot of time, a hard worker. When we first got together and went to California, we were living in the same apartment for about six months until we took the group East. We had a piano, and I had a set of practice drums I put together in another room. Whenever I came home, he would be practicing. He was always very active. Brownie goes back to what we were talking about: the man who puts in one hour. He was a man who put a lot of time in; that's why he developed himself so well at such a young age. Sometimes if I woke up at nine, I would beat him to the piano. We were very polite and respectful to each other and wanted to do something together. We knew we were involved in something and that work was the answer. Of course, everybody should know that. It was funny, I would be lying in bed and when I heard the piano, I'd look at my watch and say, God! I imagine he would probably do the same thing if I got to the piano first. Whoever got there first would lay with it, because we were not kidding. We were really trying to get something out of it. So what I'm saying is that he was a man who put in a lot of time, and that's how you developed yourself.

How do you tune your drums?

I tune them to sound as alive as possible, not to any particular notes. Naturally a smaller drum is going to sound higher than a larger drum. The drum is an instrument that has the privilege of being of an indeterminate pitch unless it's a tympani or tunable drum, which means a guy who is a percussionist and a drummer can make something happen on cardboard boxes. Trying to tune them in fifths or fourths is not what the instrument was made for. I kind of let it go for itself. If all of them sound the same, it's all right with me as long as they have life and resonance; I mean that. But they can't sound the same because one is larger than the other. That's why they're made in different sizes.

Do you have any special technique for recording?

Yes, but it's changing with the development of recording techniques. When I first started recording, the microphones hadn't been developed to the point where they could accept the total sound of a percussive instrument, like cymbals and hard mallets on skin. They would always cover the drummer and put him in a far corner of the room. However, the microphone has since been developed so it can accept all this. Before you could play open in a live atmosphere, but when you came to the studio you wanted to sound the very same, so you had to play everything much softer and more delicate; however, today you can play as open in a studio as you would in a live atmosphere, so that changes with the development of electronics.

What do you think about electronics used in music?

I think it comes from Creation. When people say *electronics,* they act like it just happened, but electronics have been in existence since the beginning of time. We have always had electricity in the atmosphere, and now mankind is beginning to harness and utilize it. It's always been here, so it's good. Man is slowly beginning to use some of these devices that have been here, were here and always will be here. I think it is an asset.

What do you think about the Beatles?

They have definitely been influenced by and owe quite a bit to the African-American musical creativity, and I've heard that they freely admit this, which doesn't mean anything. They have stimulated an interest. After they hit, people like B. B. King and a lot of other people had a resurgence, but that would have happened anyway, because that's life.

Do you think Africa is the source of our music?

We are all blessed with African blood, which is what makes us different from everybody else. The United States of America to me is a grand social experiment, like no other country in the world that I have been to; it contains people from just about every part of the world. You'll find people of African, European, and Asiatic heritage, and of course the people who are indigenous to that continent. But we were all thrown together to partake in this social experiment to see if human beings will be intelligent enough to live together. I believe it's going to happen. All the strife we have in the United States is a part of this experiment, because we are rubbing noses and shoulders with each other. I think everybody should look for some kind of peace of mind in his own way. We are of African descent. Our music is rooted deeply, rhythmically and harmonically, in African music. It's a part of us.

What do you think about the word jazz?

Jazz is a word that came from New Orleans. It came from the French. It was spelled *j-a-s-s*. A jass house was a house of ill repute. In those days they also called them bawdy houses. This was where the great Louis Armstrong and people of his caliber and those before him had an opportunity to work before a public audience. I imagine the pay was extremely small. Our music was first known as the music that came from these bawdy houses, which were referred to colloquially as *jass* houses. Therefore, when it moved up the Mississippi to Chicago, they made it into jazz. Louis Armstrong always referred to his music as New Orleans style. When someone decided to capitalize on it, they would call it Dixieland, presumably to take the taint of jazz off. There is a lot of truth in the saying that when you name something, you claim it. Like you come to this continent and say you name it America, that means you claim it. A person will say: "I'll call this rhythm and blues instead of rock-'n'-roll; therefore, I can put my name on it. Even though I am pilfering and imitating, I can still say it's mine because I have renamed it." So, they named it jazz.

They who?

The individuals involved don't matter. No one can really do anything to you but yourself and the Great One. Getting back to the subject—it was named jazz, which is why today when you hear people in a film or a television show saying: "Don't give me all that jazz," it's synonymous with saying: "Don't give me all that shit." Some of us accept this title, though there are many who don't. Personally I resent the word unequivocally because of our spirituals and our heritage; the work and sweat that went into our music is above shit. I don't know whether anybody else realizes what this means, but I really do, and I am vehement about it. The proper name for it, if you want to speak about it historically, is music that has been created and developed by musicians of African descent who are in America. That's a long way to explain it, but if you look at it analytically, this is what you have to say. If someone from Mars came here and asked where this music came from, they would have to say it was music developed and created by people of African descent who live in America. So for a title I would call it African-American music.

There are musicians who persist and say you can take something and make it good. But there's no way you can turn sugar into salt or salt into sugar. This is what Creativity said. Consequently we have to start redefining everything about us, because most of these things were given to us to claim something. Like our names, for instance. I was born in North Carolina, and I am a direct descendant of slaves. In northeastern Carolina there is a white Roach family. Roach is an Irish name. I don't want this to sound "racial," because to me slavery was only a device Creativity used to get black Africans involved in the grand social experiment I was talking about earlier. Right after the Emancipation Proclamation or even prior to that period, my forefathers worked on a Roach plantation. If one of them was caught during a curfew period visiting a woman maybe on another plantation, and he was stopped by someone in authority, they would ask: "Who are you?" His way of identifying himself would have been to answer: "I work on the Roach plantation." After slavery our people kept these names. As I said, you name it and then you claim it. So now going back to the word *jazz*, we have to redefine and rename things so that we can reclaim our religions, ourselves and everything else. That's the way I feel about the word *jazz*.

Do you prefer playing concerts or clubs?

I think it depends on the development of a person. As you develop, nightclubs are good. When I felt I wanted to play every second, it didn't matter where I played as long as I played, because I wanted to learn. But at my present age if I didn't know anything about the instrument by now, it would be ludicrous for me to go into those little joints and play like I used to. There are other people now who need that kind of experience. Today I prefer to play concerts. First of all, I have prepared myself for that. Second, it's economically much more rewarding, because you can get more people into a concert hall; therefore you can ask for more money. You can do things musically on a broader scale, because a concert hall can accommodate so many people that you can afford to add other things. However, I think nightclubs are good proving grounds for people who feel that they want to develop a sound and develop themselves. It's all good.

Do you play for yourself, your personal enjoyment or your audience?

I try to be selfishly unselfish about the whole thing. Meaning I'm selfish as far as my attitude toward treating the craft is concerned. I am very selfish and proud of our music and our heritage, so I try to do the best I can all the time. That's the selfish aspect. But I also try to be considerate to the audience and to anyone else who is involved, which makes me selfishly unselfish. It sounds contradictory, but the two go together.

Tell me something about the Putnam Central Club.

I grew up in Brooklyn, as you know, and Putnam Central was a place where we used to play. I liked the gentleman who owned it at that time very much and respected him a great deal. He took an interest in me. He was an old West Indian man. I knew him as Mr. John [Parish]. I had a studio there and moved in a piano, some vibes and drums. He had a small ballroom downstairs where we used to have sessions on weekends. I guess that played a major part in whatever I have accomplished in this business. I was trying to promote sessions and organize bands, like most of us were doing at that time. It helped us learn something about our craft. The music that has been left to us is a great, great gift. We are very fortunate indeed to have this kind of musical heritage handed down to us.

Have you ever played music you didn't like in order to get money?

Not that I can recall. I have always been involved with people I respected and enjoyed. I've tried to be honest with myself and to stay within areas where I can do best and with which I am familiar. If I can understand something about the music, I can operate in it. If I am asked to do something and I don't do it, it's not because of the music but because I'm not qualified to do it. I'll play in any situation musically because I love to play. The reason I don't play what they call contemporary is because I am not well versed in the rhythmic conceptions. I have a great deal of respect and appreciation for what young people are playing today; that's the truth. I imagine I could sit down and start practicing four or five hours a day and develop some sort of familiarity with it. But I did four or five hours a day for so many years; I just don't have the time now, and I'm more interested in other things. I'd like to grow old gracefully.

I think it was in the 1950s that you began putting a message into your music. Can you tell me about it?

Two theories exist. One is that art is for the sake of art, which is true; the other theory, which is also true, is that the artist is like a secretary, whether he is a writer, a musician or a painter: He keeps records of his time, so to speak.

Sometimes I do art for the sake of art. I am deeply involved socially, politically and economically, God willing. So I hope that my music says this, if it can be called music. My music tries to say how I really feel, and I hope it mirrors in some way how black people feel in the United States.

What do you consider to be your finest musical achievement?

Every time I have sat down to play my instrument or write or do anything else, I have given everything I had and knew at that time. To me everything I did was the best I could do, so I can't say one is better than the other. I hope that day by day and year by year I grow and learn more. I hope I am more today than I was yesterday, but yesterday was the best I could do, so that was great to me because I gave it everything I had. I hope today comes to par with yesterday, meaning I hope today I give everything like I did yesterday. I'm not qualified to say what's best or better. All I can do is give the best I can every time I have the opportunity to do something. Then that's good enough for me, and if it's not good enough for anybody else, that's his problem.

Have you ever read any bad writeups about yourself?

To simply say I don't care what somebody says is not true, because I do care, but for a different reason. Not because of me, but because of him. Anyone who takes it upon himself to be a judge and sentence somebody is taking on quite a lot. The only reason I would be disturbed is because here is a person who is really sick. If a man or a woman does the best he or she can, who can stand up and say it's nothing? I remember Charles Mingus was going to take a critic to task not only mentally but physically; he was very serious about it. He said: "What you wrote about me is affecting my taking care of my family and paying my rent." And he was correct. A critic is taking his life in his own hands. Suppose he doesn't like the guy, but the guy has given everything God has given him to do the job and he says it's nothing. He's giving that man license to kill him.

Would you tell me about any obstacles you and Charles Mingus had to overcome to get Debut Records off the ground?

The only obstacles were personal ones. We had everything going, but Mingus and I were busy developing as musicians, so we couldn't devote ourselves full-time to it. You know how tense we all were at that time, trying to play and to learn how to play. In order to start a record company, you have to put in a lot of time to develop it. We just didn't have enough time, because we both spent twenty-four hours a day thinking about music and trying to make a record company in between.

What do you think about drug addiction among musicians?

Doctors and people in the medical profession have a higher incidence of drug taking than any other group in the world. If you want to talk about professions, musicians are way down the line in that category. Drugs exist to be used in extreme cases of pain. If a person is not in great pain because of an accident or the removal of a limb and he takes drugs, it turns around and makes him sick. Drugs are a part of our life, and if they're used incorrectly, like a lot of other things, they hurt. I think if people really knew what the function of drugs was, maybe they would understand why people use them. People don't use drugs for the pleasure of it; they use them for a definite purpose. There is nothing wrong with drugs, but you have to know what to do with them.

What do you think about the concentration camps they've set up for black people in America?

It's there, isn't it? Whatever anybody does about it pro or con, that's part of life. If you want me to say what I would do about it, that's different.

What would you do about it?

I'm going to resist anything that's going to hurt me or mine physically, resist with everything that's in me one way or the other: my brain, body and mind.

How did you become interested in music?

I started music in the Concord Baptist Church Bible School. That was during the summers when both my parents worked. It was similar to what they call day-care centers today, but it was the church which took the children. That's where I started becoming interested in music, at the age of seven or eight. We had an aunt living with us who was a church pianist. She taught my brother and me the staff and keyboard harmony we could use for playing spiritual music. I became interested in drums at the same church, and I began to study formally. Then I decided to make music my profession. I continued through high school and later went to the Manhattan School of Music.

Would you tell me about the percussion ensemble?

We have a percussion ensemble called M'Boom Re: Percussion. It's a group of six people consisting of Warren Smith, Joe Chambers, Roy Brooks, Omar Clay, Freddie Waits and myself. The group got together to promote and further the understanding of all percussion instruments, whether they be instruments of determinate pitch, such as mallet instruments—xylophones, vibraphones, bells and tympani—or instruments of indeterminate pitch, such as gongs, cymbals and drums of various shapes and origins from all over the world. We hope it will bring about a better understanding of what we as African-Americans can contribute to percussion literature. We started in the summer of 1970, and the group is just beginning to jell. It's something extra that all of us have dedicated ourselves to. I might add that all the members of the group are accomplished percussion players and also very fine composers, which was why we put those six particular people together. It's been a revelation to me and I guess to everybody else involved. We are doing concerts in colleges and I hope to record with the group. I find it extremely interesting and stimulating in every way.

What do you think about my compiling these interviews?

I think we black musicians are long overdue as far as explaining ourselves musically. Now is the time for us to do it, and that's why it's being done. More and more people who are involved in our music are beginning to explain it. Before, it was always written down by people other than those who, like you, are involved in the creative aspect of the music. It's something that has long been needed, and it will be relevant because you're going directly to the sources which have been involved in creating new forms and in sustaining the forms that have established themselves in our music. I think it's necessary, and I want to commend you for taking the time to put down some of the ideas and thoughts.

The music business has changed since the fifties, when you were working on Fifty-second Street.

It certainly has changed, and so have we all. I think it's hard to judge whether changes are for better or worse. We don't have as many small clubs as we had during the fifties and part of the sixties, clubs where we could develop ourselves in spite of the fact that they were places where alcohol was sold. It gave us an opportunity to develop the great talents we have been blessed with—Charlie Parker, Dizzy Gillespie, Sonny Rollins, Art Tatum, Billie Holiday and people like that. Today we don't have as many clubs, but sometimes I view that as a good thing simply because the music itself has outgrown that environment, just as the society has outgrown that environment. Clubs cannot accommodate the profoundness of our music, but they can give musicians a public and the opportunity to make a decent living. There has been a change for economic reasons and, what is most important to me, because of how our music has developed itself.

Where do you place Louis Armstrong in the development of our music?

I think he is one of the founding fathers of our music. What came out of Louis Armstrong was untouched by Western organized musical thinking. He is one of the men who led the way to what we are today. He wasn't exposed to the organized Western way of teaching music, so what we get from him is pure. No matter how good our technique is today, with all our musical studies and higher schools of learning, men like Louis Armstrong established a pattern, a definite line that still points out the best way to use all our knowledge and training. We still have to go back to Louis Armstrong to enhance what we have learned. That's what I mean by pureness, and we have to adhere to that. Out of Louis Armstrong have come Lester Young, Lady Day and on up to the people of today who have made lasting contributions to our music. You will find the same emotional and musical conception in John Coltrane, Charlie Parker or Miles Davis as in Louis Armstrong.

Some musicians have told me that we had more control over our music in the twenties and thirties. What about that?

I can only judge what existed yesterday by looking at what exists today. How far advanced were black people politically during that period? I think the question is relevant, because the control they had politically would be the same, relatively speaking, as the control they would have economically. How much control do we have over our destinies now, as compared to the control we had over our destinies then? I think we must ask ourselves where we were as a group of people in the thirties and the twenties. Even in the early 1900s, when there were great minds like Eubie Blake, one of the forerunners of what is now called Broadway theater, how much control did black people have economically and politically then? Because on that would depend the degree of control they would probably have had over themselves musically speaking.

It's true that segregation is largely responsible for black people owning their own businesses. We had to have black theaters to go to and, because of segregation, blacks owned the theaters. The whites didn't care. They didn't want to deal with us at all. This still happens in some areas of the South today, where blacks are responsible for their own schools and hospitals, so that you can have more black doctors in the South than in the North because of segregation. Control did shift during integration in our history. I knew a theater owner in New Orleans who owned about eleven theaters in the South before 1954, which was when integration came in and the Supreme Court passed that law. Right after the law was passed, blacks knew they could go downtown to the white theaters, and over a period of maybe eleven or twelve years, this man began to lose all his theaters. People wouldn't go to his movie theaters because they could see the pictures downtown when they first came out.

As you know, the same thing happened to black hotels. In Detroit we had the Gotham Hotel and the Mark Twain Hotel. These hotels survived during segregation, and they were owned by black people. The minute integration laws were passed, black people began to move downtown to what they thought were better accommodations, and black owners lost their clientele. So in a sense, the people who told you that were right. Segregation gave black people more of a chance to be their own boss. We're going through a period of integration now, but someday we'll realize that integration threw all the black money into the hands of whites. However, I think that things are beginning to turn around.

Would you tell me about technique in relation to your instrument?

I find there are two kinds of techniques, and I can tell you a funny story about that: I was going to the Manhattan School of Music and working on Fifty-second Street at the same time. I was paying for my tuition by playing on Fifty-second Street with Bird and Coleman Hawkins. The percussion teacher at Manhattan asked me to play as a percussion major and told me the technique I used was incorrect.

This eventually made me change my major to composition. If one thing doesn't work, I go on to another, which I've found very rewarding. The percussion teacher told me, "This is the way you have to play in order to be a percussion major." That particular technique would have been fine if I had intended to pursue a career in a large orchestra playing European music, but it wouldn't have worked on Fifty-second Street, where I was making a living. There was a conflict there until it dawned on me that I was involved in two kinds of techniques. On the one hand, I was playing with people like Coleman Hawkins and Charlie Parker and emulating people like Jo Jones of Count Basie fame, Sidney Catlett, Chick Webb and Kenny Clarke. On the other hand, if I had used the technique that the percussion teacher wanted to involve me in at Manhattan, it would not have been adequate for Fifty-second Street. By the same token, the technique I was using then, that I use today, that I was trying to learn and am still learning about today, couldn't be used in European music. This is truly segregation: There's a highly developed technique for playing black music, and I imagine there's a highly developed technique for playing European music, which you learn in school. The two techniques are different. Our black technique is difficult, and it changes constantly. It's the kind of music which develops its own techniques with the times, so to speak. Each new generation of musicians has the opportunity to bring something new to the music, if they are aware of what went on before them, of course.

Where did the term be-bop come from?

"Be-bop" is the name of a song written by Dizzy Gillespie. As far as I can remember, critics called the music be-bop when they came into the club where we were playing at that particular time, on Fifty-second Street. The music was so unique and unusual, so fresh and original; they asked Dizzy what he called it, and perhaps Dizzy misunderstood their question, or maybe he told them the title of the tune. At that particular time, I remember, we were playing a song called "Be-Bop," and they just called all the music be-bop. It's another one of those nicknames like boy, nigger and jazz. In fact, the music which Dizzy, Bird, Monk and people like that created is very difficult to master technically and very difficult to play emotionally, because you have to get your emotions up to the level of the technique involved, which isn't easy. They've been nicknaming our music for a long time, and I resent terms such as jazz and be-bop.

Would you tell me something about your wire-brush technique?

My technique really developed to its present level by watching old masters like Sidney Catlett, Jo Jones, Keg Johnson and O'Neal Spencer. I had a chance to check out O'Neal Spencer when he was with John Kirby's band. To me, he was a master. Today brushes aren't used as much as they were once, but brush technique is beautiful, and some of the guys still remember these things. Lester Young's brother, Lee Young, was a fantastic brush man, too. It's almost as much of a lost technique as tap dancing now, where black people are concerned. The development of our music probably had a lot to do with it, and the attitude that musicians brought to it; sticks were more definitive, I guess. With a lot of people concentrating on volume, brushes are just out of it, unless you could wire the wire brushes in some kind of way so that they matched the sound of some of the electronics we have today.

Do you think boxing is comparable to music?

I think it is a definitive skill and that it's been raised to the level of an art form by black fighters. It's not just beating somebody but is as highly developed as fencing or tennis. Rhythm has something to do with timing.

Where, when and how to slip punches is all rhythmic. Setting up somebody is done rhythmically. I know quite a few boxers who make a point of having something to do with a percussion instrument. Sugar Ray Robinson and Johnny Bratton both played the drums. Quite a few fighters got involved in music so they could develop the kind of coordination that was required. Dancing has a lot to do with good boxing, too, because it's very rhythmic. The same is true of baseball, and you could see it in Jim Brown's running when he was playing football. The way he could slip tacklers came from a keen rhythmic sense, as did the knowledge of when to take a breath and when to make a phrase, so to speak.

Do you think the music business is controlled, in the sense that someone can take a particular artist and turn him or her into a great artist?

Not in that sense. I think time will tell which person is a great artist. But artists can certainly be promoted; it can happen, does happen and is happening. There are a lot of people out here now who are exploited and turned into stars. It's impossible in the long run to take somebody who is not really a contributor and pawn him off as a contributor; eventually it gets broken down, as has happened in so many cases we know of. It's detrimental psychologically to the person who is stupid enough to go for something like that. In this kind of society it mainly happens to white musicians. They push them up in front, because they know that whites are more acceptable on a commercial level. Then, all of a sudden, this musician will run into somebody who really teaches him a lesson as far as the craft and art of the music is concerned. It may be someone he never heard of, just a kid from the black community, and this can sometimes be a traumatic blow. A lot of people allow themselves to be put in that position. In some cases they can't help it—greed was their reason—but it always comes out.

—Paris, June 18, 1970
—New York, October 2, 1971

≡ DIZZY GILLESPIE ≡

"Unification."

Tell me, Birks, how do you like Stockholm?

There's a nice feeling up here. The political system is pretty good, too. For people who are looking for materialistic advancement, it's no good; but for people who are interested in the betterment of the whole society, it's great. Suppose you get married and have ten children; their education is guaranteed all the way through. If you get sick you can get hospitalization. If you're out of work you've got a place to stay, something to eat and clothes to wear. I think it's just marvelous. A citizen deserves that from his country, but a citizen has a responsibility, too: His responsibility is to work when he can and to contribute to the overall welfare of the citizens in the society.

Would you tell me something about your relationship with Bird?

When I first met Bird, I was with Cab Calloway. That was in 1940, I guess. I knew a trumpet player called Buddy Anderson, a great trumpet player, but something happened to his lungs and he had to stop playing. He started playing bass and went back to Oklahoma. Whenever I went to Kansas City, Buddy and I would hang out forever. One day he came to the Booker T. Washington Hotel and said: "I'm going to bring a cat down I want you to listen to." I said: "Okay." The next day he came and brought Yard. The things Yard was doing, the ideas that were flowing . . . I couldn't believe it!

His playing was cute: He'd be playing one song and he'd throw in another, but it was perfect. The chord of the song that he threw in was perfect. I did not see him again for a long time. He came to New York with Jay McShann, and we started hanging out together a little. We used to go to Monroe's and play with Vic Coulson, George Treadwell, Ebenezer [Paul], Tinney and Max.

That's when I first met Max. We used to go there and jam all the time.

Yard didn't hang out at Minton's too much, I don't think. Our music developed at Minton's, though some people have said it developed at Monroe's Up Town House. In fact, there was an established group at Monroe's and an established group at Minton's. I don't know which one had the biggest influence on the music, as all of us went to both places. Billy Eckstine got me with Earl Hines. Earl Hines also needed a tenor player, so they got Yard. From that time on we were together. It was a perfect union. From Earl Hines we used to hang together all the time. We would play in hotel rooms. When we were in Chicago, we would go to Bob Cross's room, and Yard made the tune "Red Cross." Ideas, ideas, backward and forward. His influence is layers and layers of spirit.

After I left Earl Hines and went with Billy Eckstine, it was natural that Yard should be there. After I left Billy Eckstine, I went to Fifty-second Street. Oscar Pettiford and I opened at the Onyx Club with Billie Holiday and Al Casey, and we decided to get Yard. We sent him a telegram to Kansas City and we didn't get any answer. The telegram just laid there. So the club hired Don Byas as a soloist, not with our group. We used to rehearse all the time, and Don Byas would come to the rehearsals. Don fell right in the group. He learned all the arrangements and everything. We were cookin' so much, oh man, that was bad! The people couldn't believe it. That was really bad. All the musicians from everywhere used to come, the soldiers, when the ships docked: Onyx Club!

I got a group together with Budd Johnson at the Down Beat. After that gig played out Yardbird finally got my telegram. He came, and we played together in the Three Deuces. From there we went to California. That was around 1945. At that time I got Ray Brown, Milt Jackson and Al Haig. Max had gone then, so I got Stan Levey. That was the group which went to California. I had a contract to go there for a five-piece group, but I took six because Yard sometimes wouldn't be there. I had Milt Jackson, so we always had five guys. Then Billy Berg said we weren't heavy enough and he hired Lucky Thompson to play with us, so that made seven. At that time Yard had a breakdown, and I gave him his money and his ticket back. I went back to New York and got

Sonny Stitt. Yard stayed in California, and it was the end of that phase of our relationship.

Do you use any special technique for recording that is different from playing concerts or clubs?

You can't alter it; you've got too much to think about. If possible I like to record the rhythm first, then put on earphones and do it from there. I did it on a record date Richard Carpenter produced for me called *Cornucopia*. I hadn't looked at the music or anything. They recorded the whole band with violins; then I put on the earphones. If I made any mistakes I could go over them, as it was on a different track. That was great, but it's not like an in-person performance, I don't care what anybody says. The musicians, the groove they give you, that spark is what makes the difference.

Do you play for yourself, for the audience or for the musicians?

First I play for myself, next I play for the musicians and then I hope the audience likes it. It's in that order. You might have to inspire a musician. One time a funny thing happened to me. I said to Teddy Stewart, the drummer, "You're supposed to inspire the soloist." He said, "Have you ever thought that the soloist is supposed to inspire me?" I didn't say nothing else. It's true, we're all supposed to inspire each other to greater heights.

Since I became a Baha'i, which is my religious faith, I've been much more aware of unity. Because the Baha'is are destined to bring unity to the world: unity of religion, of races, of finance, of everything. I'm looking at it like this: If you have a group, the group is like a painting, a masterpiece. Each one of the instruments represents a specific color, and the diversity of the colors makes it beautiful. You've got five pieces, and none of them sounds alike, but they must have unity. So you take red, orange, blue, green or purple: Each color in its diversity is supposed to be beautiful. Each one has a role, and when one of the colors overlaps onto another, you have chaos. Therefore, each one should be thinking in terms of the whole, in terms of the beautification of the diversity of the instruments. Paintings don't clash, like a purple going over into another color. They stay what they are, but it's the whole picture that makes for the togetherness. Unity.

Would you tell me more about your religion?

I belong to the Baha'i faith, which means "follower of Baha'u'llah." *Baha'u'llah* means "glory of God" in Persian. The one principle that holds true in the Baha'i faith is the Unity of Mankind. You must always keep that unity in mind. Everything you do is designed to bring about the unity of mankind. So that's what I'm about now. We are taught to look at things in a spiritual way. If you do an act that is not spiritual to me, that is not godly, I'm not supposed to get mad at you. I'm supposed to be sorry that you're not spiritually developed enough to see the wrong. I must say: "I wish I could help him." I must try to think of a way to help you, as you did that rotten thing to me. I will bring you a little gift and just lay it on you. That might start something in your thinking, because man is noble; man is not an animal.

We have four levels of creation on this planet. We have the mineral life, which always stays mineral. We have the plant life, that has everything the minerals have, plus the ability to grow. We have the animal life, which has every mineral on earth in it, everything that the plant has got in it, plus senses. Then we have the human life, which has all of these other things, plus intelligence, which is manifested socially, in science and building. Man is the highest of all these levels. He never goes back to those things. Man has the power to change nature; none of the others does. Like an animal out in the jungle: nature's there, and he knows what time the different seasons are coming around. He stores fruit and nuts, but he never changes. But man has the power to change these things, like flying or like going under the sea.

What qualities do you like in a drummer?

First, if the drummer can't hear the soloist, he's playing too loud; second, he's supposed to aid and abet the soloist. He's supposed to subject himself completely to the soloist and to forget about himself altogether. But to be able to do this, he must have the tools to work with. He must have the most astounding reflexes, 'cause a guy might do anything, and he's supposed to catch him. Like Sid Catlett used to play shows, if somebody blinked an eye, he got it. His rhythm ought to be impeccable. It can drop, or it might get faster, just so long as the intensity stays there. It's supposed to build. The breaks a drummer makes are supposed to be in the proper place, like a dancer. Another thing—the drummer should be equally flexible with all four limbs, as he's got to work with them all. The things he plays should not be done entirely with his hands.

I'm getting ready to write a drum book. I've been collecting things, and I've got it all settled. I'm going about showing the drummer what instruments to play on. Drum music depends too much on the artist who chooses what instrument he should play on. How does he know? If he's got bad taste, that messes it up. There should be something to show him what instrument of the drum set to play on notewise, and he can just read. I've got a technique for that. I've always been interested in drums. You've seen guys flip sticks around on your solo and play a break at the wrong place or play loud when they're not supposed to. The basic principle is concentration on the soloist: Just stay with him and lay on him. You've seen me talking to drummers while we're playing. I say: "Look, man, don't do that anymore." If I don't tell him then, I forget about it until it comes up again. It's such a personal thing. A drummer can do so many wrong things. It's the same thing as a trumpet. There are certain rules that always hold true in our music, I don't care where you're playing or with whom.

What do you think about the use of electronics in music?

I like a little of it. I like the electric bass in certain instances, for effect. I don't care too much about music; what I like is sounds. That's another thing about a drummer: He should be a sound man who can put the sound together. As for having twenty-five thousand dollars' worth of stuff like some guys have, it's not my cup of tea. I like part of it because you can hear everything. I believe in amplification, but not to that degree.

Do you listen to a lot of music?

Not much. I don't know why. I have an extensive record collection of other people. If somebody comes by the house and says he wants to hear something, I'll see if I've got it. I like to listen to African rhythms and keep up on that. It's very difficult to lose me.

Where did the term be-bop come from, and what are your feelings about it?

Duke Ellington once told me: "Dizzy, the biggest mistake you made was to let them name your music be-bop, because from the time they name something, it is dated."

They who?

Whoever named it; I don't remember who named it. I think it came from when we were on Fifty-second Street. We didn't have names for all our tunes, so I would say: "De bop da du ba di baba de bop," and they thought I was naming a tune or something like that.

Bop ba ba di ba do di la ba de bop.

Yeah. That was the introduction to "Max Is Making Wax." That's funny. I hummed the introduction, and you started the chorus. I guess it just happened from the way we used to hum things instead of saying the name of a tune. Say you play a number that goes be-bop. It just developed into that. I never thought of the term be-bop, and I'm sure Yard, Monk and Kenny [Clarke] never thought of the term be-bop.

What do you think about the word jazz?

It's no longer fashionable to say Negro, which is what the white man named us. If we want to call it jazz, we'll make them call it that. It's our music, whatever we want to call it. I don't know who made up the word *jazz*. The blacks might have named it jazz themselves, but I don't know much about it. It's a misnomer only when it is identified with white musicians. On a television program someone was asked to say who was known as the king of jazz. The answer was supposed to be Paul Whiteman. That's a misnomer, because he couldn't be the king of our music.

Take Stan Kenton, for instance: a big phony, really, because he had a big band at the same time I did. People used to walk up to me and think they were saying something nice, like: "I like you and Stan Kenton." I'd be looking at them like this, and I'd question their taste. History will either off you or make you valid. History has wiped Stan Kenton out completely. They thought he was a master, they thought he was greater than Duke Ellington,

tried to eliminate my name altogether. Every now and then he would mention a word; it was a personal thing. That was one of his biggest mistakes, because it will be a long time before they can eliminate my contribution to the music.

What were you saying before about Miles, Fats and yourself sounding alike?

All of us were looking for the same thing. I'll give you an example: I made a record date at the Monterey Jazz Festival with Gil Fuller. I was the first one to play the "Sand Piper"; it was a beautiful thing. I was a soloist, and Harry Edison was sitting in the band. They naturally wanted to get as many notes out of me as possible, as I was the soloist, and they forgot all about Harry Edison sitting there. During the record date, on one of the numbers, while the band was playing, I said to Harry: "Come out here." We played together, and when the record came out, several people said: "Man, that was a bad solo you played on the tune 'It Be's That Way.'" I said, "That was two of us; he played his part, I played mine, and it just went together like that."

Clark Terry and I came to Europe one time on a tour together, and everyone asked us what we were going to play. Since we were playing the type of music that we're supposed to represent, and as I am a leader of that type of music, one of the creators of the music, naturally they said okay, Gillespie is the leader. Clark and I played "Ow." After the chorus Clark and I played together. You should have seen both of us trying to keep out of each other's way! That's the height of love and respect. Not trying to show off what you can do, but embellish one another. It was a big embellishment. It was beautiful, man.

How about the time we had a sellout, my big band and Ella Fitzgerald? Right in the middle of one of the tunes, Yardbird walked out onto the stage with one big red rose, handed it to me and kissed me right on the mouth and walked off. Ooooow! Talking about spirit, how deep can you get? I don't care how far you go, there is no deeper. Probably his last quarter, 'cause he wasn't doing too good then.

How do you like freedom music?

I go for freedom, but freedom without organization is chaos. I want to put freedom into music the way I conceive it. It is free, but it's organized freedom. You've got to take memory from the universe. Man will never organize anything as well as nature can. It's perpetual, but so many things are happening that you always discover something else in nature. It's organized, and you find out it's doing the same thing all the time.

I'm going to do something with voices with a friend of mine, John Motley. He's been given half a million dollars by the City of New York to conduct voices. He also teaches at the Manhattan School of Music. He came on CBS-TV one day, conducting the youth choir for the City of New York, and he made me so proud. We're going to do something with maybe a hundred voices and a rhythm section. He's one of Hall Johnson's protégés and he's got all his works, so maybe we'll do something of Hall Johnson's and have some tambourines and washboards and a bass drummer. Do you know how to play the bass drum by itself? I'm not talking about playing with the foot.

I never tried.

I play the shit out of it! You remember in Paris, at the drum clinic with Kenny Clarke, they gave me the wrong stick. You don't necessarily have to have a strap. Wes Buchanan didn't have a strap in Cheraw. My first bandleader was a bass drummer, Wes Buchanan. The bass drum was his instrument. He danced around out there and he played the bass drum. You've never heard anything like it since. I wasn't relaxed with the little bass drum they gave me. I hadn't played the bass drum in thirty years, but I do know how it's supposed to be done.

In Cuba in the Comparsa, they've got one guy who plays the bass drum as well as the tumbas and the bongos. Chano [Pozo] used to tell me this cat could whip it. So I said I had one for you in South Carolina who could whip it, too: Wes Buchanan. This cat was into it, you wouldn't believe it. There was another guy who played the snare drum and that swinging cymbal, but Wes Buchanan was the leader. Can you imagine a bass drummer being the leader of a band?

Why not? Give the drummer some.

Get out of here. I always say that leaders of groups should be trumpet players. The trumpet player knows. You see, music is not music, it is a challenge, but the more relaxed you are in what you're doing, the better the performance you're going to give. The trumpet player knows better; he can give a more relaxed performance physically. I'm serious. Art Blakey is a leader, and he wants to demonstrate his leadership qualities, so he drowns out the trumpet player. When the trumpet player comes off the bandstand, his lip is raw. If the trumpet player is the leader, he's not going to do that to himself, which is very well demonstrated by me and Miles. Therefore the best leader for a performance is the trumpet player. When Max and Clifford were together, I bet you anything Clifford called the tunes. Check on it.

Anything you want to say in closing?

Well, there have hardly been any musicians in our field who have had a woman experienced enough to understand their thing, to take what they have and help them develop, as I have with Lorraine, my wife, who I've been with for thirty-two years. She has been like an anchor. It has kept me from doing a lot of things that I would have probably done otherwise. There is a possibility that I would have been a bum—a musician, but still a bum. It has been a restraining influence. When everything else was going around New York, the things that musicians did, things that were detrimental to their health, I was away from it because of that restraining influence. I'd like to talk about that, because it is very important to my development.

She was a dancer, and she says I play off time. I do play off time in the sense of what she's talking about, because she's talking about: cham ba dum ba de ba de bund. She remembers the days with Teddy Hill, when I used to make up head arrangements for the band and it used to swing, 'cause she was a chorus girl and they danced their asses off. We would have it going. We would make up a little riff behind something and they would make up a routine from that.

But music has advanced further, and I have to go along with what I think. If I'm poor with that, I just have to be poor. If it takes something else to be rich, I just don't have it. I couldn't create; I would only be copying somebody else if I were to do a thing like that. I must be a creator myself. I've been one all the time. That doesn't mean I haven't taken ideas from other people, but when I've done it, I've made a creation out of that in itself. Made a thing with my own conception.

A example of that is Chano Pozo, a creator par excellence, a real human being in every sense of the word of being aware of humanity, a composer, a religious person. He belonged to a religion which came directly from Africa. His grandmother taught him all those things. Those chants we used to do were actually in the same groove. I have always been interested in Latin rhythms, as you know . . . "Night in Tunisia." Every drummer I have seen playing ⁶⁄₈ time is playing my lick. I took that off the conga and put it on the other drums and showed it to Charli Persip. But Chano Pozo played things before he died in 1948 that I'm only understanding now. When I hear it now, I say oh, he used to play that, and I dig it right away now, because I heard so much of it then. There are so many things he did that I'm just getting hip to now. Chano didn't speak English, and people used to ask, "How does he know what tunes you're playing?" He'd look at my mouth and tell by the expression, by the movement of my lips what I had said, what tune we were going to play. It's strange, when somebody asked him, "How do you and Dizzy converse?" he would say, "Dizzy no peaky pani I no peaky engly, but boff peak African."

—Stockholm, August 31, 1970

≡ CARMEN McRAE ≡

"We were happy in the days of Fifty-second Street."

I imagine my interest in singing must have started when I was a baby. My father was a very musical man. Not a performer, but someone who loved good music. I don't remember this, but I'm told that as a child, I used to know all the popular tunes of the day, like most children do today because of listening to music that's being played constantly on radio and television. I found out later on that there were two or three relatives of mine who were musically inclined. I mean musically inclined to the point of having good-sounding voices. They could have been singers if they had wanted to be, but I guess they never did. So maybe that's where whatever musical talent I have came from.

I'm the only one in my family who is in this business. I have been fortunate; they all wished me well and they might have wished me their talent. Their talent and maybe a bit of my own has helped me get where I am today. I had to become one of two things in life: someone who was musically inclined and good enough to be able to perform or else a good audience of music. I just happen to be a performer.

When I was still in my teens, I met a woman who became my idol. She was my idol then and continued to be my idol; though she is dead now, she still is my idol. That's Billie Holiday. I met Lady when I was very young, and she was one of the most impressive women I have ever met in my life. She really scared me as far as singing was concerned. She seemed so utterly perfect to me that I felt anything after her would be anticlimactic. Consequently I was afraid of becoming what I had hoped to become at an earlier stage in my life. That was a very important phase to me. After that I had some minor experiences with Benny Carter's band, Mercer Ellington's band and Count Basie's band, just short stints which really couldn't influence me much because I was too young. What helped me was Billie Holiday, which happened at a very early stage in my life.

The next thing was going to Chicago [sings]: "Sorry that I can't take you . . ." I'm getting carried away! Anyway, I went to Chicago and liked the city. In order to stay, I had to make a living. A friend of mine who was an ex-chorus girl knew I could play and sing, which I would do just for friends, not professionally. She said: "Why don't you take a job playing and singing?" I said to her: "Lulu, that sounds great, but I don't know if I'm capable." She said: "I know someone who wants a girl singer and piano player. If you go and you don't make it, at least you tried." I said: "It's hard for a woman like myself, who is an Aries, to take a defeat. I would rather hear nothing than hear no." She convinced me, I went, and the man there was beautiful to me. I will never forget him. He gave me a job for two weeks with a two-week option to play the piano and sing. He advanced me money to join the union. I stayed two weeks, and he picked up the option.

I realized that my piano playing was very limited, because I had never intended to become a real pianist except just to play for myself or to rehearse a tune. It became essential to play better. I stayed in that job for seventeen weeks. During that time I hired a piano, and as my repertoire was very shallow, I rehearsed every day until my repertoire grew bigger. I stayed in Chicago and worked there for three and a half years, which was the greatest experience I could ever have had. I don't care that it happened in Chicago. I don't care where it happened, as long as it happened. I found out I could make a living playing and singing. My idols were great pianists like Teddy Wilson and Art Tatum, so I could not be fooled by my own piano playing at all. My piano playing was just a means to get where I wanted to get as a singer.

How important do you think it is for a singer to know something about the piano?

Going by my experience, it's one of the most important things. I don't believe I would have whatever reputation I have today if I had not had any knowledge of piano. That experience of studying music is what put me where I am today. Without it I would perhaps not even be singing, or if I had become a singer, it might not be as impressive as whatever it is I do now. I have said this for years, and I still think it is extremely important. It is important if you want to be a lasting artist. Any artist who really knows what he or she is doing musically will last. I think it's the nonprofessional professionals who fade out. They earn a lot of money in a minute, yet they don't make it somehow. After they're gone, people don't even remember who they were. That's why it's very important to know your craft.

What would you recommend to someone trying to start a singing career?

There is no set example you can give anybody. It's a combination of luck, talent and being at the right place at the right time, with the right people listening. They should have some sort of musical knowledge. It doesn't have to be the piano. It can be a guitar or a harp, but I think piano is the simplest if you want to be a singer.

Are you religious? If you don't mind my asking the question.

If I didn't want to answer it, A.T., I'd say so. If being religious is believing in a Supreme Being and that all our lives are destined before we enter on this earth, and believing that fate has a lot to do with our lives, if that is being religious, then I am. If being religious is going to church or getting on my knees and praying to a Supreme Being every night, or reading any sort of Scripture in regard to a Supreme Being, regardless of whether it be Allah or God, then I'm not religious. I'm not an atheist. I was a Catholic as a child, and to me Catholicism is a farce! I gave it up. I have not found anything to delve into other than the Baha'i faith that Dizzy Gillespie talked about to me, but I don't know.

I feel very comfortable the way I am. Rather than get involved in something that is seventy percent good for me and thirty percent not right, I'd rather not get involved in anything. I would like to embrace whichever bit of each faith suits my way of thinking. My main concept of anything we can consider godly would be to treat my fellow human beings, regardless of what color or creed or religion they might practice, as individuals. Let me put it this way: A lot of individuals are not human beings. I'd rather treat an individual the way I get vibrations from him as a human being. Consequently I have to practice it myself. I cannot expect my fellow brother or sister to be decent if I don't try to be.

You do meet people you don't like and that you're not compatible with. People meet me and dislike me, too, for some reason. I think when people feel like that, they should avoid each other, because life is too short to have to tolerate someone just for the sake of tolerating them. I don't think it's fair to them or to their intelligence. If you cannot make it with someone, then you both should go your own way. You've got to be fair to yourself before you can be fair to anybody else!

When you are onstage, are you singing for yourself, for the musicians or for the audience?

I'm glad you asked me that. That's one of the most important things in the world. I can answer this question better than a lot of other questions. I have to sing for myself. Let's look at this thing in the proper light. I am involved because I'm the one who is doing what I'm doing. Right? I'm only doing what I do because I want to please the people who have taken the time to come and hear me. I have to do it for somebody, because that's the only way I can find out whether I was right or wrong to feel good about whatever I've been doing. Consequently I sing for the musicians, too, because I need them playing competently behind me, doing what I want them to do for the people that are sitting there. So it really is a combination of doing it for everyone. If the musicians are good—and they have to be for me to feel good—I'm going to do my best for the audience; so it's really a combination of musicians, myself and audience.

I want the musicians to like it, too, 'cause if they don't like it they're not going to be able to play for me, even if they are competent. If they don't like what I'm doing and if they're only playing for the sake of the bread, it's no good. They've got to dig me. I dig them, 'cause I'm hiring them. Right?

Of course, my main way of earning a living is pleasing my audience, so that I can pay the cats and get paid, too, so I can go home happy. Actually it's a combination of pleasing everybody. If you can start out onstage pleasing each other, ninety-nine percent of the time you please the audience, too. Audiences know who you are, they know what you do and they have come to hear you in person. You have those three things going for you before you open your mouth. You only have to do your thing, 'cause that's what they came for. If you do it well and you're not inebriated or under the influence of anything, you'll be sincere, which is all you need.

It's such a beautiful business we're in, A.T. I guess all the arts are beautiful, but I think we have a better chance of feeling good about ourselves, and we have more incentive to go on, because we get confidence from the people who come to listen to us. The music business is one of the finest businesses in the world. You make contact with people immediately, and they tell you what they like and what they don't like, and that gives you a sense of what you're doing. You might want to go in one direction and they say no, they like the other way, so you go in the other direction. That's what you're really there for, to entertain. If I had to sing for myself, I would never hear a note, because I'm not here for that.

Do you consider yourself a jazz singer?

That's a question I have been asked many times. I am jazz oriented; if it weren't for jazz I wouldn't be anywhere. I only want to be categorized as a good or a bad singer. I originally started as a so-called jazz singer. I was dubbed that somewhere along the line, and I never really thought about it. I really didn't start out to be a jazz singer; I just started out to sing. But it was awfully hard, as it is for any musician, to play and not to improvise in some sort of way on the melody. If doing that made me a jazz singer, then yes, that's what I am. I have also done many tunes that couldn't possibly be called jazz tunes and made many single records that were not jazz.

Either people like what I do or they don't. They can say: "She has a good voice, but I wish she wouldn't do . . ." I don't care, but they must not categorize me. I know what people expect when you sing a song, and if you scat, that's jazz; that's understandable. I hear people who are not categorized as jazz singers, such as Ray Charles, Nancy Wilson, Tony Bennett, Frank Sinatra and many others who are all making exorbitant amounts of money. I haven't heard them sing one song the way it was written yet. If they can deviate from the melody, which is what is categorized as jazz, where does it begin and where does it end? What makes one person a jazz singer and another one not a jazz singer? Is it a question of how much improvising they do? I don't understand it.

Today we have contemporary music, a lot of which is fantastic.

A lot of it is also garbage. I'm very happy about contemporary developments in music, because to keep doing all the rest of my life eight bars and a channel and eight bars, and ¼ time and ¾ time, would have driven me crazy. I'm happy we have ⅞ time and ⅝ time; I'm happy we're saying something different than moon june and love dove. I love what I'm doing now. I do Beatles tunes. Incidentally, I think they are excellent songwriters. I don't think they are so great singing or doing their thing, but their songs are fantastic. If they want to call them jazz, I don't mind just as long as they call me to do it.

Have you ever had any bad writeups?

Well, you don't get all your writeups everywhere you go, but I don't remember having had a critic that really spoke ill of me completely. I've seen what I consider bad writeups. I have had critics who didn't particularly like a certain thing I did but who really loved something else I did. The only thing I find wrong with critics is that they are inclined to describe what the singers had on and what their hair looked like. I'm sure that's important, and I'm not saying that's not good, but I don't think it has anything to do with the music. I think it's the singing that should be described. If it's criticized it should be criticized by someone who is an authority on the music you're playing and not someone who comes up to you and asks you the name of your latest album. Then they tell you about an album they had ten years ago. How can they judge an artist if they're not aware of what he has accomplished up to that point?

Everybody in the world wants good writeups. If somebody is going to criticize, let him be someone who knows his subject. I'm sick of people who are critics for a newspaper and who don't know a thing about what the artist is concerned with. Everybody gets a bad writeup now and then, so at least let it be from someone who is really nonbiased. It's not easy, because human beings have traits they cannot live without, and one of them is being biased.

Let's say I'm a critic and I've come to review you; before I walk in through the door, I'm in love with your playing anyway. So you're ahead of yourself, and that isn't truthful either, any more than when someone who doesn't like you walks in and you've got two strikes against you. It's awfully hard to find someone who is really down the middle and unbiased, walking in to do a completely truthful criticism of someone's art. You also have to remember that however good or bad criticism is, it's only done by one person—his own opinion, that's all you'll get.

What do you think about the Black Panthers?

I have a second cousin, a young lady, who is a Panther. Oddly enough, I'm very proud of her, because she believes in what she is doing. If a lot of us believed in something, we would be better off. In my view, in my eyesight, in my opinion, the Panthers are young men who are trying to right a wrong that's been wrong for a long time. But they're trying to do it in the shortest space of time, which is fruitless. Now that's my opinion, but I think they are more manly than a lot of men I've met, because they are willing to either get things right or to die. There is nothing more beautiful to me than people who believe in something, who have been in slavery for so long and who want to come out of it, wanting to do it and getting what they want or else dying for it. There are a lot of people who want a lot of things but who are not willing to die for it. They'd rather compromise, and there is no compromise with the Panthers.

They have gone about doing a lot of things that I don't particularly condone, but then I say to myself, if I were their age, if I had their knowledge . . . I found out that they were superintelligent young men when I did a benefit for them to help raise money for Panthers who had been arrested very unjustly and had not been given bail because of something they thought the Panthers were going to do.

These Panthers were indicted for planning to blow up something. Well, that's a lot of nonsense. Say the government was right to arrest them, but they left them without bail or with exorbitant bails. It was like they were complete saboteurs of their country. I don't believe that. They are only looking for their rights, because they know life is short and we all need to live as human beings. In our country, the country we're born in, the country we pay taxes in, the country they want us to fight and die for, it's only right that these youngsters and everybody involved who are Americans should all enjoy the same benefits, I don't care what faith, creed or color. Why should some of us be expected to die for our country and then live in our country and really literally die in it.

A lot of young people tend to be violent and maybe they have a right to be; I am not here to judge them but only to judge what I feel is right for me. I can't say what's right for you. If you think you ought to go out and kill seven people and I can't talk you out of it, go ahead, as long as I'm not one of the seven! I think the Panthers were treated very unfairly, and I wanted to do something for them, however little. I did it, and I'd do it again if they were right. If they were wrong, I wouldn't do nothing! I wouldn't care if it was my mama. Wrong is wrong!

Do you find traveling for your work a strain?

Yeah, it's a drag. I'm getting tired of it now because I've done it for so long. I loved traveling when I first started, but it's like anything else. I don't want to sit home too long, either. You try to find a happy medium, which I guess doesn't exist, anyway. I like to travel and I don't like to travel; I do it and I don't think about it. After I get where I am going, it's all worth it if the music is good and the people like what I do.

Tell me your impression of Bud Powell.

It's funny, but I think I got to know Bud better in Paris than I ever did in America. I don't know why. In fact, I don't think Bud and I ever exchanged more than fifty words in the many years that we knew each other. Sometimes I wondered if he even knew who I was. It really didn't bother me, because I knew who he was. I always loved him, and I still do. He was a phenomenal pianist, a cat whose potential never really got where it could have gotten to. I think our way of American life has a lot to do with it. Bud was looking for something and he didn't find it. If he had lived a little longer, he would probably have found what he was looking for. His piano playing to me was always a little frantic, never relaxed. He never relaxed, as though he was trying to do so much and get it all out because he did not have enough time to fool around. Even in ballads he had to get in so many notes, as though he might not get another chance to play the same tune again. He always gave me that impression. Art Tatum, great as he was and 93,000 years ahead of his time, was always relaxed when he played a ballad, however many arpeggios he made. Bud gave me the impression he had to get it all in right now. Every time you heard him it was another artistry, something else. I loved him; I hear things of his today being played and I ask who it is and they answer Bud Powell, and I say yeah, that was beautiful!

What were your impressions of Charlie Parker?

Yard was without a doubt my very favorite musician of all time. My favorite musician now is Dizzy. But Yard, I still hear things of his today that are so phenomenal I don't believe it. If they could take the background out of some of the things he did with strings or big bands and just put in a really up-to-date group, it would sound as though he had recorded it last week. In my estimation no one has caught up with this man. If he were still alive and doing what he did some twenty years ago, even if he never played anything other than what he was playing then, he'd still be up to date. He was one of the biggest musical influences in the world.

We were talking about Muhammad Ali earlier, and you got excited.

Let me tell you about this cat. Muhammad Ali is one of the nicest men I've ever met in my life. I met him for the first time in London, when I was doing a show called the Eamon Andrews show. On the show were Lucille Ball, Noel Coward, Muhammad Ali, Tom Jones and myself. People in London love Muhammad Ali to death. He sat on the panel and talked and he was extremely amusing with his answers. After the show, when we all went upstairs to have drinks and eats, that's when I really got to talk to him. This man is not at all like his public image. It's like a play or a mask that he puts on for certain things and then takes off as soon as he can be himself. He is a beautiful, soft-spoken, humble young man, besides being one of the greatest athletes I've ever had the pleasure of feeling. I felt his arms and legs and I have to say it was out of sight. It was just marvelous! He was a beautiful man who first of all respected women and particularly black women, which I loved, I adored that. He was very attentive and not fresh, but just as a man and a gentleman should be.

And then I saw him again when I did a thing called Operation Breadbasket in Chicago for the Reverend Jackson. He was there and we talked. I'm so happy they agreed to let him continue to do his craft, which he does so well. He always has been the champion, as far as I'm concerned. When they took the championship away, it wasn't taken away by another man, so consequently he was still champion to me. I hope he can continue to do his thing, because it helps so much to see a black man be champion and honestly be the champion, because that's exactly what he is.

What did you think when I asked if I could interview you?

I was really very pleased to know you were into something that we needed. To do what you're planning to do is really necessary, so that people will be enlightened about us, the things we do and think. I don't give a damn about older people, because they're into their thing and their minds are made up. What I'm interested in are the kids. I find the kids today so beautiful; they fight for anything they believe in, they're in sympathy with all the minorities, which is what we are called. The young kids are for anything that's right, and they'll get out and help you fight for what is right, for what you believe you should have. They are the ones I'm trying to get to. One of the greatest compliments I've had in this business is looking up and seeing young people in my audience.

I have always thought of myself as being a very sophisticated type of singer, talking only to people who have lived a little bit. But sophistication, I found out, is not for those who have lived any particular length of time; some of them are the dumbest people in the world. Sophistication has to do with the way you think, the way you want to live. It has to do with people thinking the same way about the same things. If it happens to be a teenager, then right on!

I have done a lot of things where I've had college kids who were so together that I was curious. Let me give you an example: I did a couple of one-nighters in the Catskill mountains, which caters mainly to vacationers. When you work at one of those places, you have a captive audience; in other words, they come on Saturday night and that's when the entertainment is. They come whether they dig you or not. I got compliments, of course, from the mothers and the dads who were in their late thirties and so on. But the thing that thrilled me most was having their fourteen-year-old kids come up to me and say, "Miss McRae, I really enjoyed that. I have two of your albums," and they could name them. I wonder what I do at my level that can get to a fourteen-year-old. Today I do some rock things and what we call contemporary music. I only do the ones I identify with. The kids say to me: "We love you because you're so sincere." I can't ask for anything more than that. I try to be sincere, but how do they realize that at fourteen? You see, that's the thing about kids today.

They come out of their mother's womb so completely together and so much more intelligent. Who knows; when we were kids, if we had seen what they see, we would perhaps be as active as they are. Times change, things change and people change. If we had not become aware of fighting for civil rights in 1954, which is not so long ago, who is to say that we would actually have felt so vehement about it. I think certain times breed certain things.

We were very happy in the days of Fifty-second Street. We didn't think of the things we think about today, did we? The one who really made it prominent was our Martin Luther King. He changed the whole economic structure of Alabama. That was the beginning, and it all stemmed from that. We all knew then that it wasn't right, the things that were being done to us. But nobody really got up and said let's sit in, let's picket here, let's boycott this. I'm sure we all thought of it, but we didn't do it en masse. It was never discussed like it is today. Today it's prominent, not only with black people but with every living human being. That's the trend. If it had been the trend of yesterday, we would be doing something else today; I just think it's the kids' world, really. We have lived in it and we have really done our thing in it, and we were lucky. Whatever we've done and whatever we're doing now will be somewhere in time, in a book of posterity, that we were alive and that we contributed something.

Today there are a lot of kids who have died for what they believe in, and you will never know who they were. They died valiantly, not from dope or somebody shooting them, but because they believed in what they were doing for this world. They either wanted to change the world or die, and they died. They really have beat the game.

What do you plan for yourself in the future?

I would like to do some acting. I would love to try something else that is still a part of what I do, only without music. I wouldn't particularly want it to be a musical—not that I would turn a musical down—but I would prefer something dramatic or in the comedy field. I don't know if I can do it, but I sure would like to try.

Singing is a natural road to acting, yet none of our great singers, including yourself, has gotten into acting. You should try.

A lot of people have told me the same thing. First I would like to convince myself that maybe I do have a knack for it, but I'll never know unless somebody comes along and offers me an opportunity.

Do you listen to music when you are at home?

Yes, I do. I listen mostly to instrumental music. Being a lover of the piano, Oscar Peterson happens to be my favorite all-around pianist. There are many other pianists I love, but I won't go into it because there are too many of them. Oscar is my favorite because he encompasses everything. There are pianists I like because of one thing and pianists I like because of another. But overall I like Oscar best.

Since we are talking about pianists, what is it you look for in a piano accompanist?

That's a hard question. Accompanying someone cannot be explained by a singer to a pianist. He either knows what to do or he doesn't. An accompanist and a guy who can play the piano are two different things. You have to find someone who is completely sympathetic to the soloist as a singer and not to a soloist as an instrumentalist. It's a completely different thing. Even if a guy can play his buns off, it does not necessarily mean he can accompany a singer. There are some guys who can accompany a singer and who can't play worth a damn as far as soloing is concerned. That is the difference, and it's a vast difference. A guy must really love to do it. He cannot do it because he has nothing else to do.

Getting back to the music you like: what else do you listen to?

Of course, I listen to John Birks Gillespie, and to the Kenny Clark–Francy Boland band; I listen to Miles, to Freddie Hubbard, to Cannonball Adderly and to Blood, Sweat & Tears. These are my favorite groups I'm mentioning to you, and I know I'm going to leave some out. I love music only when I can communicate with it. If I can't communicate with it, it leaves me cold.

You asked me about avant-garde music. Well, that's what the avant-garde does to me; I'm sorry. If there are six people in a group and all six are playing something different, there is no way for me to know who to concentrate on or what's going on. If I go to a club to hear somebody, I'm going there primarily because I believe that they're going to play the kind of music that brought me in there in the first place. I believe if it's more than one person, there has to be some kind of discipline. It mustn't get to the point where there is no discipline. If you're playing by yourself, right on, anything you want. But when you've got three, four or five people, you start off with a mode of some kind or a set pattern of chords for all of you to play for the first chorus; then after the first chorus what happens? Where do they go? Why do they all have to go in opposite directions? When I find out how I can get some musical satisfaction out of it, then I'll say, great, avant-garde, I dig it. But for the time being, I cannot.

What do you think about the vast publicity surrounding the use of drugs by musicians?

Well, I'll tell you, you've got to use something to be in this business. It's very hard to get by without drinking or smoking or whatever people feel they physically need to make it. This is not always because they had a bad upbringing and their parents weren't this and their mother was a whore and their father a drunkard. You can come from a completely normal family and have had a very normal and beautiful childhood, and when you get into this business, it's like something else. I think it's foolish for someone to try to destroy himself, but I do believe some sort of stimulant must be used by those who feel they need it in order to survive. If I feel that I need something and somebody else feels that he needs something stronger, then that's his thing. I can't say it's wrong. I just hate to see people—and it's usually the ones with great talent—who utterly destroy themselves by wanting some-thing to stimulate them; after a while it's not a stimulant, it's a necessity.

It becomes a sickness because of what it does to you physically. But I'm not thinking in physical terms. I'm thinking in mental terms. If you feel you have to do something, I think you must be stronger than the will to destroy yourself. You must try to find something that you can cope with, that you can rule, and not something that rules you. That something, just the will to get out of bed, you must have from the start almost literally before you take your first breath. If you can't rule yourself you should go and take a gun and kill yourself, because that is better. You're putting not only yourself but the people who love you through all kinds of mental anguish, and that is not fair. If you were only doing it to yourself and nobody else cared, then I'd say right on. But not when people love you and have to sit around watching you destroying yourself . . .

I'll tell you this in regard to drugs, I am so proud and happy and love the cats I know who were so deep into it and have come out of it and are beautiful individuals. Maybe it sometimes helped to make them the great individuals they turned out to be. So how bad was it? But they are exceptions to the rule. I have known too many great cats who have died from it. That's when you wonder how it can be good. Then you look up at a cat that's been through it and licked it and come through and been a better man than before he tried it, so what do you say?

Do you use the same technique if you're recording, doing a radio show, at a club or at a concert?

You have to change according to where you are. If you're doing a radio show and there's nobody there but you and musicians and technicians, that's one thing. If you're doing a broadcast or a TV show in front of an audience, that's another thing. Doing a concert with nothing there other than the people you're entertaining is still another thing. If you're cutting a record in a studio alone with just the musicians, that's another thing again.

First of all, TV I can do without. I never feel too comfortable on TV, mainly because I can't see all those twenty or thirty million people that I'm supposed to be singing to. Consequently it's like singing to the audience in the studio. Right? Which doesn't make up one iota of the people who you're being seen by and who are the real judges of the show; that leaves me cold. I don't mind because eventually I can sit down at the panel and talk, and I hope I can make up whatever I lacked while I was singing with some intelligence.

I really prefer to sing in concert for people who have paid

admission to hear me. I think I do my best in that atmosphere. I never do my best recording, because I never know the song until I record it and start doing it, and six months later it's right. Somebody says to you two weeks from now or four weeks from now, we're going to do a record; here are twelve songs. You learn them and you learn them, and you really learn them. But you don't know them until later.

You've never tried to do the numbers long before, say, in clubs?

I've never had the opportunity, unless it happened to be a song that I did with my trio and that I decided to put in an album with a big band. Then I know the song and I can do my thing. But not the songs that we sit down and pick out two weeks before the session. Some of them are utterly unfamiliar. I've never heard them before. Some of them I might know but have never sung before. It isn't really done right unless I dig the song and take out the rhythm-section parts after the session. Then we'll start doing it in clubs, and by the time the record comes out, I'm doing it completely different.

Carmen, I think we have a beautiful interview.

We've been talking for days, A.T.

Is there anything you want to add?

I think this is a fantastic idea of yours. I love to voice opinions and to be among such people as I'm going to be involved with in this documentary that you're putting down in book form. I'm very flattered that you chose to interview me. I just hope I will be worthy of all the other people that you've interviewed and that I'll have contributed something to somebody.

—*Cologne, Germany, October 30, 1970*

"I'm always interested in a love song."

How did you become interested in music, Nina?

It wasn't a matter of becoming interested in music; music is a gift and a burden I've had since I can remember who I was. I was born into music. The decision was how to make the best use of it.

What would you say was the major thing that helped in your development, and how did the piano help you as a singer?

I started out playing the piano at home and at revival meetings, which was a joy. I sang a little bit, because everybody in my family was musical. Every day there was singing and playing after dinner. My sisters and I formed a trio when I was about eleven, and we would go to churches and sing. I could harmonize without having learned, and I would always take the bottom part because my voice was very limited.

I started singing because it was the only way I could keep my first job. This was in an Irish bar at Atlantic City. I was playing the piano there, and the owner said to me, "If you want to keep the job, you must sing." I needed the ninety dollars a week—I had never heard of that much money in my life—so I sang. It's as simple as that.

In spite of my limited range and limited voice, I sang everything I heard. The piano helped because I have perfect pitch. I would play the songs in the easiest keys to sing in, so that nobody could detect that my voice was limited. By the time I got into show business, I had studied the piano seriously for fourteen years, practicing for about six hours a day. I never studied voice, but I had been around people who had studied voice, so I knew a little about it. I just used whatever came naturally to me.

So you had no formal voice training?

None at all; just piano. My mother and the white lady who

taught me classical piano had wanted me to become a concert pianist, so that's what I was preparing for. Then the harsh reality of making a living hit me when I went from North Carolina to Philadelphia and New York. I realized that if I didn't sing I couldn't keep a job; then I became known as a singer. The truth is that I'm a pianist; but I'm not only a pianist, I'm a total musician. The voice is one segment, one of my instruments. My piano training has helped me immensely, because at first it could hide all the things I couldn't do with my voice.

Were you influenced by anyone?

I was and still am influenced by everything I hear that is musical. My family was very religious, so we weren't allowed to listen to worldly music, but I got tastes of it. I might hear a record made by Ella Fitzgerald, Buddy Johnson, Ivory Joe Hunter or Louis Armstrong; on the classical side there was Marian Anderson and Bach, who I fell in love with. There were the pop singers on the radio. I had been playing what we call blues and gospel from the age of three, so I was very influenced by that, too. Bach was my chief musical influence. He's a great composer who had a perfect form in which he wrote, and he influenced me as much as the blues did. I didn't understand the blues form until much later, even though I was playing it all the time.

Have you modified your style in any way?

Yes, in a sense. The first thing I'm always interested in is a love song. I'm an eternal romantic. When my people began to make strides in getting equality of a kind, I found that I could come out of hiding. Ever since the age of three or four, I had known what the racial problems were; I also knew that I couldn't say anything about them. As time went on and I became older, my development and the direction I took musically were completely relevant to what black people were doing around the world. The more they asserted themselves, the more I was free to say right on! During the sixties my people started having riots and saying, we want this and we want that. I said, well, okay, now I can change my direction from love songs and things that are not related to what's happening, to something that is happening for my people. I can use my music as an instrument, a voice to be heard all over the world for what my people need and what we really are about.

It's just like a person being an actor every day and no one knowing who he really is. All of a sudden someone says, "I want to know who you really are," and the actor says: "All right, I can relax just a bit." I can't relax that much yet, but as my people make progress all over the world—Africans and my folks in America—I can come out of hiding a little more. I think it's my duty to express in music what they're feeling, and I'm privileged I can do that. Tomorrow I could compose a love song which would take the scab off the terrible sore that has to do with black men and black women's relationship with one another. Every black person who heard it would understand; there's no more hiding, because music is a universal language. You can be a complete politician through music. Just sing it; if the lyrics and the music are right, everybody knows and everybody feels.

I have become more militant, because the time is right. It always bothered me when I was a child that I could play certain songs at home, then go across the railroad tracks and study classical piano, and it was like two worlds all the time. To me at this point the subject of love between men and women is not as important as getting our people to become completely unified, to forget about their arguments with each other, to come together and see what they can do about getting their rights as human beings. This supersedes love; it is a supreme love and it must supersede love songs. I hope that explains the direction I've taken in the last eight years or so.

Yet I want to go back to love songs someday. I don't get a kick out of going onstage every day and singing protest songs; I love love, but I'm a voice and I influence millions and I know exactly what we want to do. I know a good protest song will make a man or a woman feel, I could be doing a little bit better every day. Music is one of the strongest elements we have.

Will you be singing protest songs in the future?

Well, I stopped singing love songs because protest songs were needed, so the direction I'll take in the future depends entirely on what happens to my people. If my people go back into hiding, perhaps I'll start singing love songs again. If we continue to make more strides, then I shall go on singing protest songs—protest songs that are acceptable, however, because I don't particularly want everybody to die, I just want everybody to know who we are.

I think women are eternal mothers, and the first thing that hits their mind is a maternal thing. They always want to know how they can help, how they can be in it and what they can get from it, though not necessarily for themselves; they want to control you, just like they want to control a child. It's maternal, and I don't think there's anything negative about it. I think it's a dominating force that must be harnessed. A man only has to say, Now look, just leave me alone. Women are impressed by things that they can be a part of in some way. That's the strangeness of women.

Most people don't realize how much of the mother there is in our black women. They are intuitively kind and instinctively want to help. In the United States the first thing a black woman will do when you enter her house is ask you if you're hungry. Then, when you eat her food, she wants to know if you liked it, and you better say you liked it. She just wants to be noticed, to be a part of your existence. I could talk to you for five hours about black women, black men, white women and white men, but I won't, I'll just say to those of you who haven't read Eldridge Cleaver's *Soul on Ice* and John H. Williams's *The Man Who Cried I Am,* that when you do read those two books, you'll know exactly how I feel about the whole situation.

Are you religious?

Oh, yes, but I have no particular religion.

Can you find God in your music?

Of course, all the time.

Can you explain that?

How do you explain what it feels like to get on the stage and make poetry that you know sinks into the hearts and souls of people who are unable to express it? How do you talk about that? There aren't many words, but in some way you know that tonight was a good thing, you got to them. That's God. I am very aware that I am an instrument. I have fights with God every day. I tell Him, "Unless you do such and such a thing, I'm not going to play anymore; I'm not going to sing anymore; I'm not going to let anybody know I'm around." It's because I know I've been given the gift of being able to play by ear, having perfect pitch, having things that ordinary people do not have. What perfect pitch is or how a person gets it is unexplainable. When you have this gift, you must give it back to the world. That's the only way you're going to get it off your back. I don't know if I can explain any better than that what God is.

Does your technique vary according to the type of performance you do?

No. My voice, as I told you, is very limited, so I can only do so much with it; my pianistic ability is not too limited, but what I do change is this: At each concert, each television show, each performance, I psych out the situation. Every room is different. The people in it are different, their mood is different, the time of day is different; all that goes through me before I perform. That determines what I'm going to sing and what mood I'm going to try to develop.

Sometimes I go to the concert hall earlier than usual, and I've done things like count the seats, try to get into the mood of the place. I'll know what kind of people come here if the seats are very lush; I'll check the position of the stage, the intelligence and education of the light and sound men, the mood I'm in, the mood my musicians are in and what I want to say. All that is influential and will certainly determine what I'm going to play.

I never make up a set or a concert until about thirty minutes before I go onstage, sometimes less than that. The musicians working with me know they must come to get the list of songs or the order of the concert; they sometimes cannot get it until five minutes before we're going onstage, because everything until that moment has influenced my selections. By that time I'm feeling completely different from the way I felt when I first entered the place.

Do you usually know your music well in advance of recording an album?

I never do it cold. I can't unless I'm going to do it by myself. If I'm going to play the piano with a musician I know, then I may do it cold, but the truth is I have not. I arrange most of the music I record personally. Weeks in advance I take the songs we have agreed on and I have the final say about the arrangements; then it's taken to an arranger, who orchestrates it.

The only thing close to cold I ever did was an album called *Nina Simone Sings the Blues*. We got the best musicians we knew, and we chose the songs, but we didn't do the arranging until we were actually recording. I must say, though, that I have done many concerts cold that have accidentally become albums. Like the second album I did at Town Hall. I hadn't seen the musicians who played with me that night until seven o'clock; we went on and did the concert cold, and it was recorded. If I had had a choice in the matter, I would not have done it that way. Fortunately, Wilbur Ware was on bass, but I get much too nervous to do anything cold, because jazz musicians like Wilbur Ware are rare! Most of the youngsters don't know beans about music, and I would never trust myself to do anything cold with them.

What do you think about electronics in music?

I went to a place called the Electric Circus in the Village, and I heard a violinist doing a solo there; it was a classical piece, a suite, I guess. He was playing with an imaginary orchestra; it was not completely imaginary, but it was done electronically. I was intrigued by that. The sounds weren't completely true, but the fact that it could be done intrigued me. I think that electronics can be used effectively, but you must know how to use them.

I suppose you're also asking me what I think about those loud rock groups. They have great equipment, but they haven't the intelligence or the experience to know that if you play too loud you puncture someone's eardrum. They have no taste or judgment. To be effective electronic instruments have to be used by people who are fully acquainted with music and its effect on the listener. Otherwise you run into what we have with these rock groups: They just play loud for the sake of playing loud.

How do you like the Beatles' music?

Well, we're in the seventies, and I can hide a little less. I think that my entire life consists of me coming out of my hole a little more. The Beatles were good inasmuch as they drew attention to our music in the white world. They made white people listen to our music with a different attitude than they had before. It could be that they give their respect only to the Beatles and that they are as racist as they've ever been, but I think we are listened to more and given more respect than before the Beatles. I do not know if this is true, and if it's not true we're in worse shape than we were. Because that would mean the Beatles had come along and distorted a part of our music while admitting they got their inspiration from us. It would mean that whites are only listening to whites, as before, and that youngsters who listen to the Beatles' music don't even know what good music is. Only history will prove whether the Beatles were a good thing.

What do you think about the so-called narcotism in our business?

I remember a time when drugs were thought of in the same breath as a musician. This is no longer true. Drugs have invaded the entire world, unfortunately; you get junkies of eleven or twelve now. Musicians have always known how to use drugs, unlike the youngsters today, who just use them because they're there. I think the drug problem is over in terms of us having to deal with it or think about it or having to justify it. Youngsters who know nothing about music are dying every day from drugs. It's an epidemic and a universal problem.

Do you think a musician could need a stimulant like that?

Yes, I do. Words do not tell people how you really feel. You have experiences and find yourself in situations that you can't tell anybody about. If they haven't got it here, where they can feel it, you can't tell them. I think that drugs have a function, but don't get me wrong, I think there's a limit to that, too. I can easily understand why musicians drink or smoke. I won't talk about heroin, because that's out of my thing. When you become the slave of anything, you better leave it alone. It's just like drinking; if you drink too much, it's going to do you in; if you drink moderately and it helps you do your work, then why not drink? It's only when it's taken to extremes that it's bad. If drugs are used for a particular purpose and you know what that purpose is, then you're the master of it.

Have you ever had any bad writeups, and if so, how do you react?

I got a bad writeup years ago in *Downbeat.* When I read it, I said, "This cat don't know me from beans." The critic didn't hear what I was trying to say, so I said to myself, Nina, you must say it more clearly next time. My attitude is that if a critic hits me in the gut and picks up something that I knew was bad, then he becomes my friend, because I know he heard me. But if a critic says things about me that bear no relation to what I was trying to do, I either think he doesn't know what he's talking about and that may be because I didn't make myself clear, or maybe it's because he's too stupid to know.

Have you ever run into a situation where you got a very fine review for a performance where you felt you weren't up to top form?

Yes, I've run into that. What happens then is that I call up the critic to say, "Look here, I'm glad you liked the show, but such and such a number wasn't that great." I don't respect him any more than I do a critic who didn't know what a fine performance was. I try to deal only with the truth. A critic who praises you when you shouldn't be praised is almost as bad as a critic who doesn't know what you're talking about and who gives you an X when you did well.

I haven't received many bad writeups. When I made *Mississippi God Damn,* we sent a box of records to one of the radio stations in North Carolina, and they broke up all the records and sent the box back. Of course, that was to be expected. It's the worst thing that's happened to me.

For some reason I can get away with saying the things I've been saying. I've been able to get away with it so far, but believe me, I know that the web gets tighter. I know that I'm being watched and that in the end, when the deal goes down, I'll be taken seriously; for in many ways I have not been taken seriously by the white world until now. Time is running out, though, because I'm sick and tired of my people being beaten and stepped on; I'm sick and tired of my people thinking they're nothing. So I'm just a blind person saying, all right, you did this and that, well, you're going to pay for it. Life is a balance, and justice is blind. Whoever it hurts, I'm sorry, and I may have to die feeling like this. When it comes to black people in the white world, I would rather die at the hands of a stupid black than at the hands of a knowledgeable white who's doing me in because I'm black. Let me die for a simple reason, an argument between blacks or an argument over five cents, as happens sometimes in Harlem when they're gambling. Let me die for something as stupid as that, but don't let me be killed by the establishment.

Have you ever been categorized as a jazz singer?

They can't seem to decide. Some critics say I'm a jazz singer, others say I'm not. Still others will say I'm a jazz singer plus another kind of singer. The truth is that they don't know what I am, and I'm glad.

I would like to know your feelings about the word jazz.

Max Roach defined the word technically. Jazz is not just music, it's a way of life, it's a way of being, a way of thinking. I think that the Negro in America is jazz. Everything he does—the slang he uses, the way he walks, the way he talks, his jargon, the new inventive phrases we make up to describe things—all that to me is jazz just as much as the music we play. Jazz is not just music. It's the definition of the Afro-American black.

You were telling me that you practice yoga. What is the reason you started, and how did you get involved in it?

I have always wondered how I could stop thinking about music. Sometimes at night I would be unable to sleep because a tune would be going around in my head for hours. I didn't know how to relax. I met this wonderful man, a swami from the Himalayas, and he taught me how to relax in any given situation; it had to do with breathing and was so interesting and simple. This led me to doing the exercises which keep your body supple, firm and young and also relax your mind. To me it's one of the greatest ways of getting high without getting high. I do about twenty-one exercises; the meditative exercises are the hardest, because you must be quiet. You can get high off air if you know how. It was an eye-opener to know this and to learn how to do it.

Do you find that it stimulates your perception of your work?

Yes, it does, but it also makes one feel tremendously lonely. The loneliness is not deeper or more intense than before I did yoga, but it hasn't helped make me feel part of any group. Yoga always makes you feel kind of apart from everybody, which is my problem anyway. It makes you terribly objective; it makes you create beautifully, but it makes you so sober and so apart from the situation in which you find yourself that everything is away from you; you're not a part of anything. I don't like that feeling.

When you're performing, where are you directing your art? Do you feel you are singing for your own pleasure, or are you doing it for the audience or the musicians?

At all times I try to play for myself if possible, and I hope that it pleases the audience. I will not do anything for them at the expense of myself. But I try not to please myself at the expense of the audience. I'm really always striving to do both—to have a good time and for the audience to have a ball, too. As for my musicians, they are an extension of myself or they don't play with me.

How did you like the Panthers?

God bless them. I'm so glad they existed. The Black Panthers and Angela Davis are an inspiration to young blacks who have never known anything about black people except that they were pacifists, in the sense that they took all the mental and physical cruelty inflicted on them by whites. That's all black children ever saw. The Black Panthers made these kids realize that there are black heroes who will fight and die if necessary to get what they want. That's what I find wonderful; they scare the hell out of white folks, too, and we certainly need that.

Have you ever had the opportunity to do any acting?

I have not had the opportunity to do any serious acting, but I'd like to do just one film or play before I die. I would want it to be something memorable; it's not that I want to become known as an actress, but I'd love to try my hand at it once or twice if the material was fantastic and if it was the kind of thing that I felt kin to.

What about women's fashions?

That's part of my breathing, part of me. I showed you this month's *Essence,* and I told you that it had been a dream of mine for fifteen years to be featured in some fashions. That's a woman's thing. Black women have to feel beautiful, and it's very hard when everything around you says that only blue-eyed blonds are beautiful. It's an intense interest of mine, because it's directly related to what people think of as beautiful. Fashions themselves are not beautiful, but if you know how to use them to enhance your own thing, your image changes. For instance, people thought I was fat for many years, and I've never been fat in my life. The truth was that I didn't know what clothes to buy. I didn't know that clothes were so important, that they could make you look fat or skinny. If you wear a white dress with big puffed sleeves, it makes you gain ten pounds. When they meet me, people say to me, "I thought you were fat," because of the photographs they have seen. If you know anything about fashion, you know that you should have been wearing a dark dress with long, slim sleeves. Anyway, the fashions you see now in all the magazines—*Vogue, Bazaar* and the black magazines as well— enhance the beauty of black women. All of a sudden the bandanna is fashionable. Most of the fashions now look better on black women than on white, so that makes it easier for us to develop our image.

What impression did you have of Charlie Parker's music?

I only saw him and Billie Holiday once in my life before they both passed away. Charlie Parker and Billie Holiday are our father and mother. Charlie Parker was so complex, his music was so superb and ahead of time that he reminds me of Beethoven, in the sense that he was one of those geniuses whose music will be remembered and understood long after their death. He's the father of modern music. As for Billie Holiday, every time I listen to her I hear more in the music than I heard before. I can't pay her a greater tribute than that. How do you talk about genius, 'specially when it's extraordinary genius? My God, how do you talk about Charlie Parker? Hundreds of years from now he will be understood and accepted much more than he is today. I expect a Charlie Parker cult to crop up years from now. It will grow and grow. It's got to happen.

Do you find it easier talking to someone like myself than, say, to a journalist?

Not necessarily. You're a terribly good interviewer, but I don't find the fact that you're a musician makes any difference. Your questions are more pointed, they're human, but I've also been privileged to have good interviewers before. It depends on the intelligence of the person who's doing the interviewing. If you mean do I feel a rapport with you because you're a musician, the answer is no.

Have you been to Africa?

Yes, I've been to Nigeria and Morocco. I'm going to Guinea very soon on a holiday. That's the only way that you can get to know a country. I've got friends living there, Miriam Makeba and Stokeley Carmichael. I'm looking forward to going there because I want to feel part of the people. Barbados is a black island, and I've been there five times in a year, so that tells you how much I love it. I'm planning to buy land there. It's heaven!

—Paris, December 14, 1970

≡ TONY WILLIAMS ≡

"Circle 45."

Tony, how did you become interested in music?

I guess it was going to gigs with my father all the time and watching the cats play. He started taking me about the time I was old enough to walk.

Your father's a musician?

Yes. He's a tenor and an alto player. One night, if I remember correctly, I said, "Dad, can I sit in?" and he said, "Sit in doing what?" I said, "Sit in playing drums." He said: "Okay," and that was the first time I ever played the drums in a club with an audience. Child wonder!

Where was that?

In Boston or Cape Cod.

Where were you born?

Chicago. When I was about two, we moved to Boston, Cape Cod and all that.

To what would you attribute your development as a musician?

Work. Hard work.

Do you do a lot of practicing?

Not a lot. Not as much as I'd like to.

Did you when you first started out?

I used to practice eight hours a day, every day! From about 1956 until about 1962. It was a whole thing, a whole period in my life where nothing else was happening.

Betty Carter. *Bob Richards*

Thelonious Monk. *Arthur Taylor*

Miles Davis. *Jimmy Cobb*

Dexter Gordon. *Arthur Taylor*

Big Sid Catlett.

Don Byas and Erroll Garner.

Above, J. J. Johnson (trombone), Duke Jordan (piano), Carmen McRae (vocalist), Kenny Dorham (trumpet), Sam Gill (bass), unknown conga player, Arthur Taylor (drums). Taken at Tony's in Brooklyn, New York, in the 1950s; *Below,* Charles Mingus (bass), Miles Davis (trumpet), Max Roach (drums), Gigi Gryce (saxophone). Taken at Tony's in Brooklyn, New York, circa 1953. *Jim Morton*

Joe Newman (hands on belt), Charlie Parker (alto saxophone), Shubert Swanson (seated in background), Lou Donaldson (holding saxophone), Walter Bishop, Jr. (piano), Ron Jefferson (seated in booth next to piano). *Courtesy of Walter Bishop, Jr.*

What do you think about the word jazz?

Sometimes I hate it and sometimes I love it. It all depends who I'm talking to. It's weird because I've gotten to the point where it's just good or bad. Jazz is like a life-style. Sometimes I feel if jazz ever became successful and the musicians really started making money, it wouldn't be jazz anymore. Because jazz has always been down in the basements. Other times you feel you're supposed to get what you're worth; everybody should have some bread, sell a lot of records and be successful. It's all moods; it depends on how I feel. I'm an authority on nothing.

You're an authority on you. Right?

That's about it, but sometimes I don't even know about me. I come up square sometimes.

Do you play for yourself, for the audience or for the musicians?

I'm mostly playing for myself and the musicians, 'cause if that works, then it's got to go over with the audience. That's my main concern.

Were you influenced by anyone when you started out?

Sure. Max Roach, Art Blakey, Jimmy Cobb, Art Taylor, Philly Joe Jones. All the cats, 'cause that's where it was and is.

Would you tell me about the group you have now?

It's another extension of me; it's all kinds of influences. I'm not that snobbish to rule out any influence. If people think you're playing rock or trying to play rock or trying to make money, that's their problem. I'm not going to rule out any possibility of making music. I use electric instruments because it's there; it's another sound. I can't play the same thing all the time; after playing with Herbie [Hancock] and Wayne [Shorter], I can't play with any horn player right now. After playing with Miles there aren't any trumpet players for me to listen to right now, so I go somewhere else for something else. I try to be stimulated. It's just stimulation for me.

Where did you get that energy from?

Oh, man, what energy? I'm tired as hell; last night, boy!

Where did you hang last night?

Over on that weird Left Bank. I'm ready to go back to New York, man.

How do you tune your drums?

I don't. I just get them till they sound resonant. I don't look for no sound, I just get them resonant where they carry, so they don't sound flat and soggy and won't carry over the other instruments. I try to lift them up over the bass and the bottom of the organ, so they're not all in the same register. You do that. Sometimes you tune them real high.

I think I tune them too high sometimes.

You might; I might, too. After a while they don't feel right. They're so high you can't hear them.

When did you start singing?

In 1969. You know, when you're a kid you stand on the corner with the cats. I figured I'd try it again because it's a sound. It's not like I want to sing songs; it's just something else to do. It gives another flavor to the music.

What was that tune you sang tonight?

"There Comes A Time."

Is that an original of yours?

Yeah. It's fun, man; if you're taking yourself too seriously . . . people take themselves too seriously.

Everybody does. Even you, maybe.

Right. That's one reason I've got other drummers, 'cause I can stop playing sometimes and the music can do something that I don't have to be a part of. It changes the sound of the band. I stop in the center, all the attention goes to the other musicians, the people aren't looking at me. One drummer on each side of me; that's a stereo kind of thing. It does all kinds of things. There are all kinds of things you can do on a stage. You can sit home and play, but when you get onstage, you want to do something extra, so the people come back. So that when you come back in town they say, yeah, we had a good time, so let's go back. Might as well!

What about all the strife going on with our people?

Yeah, what about it? It's going to take a long time. We're not going to see it; we're going to be long dead. All we can do is hang in there and keep fighting. That's the way I see it right now, 'cause it's really mean. In some areas like TV it's getting better, though it's kinda sad to say that. Some places people are starting to realize if they keep going the way they're going, none of us are going to be here. It's not just black people, it's all over the world. The Catholics and Protestants in Northern Ireland, the Portuguese are still fighting the Africans, Arabs and Jews, Americans in Vietnam. Right now there's more to think about than just your own thing. It's too much, man. It's too much.

Does that affect your music?

No, because I don't play political music. Music is hipper than that. When cats in the press ask, Does your music express your people's conflicts? I say no, it's just there. Anything I do politically is too personal. I don't need to use my music to do that. That's cheating. I really don't dig political music, using music.

What do you plan for yourself in the future?

To keep working as much as possible, and get it on, and show people that the music isn't dead. Try to bring back the vitality that has been lost. They've made jazz an art form, put it in concert halls, made it intellectual, and that's one way they killed it. So did the rock. I would like to see the vitality back that used to be there. Even though Birdland was a drag, at least the cats were playing and there was vitality. There isn't any vitality in the cats anymore.

When I see you, I see it, I feel it.

I hope so. But when cats start playing music they call political music, avant-garde and everybody's out, they're doing just what whitey wants them to do. That's the way I feel.

What do you think about the widely publicized use of drugs in the business?

I don't think about it, man. What do you mean? Do I like cats using drugs, or do I like the publicity that it gets?

The publicity.

It gets the publicity because the cats are in the limelight. Doctors and lawyers have been doing it all the time, and they don't get that publicity because they're not in the limelight. Plus they have the bread to maintain theirs, so they're not exposed to getting busted. It's no different; everybody's using drugs—pills, coffee, tranquilizers.

Are you religious?

Yes, music. That's enough. I don't believe in astrology, none of that. You got it, 'cause it takes up too much time to be wondering about all that. I don't think it's going to help me play any better right now. Maybe one day if I need something that's going to make me play better . . . I believe in real hard work. I can't find time for religion.

Has the publicity you have received affected you in any way?

Only inasmuch as I want more, because of what it does, because of what you see publicity can do for other people. Publicity helps, and the record company has been good in that respect. This whole tour is a promotion tour through the record company. We were brought to Europe by the record company. They're paying all expenses, plus we get paid for the gigs. In New York I tell them, "If you want me to sell records like those other groups do, like those rock groups, then you've got to do for me what you do for them. I don't want any more than you do for them. I'm not asking for the world. I don't demand it. But just give me equal treatment." Then it's up to me. If we don't sell records then, it's my fault. Then I don't have to turn to the record company and say, "You jive . . ." 'Cause they don't want to hear that and I don't want to hear it.

How do you feel when people, after a performance, say how beautiful and how wonderful it was?

It all depends. If I don't think it sounds good, then it's a drag, but I appreciate people who dig it. Though I might not have dug it, I appreciate somebody saying they dug it, 'cause that's one reason why you're out there—you want to play for the people. 'Specially when you write and arrange the music, you worry about it and hope it comes out right. Before you go on you're tense and drop sticks. Then someone says, "It's great." I say, *"Oh."* It works differently all the time.

Have you ever gotten any bad criticism?

Yeah.

How does it affect you, or how do you take it?

The first hour, I'm arrrrrr. But I say, as long as they spell my name right.

What about when they say something very flattering?

I try to ignore that more than the other thing, because that's easy, those writers. After a while if you become a fad you can do no wrong, and I don't like that. I don't want that. I don't look at the reviews, anyway. I don't even listen to the records after a while.

You never listen to your own records?

About two weeks after they're made I listen and enjoy it. After that it's over, 'cause you can get too attached to what you just did and you can't go on.

Would you tell me what you think about Charlie Parker's music?

Oh, man! That whole thing is like . . . we play a tune called "Circle 45," and it means 1945, that's when I was born. I wish I had been born earlier because of that whole period with Bud and Bird. I'm really sorry I missed that. That holds a special place in my heart, really. That's what I think about Charlie Parker.

—*Paris, June 17, 1971*

≡ SONNY ROLLINS ≡

"I get the vibrations and go from there."

How do you like Scandinavia?

I think it's nice, but when I'm around in Europe, I get the feeling after a while that I'm somewhere that I'm not supposed to be. It's nice if you're here a short time for business. As far as staying around, I think I would feel like I was trying to come into someone else's domain. I don't like to be places where I'm not welcome. I don't want to feel that kind of draft! I was talking to Mal Waldron and he said, "Why don't you come over here and lay," but I don't know how it would be if I were to try to settle in a place like this; I'm not sure I would be able to feel right and get into it.

How did you become interested in music and the saxophone?

I liked listening to music. We always had a piano in the house when I was growing up. My brother was a very good violin player. He went with the Pittsburgh Symphony when he left Music and Art High School. He was really great. I used to hear him practicing all the time. My sister plays piano and was singing in the church. Naturally I liked it and took to it. They got most of the training, and me, being the youngest child, I picked up on all the vibrations and came into it without having to go through a lot of training, just as a natural thing. As you know, I'm more of a natural musician than a trained musician like my brother. So I fell into it like that.

How did you develop yourself?

I practiced a lot, but I think when I first started playing, I had a certain thing. It was something that I could express through the saxophone. A lot of my ability, whatever it is, is a gift. Of course I developed it, and when I went away to the bridge that time, I did a lot of practicing and studying and took piano lessons again, harmony lessons, and I tried to get up on those aspects. But basically it's just a gift. That is what I imagine gives me the individuality I have.

Do you play for yourself, for the musicians or for the audience?

I would say I'm playing for the sake of music. This is my first appearance since 1969. One of the reasons I stopped then was because things had got to the point where I found that playing was getting to be a real job and a chore, which I didn't dig. I spend as much money as necessary to get equipment, clothes or whatever I need to make an impression and to be into the music. It's all done for the music first, regardless of what it costs me. Many people have said that I have a lot of energy, which I do, because I'm playing for the music. For instance, I played a three-hour set one night in a nightclub, and they were trying to get us off the stage to turn the house over. In other words, I'm playing and thinking about trying to get the music across and nothing else. Time doesn't matter. Maybe a lot of the younger cats might not have that same energy. I've found that a lot of musicians I played with don't have the same kind of incentive. I thought it might be because I was who I am and they were working for me, so I was supposed to have more incentive than they did.

Tell me something about Bud Powell and Charlie Parker.

Of course, you and I knew Bud when he was living in our neighborhood. In my opinion, Bud was a genius just like Bird. They were untouchable as far as their musicianship was concerned. They could do no wrong in anything they did, which was a hell of a mark for a young cat to try to achieve. I'll never achieve that because I'm not as great a musician as Bird or Bud, but playing with them and being around them perhaps helped me attempt to reach that level. They were both great.

Bird was not only great to me as far as music goes; he also befriended me at a very important time in my life. You know that Bird helped get me off drugs when I was younger. That was a major turning point in my life. When I made that record, *Collector's Items,* with Miles and Bird, Bird found out that I had been indulging. He really didn't like it. I saw for the first time that he didn't dig my doing that. I realized I must be doing the wrong thing. Up until that time I had thought it was all fun and games and that it was okay to use drugs. I subsequently got myself off drugs, when he showed me that wasn't the way to go. Unfortunately, when I did get myself straight, I was anxious to let him see I had dug his message, but as life would have it, he passed away before I was able to meet him again. Still, he provided the impetus at that time to get me off drugs.

Since you mentioned drugs, what do you think about the vast publicity musicians get through the use of drugs?

I'm beginning to think it's overplayed, because with the conditions in the United States for musicians, the type of life they live, being around late hours and nightclubs, it's a natural thing for them to fall into the use of either whiskey or drugs. I don't think it's an integral part of the music or that it has anything to do with it. It's a fact that when you work around these environments, you're susceptible to get involved in these things. But to go from that point to say that drugs are an integral part of the music or that everyone in music is involved in drugs would, I think, be a wrong conclusion.

What do you think about the word jazz?

I've been talking to Yusef Lateef, and he's really death on this word *jazz*. Sometimes people say, Don't talk about all that jazz, not meaning anything connected with music. It has been used in a lot of different ways. At one time it used to mean fornication. It is an unfortunate word, but how are you going to eliminate it? I don't know. I think it's almost a losing battle to try and eliminate the word *jazz*.

What do you do in your leisure time when you're not playing?

I do a lot of yoga to keep my body together. I used to be very interested in philosophy, but in the past years I've read so many books on philosophy and I've been to India studying yoga, so that I very seldom open a philosophy book and read it. I really have to be in the mood. I'm now ready to live a little bit more, and perhaps I'll reach another period when I'll do some more reading. I don't do anything outstanding besides that. Yoga covers it as far as exercise goes. I used to do a lot of weight lifting and more strenuous things, but I found that yoga combines it all, and I can do it in the privacy of my room.

Do you think it affects your music?

It has a great effect. In fact, I read what Miles said in his interview about why he does exercise; I think this is also why I do it. It's good for your wind and it keeps your stomach flat so that you make a good appearance. This has a lot to do with the way you feel. It makes you feel better, and it is also good for stamina. If you do the physical thing, it's going to affect your mind and make you feel happier with yourself; automatically your mind becomes more serene. I don't want to let myself get fat and out of shape. I've seen some cats get a big stomach and they're puffing on cigarettes; I don't want to get like that.

Have you ever received any bad writeups?

Yeah, I've received a lot of bad writeups.

Does it affect you?

Yes, it does. I don't have the greatest opinion of myself; I recognize a lot of my faults. They might contain something that's accurate, a good point that I can dig. But as a rule, I don't like a bad writeup because it would affect my name, whether or not it's right. They might say Rollins did this bad or he can't do that, which might be true, but at the same time this is affecting my economic life. I have to kinda get a good review in order to be able to work. This is the main reason I'm against it. It's not that they might not make a true point; they might; but those guys are not right most of the time.

Do you think our music stems from Africa?

I think so. I'm glad to say that in my music one of my strong points is rhythm. I've had a lot of schooled musicians come to me and say they've tried to transcribe recordings of my work and they couldn't put it down. This makes me feel good, because Africa is the king of rhythms. I know there is a connection, especially in my case. As far as saying that all of the music comes from Africa, I don't know.

Are you religious?

I've been religious at times; then I found I might be on the wrong track when things went against the way I thought they should be. I am religious, but it's hard to describe because every time you try to say, yes, this is it, there is a God or there is a reason, there is good and bad, there might be a circumstance in life which could shake that. I haven't met anyone who really knows anything about religion. No one knows. I would like to believe, I would like to feel that there's something worthwhile and that there is a God. I have to say at this point in my life, I don't know. My innermost feelings are that there is, but it is so deep I can't talk about it.

What do you think of electronics being used in music now?

Some of the sounds are good. I have a feeling that as long as the artist himself is involved in it, it's okay. I don't want to see things get to the point of push-button music. This might be what's coming, but it would be adverse to what I'm doing, so I can't buy that. I wouldn't like to get into any era of too much of that. The use of an electronic saxophone or piano or guitar might be a legitimate form of expression if someone can use it in a good way. I would like to feel that it was the person and not the electronic thing. As long as the guy is doing it and he uses that as a way of expressing himself, okay.

Say you were playing a concert and another time you were in a recording studio—would you change your technique in any way?

If I were making a recording, I might try to condense everything; at least I did back in the days when recordings were very short. Now you have more time. If it was a three-minute track, I would perhaps try to put everything more closely together. As a rule, my playing is a spontaneous thing. I just try to get the vibrations and go from there. As it's not planned, my technique wouldn't really change. I'm always on the same level.

What do you think about the strife black people are engaged in all over the world?

I would go back to America, because I think that's the base. It's a drag. I mentioned to you before how I feel when I come to Europe; I feel I'm in another man's country. In the States it's difficult, and I'm the type of person who can withdraw into myself; so a lot of times I choose to withdraw and not to go out and get involved with hostility from white people. If you go downtown to buy a pair of shoes or whatever, you know you will run into a lot of jive. It's a bad thing. Of course I know you have to get out in it; you can't just withdraw and try to forget that it exists.

I'll say this—about ten years ago I used to be very much in favor of trying to bridge all the people in the world together and trying to bridge the gap between white and black. I used to read a lot of philosophy and look for ways of bringing everybody together. I would go out of my way to try and make friends. But now I know that this is redundant on my part as a black man, because it's not up to me to do it; it's up to the white man to be friendly with me. If I do it, the white cat can say it's because I want to better my position in the world. It can be looked upon as a selfish thing. I can't go around to the guy preaching love and let's get together, because it can be looked upon as being suspect coming from a black cat. Do you understand what I mean? It's a white person's prerogative to do all of these things; I can't do it. I had to give up that idea because it really doesn't work. It's up to the ruling class, so to speak, to do all of these things. It's probably to the advantage of a white person to keep himself on top and the black below, so I honestly can't see why a white person would want to change things.

What do you think about musicians giving political aspects to their music?

I read a book recently by Frank Kofsky. It's called *Black Nationalism and the Revolution in Music.* It has a picture of Coltrane on the cover. The book documents some of the things that have happened up to now in the political sense you're speaking of. It cites the fact that I was one of the first guys in the modern era to bring the political thing into music. My composition "Airegin," (Nigeria spelled backward), also the *Freedom Suite.* I don't know if you remember that.

I do remember. Oscar Pettiford was on that.

And Max. I had written on the back cover of the album about what a drag it was that black people didn't get their due. That was the reason for the suite. I wrote it at a time when I was beginning to get a lot of good publicity, and everyone was hailing me and saying how great I was. Yet when I went to look for a good apartment, I ran into this same old stuff. Here I had all these reviews, newspaper articles and pictures. I can look back on it and see that it was a natural thing we all go through. At the time it struck me, what did it all mean if you were still a nigger, so to speak? This is the reason I wrote the suite. I also wrote a comment on the back-cover liner notes: "America is deeply rooted in Negro culture: its colloquialisms; its humor; its music. How ironic that the Negro, who more than any other people can claim America's culture as his own, is being persecuted and repressed; that the Negro, who has exemplified the humanities in his very existence, is being rewarded with inhumanity."

Kofsky's book relates the fact that I was one of the first people to begin to talk about these things and relate them to the music. Now that I look back on it, this is true; they were some of the first things that were said about the subject, although it was on everybody's mind, of course. Yet in a way I think music should be judged on what it is. It should be very high and above everything else. It is a beautiful way of bringing people together, a little bit of an oasis in this messed-up world. If I look at it like that, then I have to reject the idea of trying to put politics in music. At the same time, a lot of things that happen are political. I don't know what can be gained from dwelling on that fact, except as a way of going back to African roots or trying to get a black sound. This is one question you asked me which I would have to think a bit more about.

Do you prefer to play at concerts or clubs?

I prefer to play anyplace where I can have a nice dressing room. 'Specially if it's a club, I like to be able to relax between sets. A lot of times I come off and I'm drenched with sweat. At a particular club in New York, when you come offstage, you're right there with the people. Concerts are good because you have a chance to come out, perform, then go back and refresh yourself.

Am I right in thinking you were originally influenced by Coleman Hawkins?

I would like to think so, because he was one of my first idols. I was very much impressed with his playing, his musical approach and the music he was playing on his horn. He was playing music!

Do you still have an interest in spectator sports like you did years ago?

Well, boxing I'm getting away from, because I've seen a lot of matches where guys would get beaten to a pulp. If it is a good match where the referee stops it if a guy's getting beaten too much, I like that. I used to be a hit 'em, hit 'em, but I'm not into that anymore. I like baseball; it's got a certain slow pace to it; it's sort of an American thing. I grew up with it and I still enjoy it. I would go more often, but in the past few years I haven't been going out much. I would if I could get back into that groove.

What do you think of Muhammad Ali?

As a boxer I guess he's okay. At first I didn't like him because I always liked a cat that could put a man out with one punch, a heavy puncher. I guess his being so fast is great for a heavyweight, but I always liked the flat-footed type of fighter. Other than that, I like him very much; I dig the way he puts an extra dimension into everything he does. The fact that he could come back after being away for so long is beautiful. This way he has of doing the extraordinary is what I dig in people. They say he can't do it, and he does it in the face of odds. That's what I admire in him. He's got some great strength someplace.

What did you think of Malcolm X?

I can relate to Malcolm X in many ways, because I came up on the streets in the same way he did, and as you know, I got into scrapes when I was younger. I think what he did was great. Like him, I tried to straighten my life out and avoid getting into a rut and getting on the wrong side of the law. In that way I can relate to him. I thought he was an extremely articulate cat. Perhaps he should have stayed more with the Islamic movement. It might have been a bad thing when he began to put down Elijah Muhammad. I don't know whether Elijah Muhammad is good or bad, or if what Malcolm said was right or wrong, but when you're that close to a person, you can't turn around and put him down. I think he might have had a little too much ambition. Of course, I loved to hear him speak, but I also like a stable thing, and I dig the Muslims. I dug Father Divine, this type of setup where you get a group and they stay together. In that respect I don't dig some of what Malcolm did when he broke away and then put Muhammad down.

In closing, I would like to know what you plan for yourself in the future—musically and socially—if you could just wrap it up.

Well, in regard to music, now that I've been away for a while I want to get back into playing a little more, and I also want to try to fulfill myself. I've left a lot out. I've done a few things, but I think there is a bit more that I could actually do in my music. I'd like to make some more recordings; I haven't recorded in a long time.

As for my personal life, I'm getting into a phase now which I think might be very good, where I'm beginning to just want to be in a natural state all the time and not have anything to do with alcohol or any kind of stimulant. I'm also reaching a stage where I can really dig life as it is. I've always heard people ask, Why can't you dig life the way it is? Why do you need to get high? I couldn't relate to that at the time. I felt I wanted to get high before playing. I'm beginning to find that I can make it without stimulants—not only that I can but that I want to, and that I can enjoy life the way it is without using whiskey or anything. This is the first time that this has ever happened to me. Maybe it's because I'm now forty and this is the time when you go through that; I don't know. If this is true it means that I will be able to get into a lot of other aspects of life. It might open the door for me to a whole new approach toward life. It's a little early to say now.

—Kongsberg, Norway, June 24, 1971

☰ DON CHERRY ☰

"Education should open you up."

I was raised on music. My mother played the piano, and my grandmother played the piano for silent movies. My father had a club in Tulsa, then he was a bartender at the Plantation Club in Watts, Los Angeles, where I was raised. We were Oakies who had moved to California. We always had a piano in the house. I took a few piano lessons, then I started playing the boogie-woogie and got off lessons. In 1950 my mother bought me a trumpet. My father was always down on me about playing music. He connected playing music, especially jazz, with taking drugs. He knew how drugs can control your life.

I also became interested in music because a lot of my relatives were members of the Baptist Church, and I would often go to the church and listen to the choirs. I saw how the spirit would enter the room, and everyone would become very happy. To me that's what music has always been about—stimulating that sense within us which only music can stimulate.

Someone in our neighborhood had all the records of Charlie Parker, Monk, Fats Navarro, Leo Parker, Lady Day and Bud Powell. We couldn't buy the records, but we could listen to them and borrow them. When I say *we,* I mean myself and an alto player named George Newman. We would listen and learn the tunes. The first be-bop tune I learned was Bird's "Perhaps." Then I learned a lot of Bird tunes like "Klactoveedestene." On reaching the level of "Klactoveedestene," I tried to reach the level of "Donna Lee" and "Confirmation." These songs open up a young musician by showing him how the notes can become sound. The sound of be-bop was fascinating, and you wanted to reach that sound. You have to know these melodies to see how they move, how the notes are moving within the chord structure. You learn about a bridge, and you learn to remember that the bridge comes again, because there were always some musicians who couldn't conceive that form.

I was always interested in form. George Newman and I started playing in the high-school band, which was taught by Mr. Samuel Brown. Frank Morgan, Art Farmer and a lot of other musicians studied with him. We were playing some of Dizzy Gillespie's big band things like "Things to Come" and "Manteca."

I went through that until I quit school. I quit because education always seems to vacuum you, to close you up and to indoctrinate you. Education should open you up, draw things out of you so that you realize they're in you. The grade school and junior-high school I went to were interracial. I could never play first trumpet even though I think I had the ability, because there would always be someone white playing first trumpet. The teacher was in that groove, thinking that way. That's why I tried to play other instruments, so I could have the melody part. I would play baritone horn, which was good, because I learned other voices. I really liked phrasing melodies. I could read, count and play something the same way twice, but when I heard how Bird, Bud and even Lady Day could play the same thing differently each time, I realized how important phrasing was. First it was form, then phrasing and then sound, always sound.

How would you classify your music?

Jazz started as Dixieland, then it went to swing, to be-bop, then to what they call avant-garde or whatever. Some people say it's development, but I believe that it's the quality of Dixieland and swing which is really important and must be preserved. It is this quality of purity, pitch and sound which must be retained, this quality of improvisation. Even in the West they used to improvise when they played the classics. Today there's so much pressure to become professional and commercial that you try to get a thing going which everybody recognizes as being specifically yours. That's what stops high-quality improvisation. People who live in nature and with nature in Africa, China, or in the woods give their music a quality which is both earthy and godly, and that's what I think should be preserved: this quality of earthiness.

What do you think of the word jazz?

If we're going to speak about words, we could talk about a word like *aum*. Because you don't say the word *aum*, you sing it. And you have to sing it where you use the *a* as *ah*, which is the throat. Then you're singing, sustaining the tone *ah*. Then you go to the *u*, and then you reach the *m* and you've liberated the body. That's a word. In the Bible they speak of the Word. First there was the Word. And then they speak of the word that was lost.

But do you consider yourself a jazz *player?*

I consider myself a jazz player because I have been around some musicians who I felt had been sent here as messengers. They were called jazz musicians and they have showed me the way.

But what about the word?

You're speaking like Webster's or the Oxford dictionary or like something commercial. What do you call those people who feel they have control and who put that word on the music? There can be so many different qualities in our music; it can be intellectual music, it can be spiritual music, or music just for joy, or celestial music. John Coltrane was one person who attained this celestial quality. When he came on the scene, he realized that he had to carry the message, and he carried it very well. His thinking was spiritual, but instead of speaking of it, he would play and you could feel it. You could also feel it in the way he lived and carried himself as a human being. Albert Ayler, too. That was a very special period in jazz. I thank God for having been able to live during the time and period of their presence.

I would still like you to classify the music.

But that's canning it if you put a label on it like jazz. Maybe we could say that jazz is a truth we realize because we are living it. That brings me to the point of when I met Ornette Coleman. Here was a person who not only taught himself to master an instrument but who also realized we had a system of music that contradicts the Western system while still having the intelligence of the Western system. I'm speaking of the way Ornette writes his music. He has a fantastic system. It's not bar lines, it's more or less where each note creates a melody of a wholeness. It's basically the same system as be-bop.

What is your reason for living in Europe?

We live on Planet Earth, and I'm at a period in my life where I have to come close to Mother Earth and live in the rotation of the seasons. I had lived in cities most of my life, and I reached a point where I had a polluted brain, a polluted soul. The only cure for me was nature. I settled in a forest, on the earth, without boundaries. It's like you asking me about this word *jazz;* I feel the same way about boundaries. Like there are all kinds of different people and languages. But there's one universal language: the language of music. When people believe in boundaries, they become part of them. When did they first start having passports? That's the only way I can categorize music. I have read different books on jazz. I have never been to New Orleans, but I know a drummer called Edward Blackwell who's from New Orleans.

When I came to Europe, especially France, I heard a lot of records I had never heard before: Bubba Miley, old Duke Ellington, Freddie Webster and a lot of Louis Armstrong. I've been raised in the environment of Jimmy Lunceford. Jimmy Witherspoon was a good friend of the family. A few musicians my father knew had different records of Pres [Lester Young] and Django [Reinhardt]. Django was incredible, and he was in Europe. All of us should write a book to record these things. I have been very close to and studied with Dollar Brand. To me he is a very important person, as are his music and melodies. I have been where people have taught them to other people and could sing these melodies. It feels so close to when I was going to the Baptist church or hearing someone playing the piano. Also studying music from India, which has been beautiful for my concentration. If we're categorizing jazz, we can speak of different systems of music. Like the music of China, of the Orient, from Bali, or the music from north India, south India, the music from the Congo, the music from the Dagoons. Each one has such spiritual quality to it. Playing music for money is one thing, but playing music to reflect God is a whole reality that holds the truth. That's it. I don't want to talk too much.

—Kongsberg, Norway, June 26, 1971

≡ HAMPTON HAWES ≡

"I wouldn't care if she was green and had red breath."

I became interested in music via the church. My father was a minister, and my mother used to play for the choir. There was always singing in the church, and she used to take me there when I was a baby; the first thing I ever saw was a piano, because she used to sit me on her lap while she played. I used to listen. At first I listened to church music and spirituals. The first record I heard was by Earl Hines. He was playing boogie-woogie on the "Saint Louis Blues." I was self-taught. I listened to Nat King Cole and I dug him. I would also listen to Fats Waller and Art Tatum, and I was just drawn to their music. I started practicing and trying to play the boogie-woogie. I listened to James P. Johnson and to Albert Ammons, the father of Gene Ammons. I was in junior high school with Eric Dolphy, and one day he asked me to come to his house to hear some new stuff. Then I heard Dizzy Gillespie, and that did it. I said, "This is what I want to play!" It was the hippest music I had ever heard in my life. Dizzy, Don Byas and J. C. Heard playing be-bop. I knew that was the way I wanted to go.

What do you think about electronics being used in music?

I'll tell you, man, I don't put nothing down. If somebody wants to play a cabbage, it's all right with me. But I'm going to stick to the wood, because those are my roots, that's the way I came up. A lot of cats are playing electronics; I don't know if it's a fad. I like some of it. I was going to play electric piano at the Montreux Festival; they had set it up and then, when I started playing the concert, I said, "Fuck it!" and stuck to the wood. I don't think niggers need to play anything electric, because niggers are electric! They don't need to plug instruments in. But if some musicians want to do it to make some money, that's cool with me.

What do you think of Charlie Parker and Bud Powell?

I think Charlie Parker was the most important cat born in this century. I feel fortunate that when I was coming up, I had the opportunity to play with him. Bird influenced me more than anybody, even more than piano players. Bud Powell was the greatest be-bop piano player in the world. Nobody could phrase like him. I met Bud, but I didn't get to know him well. I really knew Bird; we used to hang together, and we both played in Howard McGee's band. All I have to offer came from the inspiration of Bird. Maybe someday they will put up a statue of him. I think all the other great musicians like Trane and Miles came out of Bird. It's not that they sound like him, but consciously or unconsciously, their spirits came out of Bird's spirit.

Do you do any kind of physical exercise?

I used to swim a lot. I did a lot of exercise when I was in the army and in the penitentiary. I don't do enough now; I walk a lot and that's about all.

You mentioned the penitentiary. You were arrested for using heroin, right?

Right. I went to the penitentiary in 1959 and got out in 1963. I got executive clemency from President Kennedy on August 16th, 1963, and they killed the motherfucker three months later. I was next to the last cat he let out. The last cat he let out was a Japanese general who was in for war crimes.

How did you become involved with narcotics?

All niggers are involved with narcotics. All niggers have to get high because they're so fucked up from having been oppressed all their lives. I've been nervous since I was three years old, when I first became aware of the fact that there were different people on the earth and it seemed like whites controlled everything. You had to act a different way around white people, and it was all that fear and oppression which made niggers get high. Especially musicians, because if a musician wants to play what he feels, he has to escape all that shit. It's happened to damn near everybody I know. Some have survived, some have died. I just went right along because I was another nigger trying to play. Unfortunately, I got caught.

Did you go back to it after you came out of prison?

No, I didn't. I broke the habit in prison, cold turkey! I was so sick that I used to stick lit cigarettes against my arm to change the pain! I had been fucked up for nine years. When I came out, I said, I don't want to get fucked up anymore, so I didn't. A lot of cats who were fucked up at the same time as I was cooled it out.

Did they try to rehabilitate you in prison?

Listen, man, that's something I want to tell you about. In the first place, I talked to three or four psychiatrists there, but there's nothing a white psychiatrist can ask a nigger about what's wrong, because he has no understanding of what a nigger is thinking. He wasn't brought up that way. He hasn't had the years and years of depression, the feeling of being left out and of frustration. They tried to do a good job, but I canceled them out because there was nothing they could ask me that would make any sense, as they weren't black like me. They would have to live in that shit, then they could have asked me something. You could ask me something, but they couldn't. You should have been the psychiatrist there, not them. And I'm not trying to put them down, because they wanted to do a good job, but they just weren't happening.

What do you think about all the strife going on with our people in the States?

It's like a pregnant broad. It's going to be a birth into something beautiful. I don't know if we'll see it or not, but I think it's growing pains. People are waking up; black people are waking up. You notice how they're saying black is beautiful. When I was growing up, black was ugly. Niggers were so nervous that they didn't even want to marry black people; they wanted to find a high yellow bitch to try and identify with whitey. Niggers were getting conks, bitches were getting their hair done, looking at *Harper's Bazaar* and all that. Now niggers are just being themselves. Today some of the white kids are so nervous that they don't know what they're doing, either. They grow their hair long and are crazy, too, because they see their fathers are fucked up. It's all a pattern, and this pattern is going to develop. After all the

strife I believe the US will be a better country. It may even end up
being the greatest country in the world. But they're going to have
to burn the motherfucker down and rebuild it; then it's going to
be cool.

What role do you think musicians can play in that?

I think we have been playing a role for a long time. As they say
in the army, we were the advance guard, though nobody knew
what we were doing. Back in the fifties when cats like Dexter
Gordon and Miles were coming up, cats were getting high trying
to express themselves, protesting in their own subtle way. But
everybody put us in a bag, because we were just supposed to be
happy little niggers playing music for white folks. But we
musicians were the first to pay the dues. Charlie Parker died long
before Huey Newton. Huey Newton didn't die, but Charlie
Parker was crucified. The younger brothers are coming up in the
political shit now, but we were into the shit before that. They're
talking about Black Panthers, but we were the panthers then. We
were trying to bring love and understanding, though; we weren't
just hostile. The role we played laid down the foundation; it all
came out of that. I believe that when they look back one day and
see cats like Bird and even older cats like Sidney Bechet and Don
Byas, they're going to realize that musicians were the true
revolutionaries in their own quiet way.

Do you play for yourself, the musicians or the audience?

I try to play for God, man! I play for the Creator. I feel that if I
play and let everything come out of me, like my body is a tool, if I
think deep enough and try to let the truth come out, then I can
bring something to the audience. Because if they're thinking
deep, the same shit will be coming out of them. I try to play for
the Creator, because I believe that's how deep the music is. Music
is that deep. To me music is God, so I play for God.

Are you religious?

Not in the usual sense. Fuck a cross, a church and all that! I'm
religious insofar as the earth and all that mean something to me,
but not the Bible, because that's manmade shit. I'm religious
about nature, the universe and human beings, but I don't claim no
one motherfucker as anything. I believe everybody is God,
everybody has God in him, so just let it come out.

What do you know about the history of our music?

It probably came from the South. I saw a movie once which showed some cats sitting humming in a cotton field, and it sounded real close to what I used to hear in my father's church, where they would be humming on Sundays. Then I heard Bird hum on jazz, and it all sounded alike. They brought the Africans here and put them to work in the fields. The motherfuckers were tired and their feet were hurting, so they started moaning, and the shit just passed on down to us. We're moaning, man! When we play, we're moaning. I think it came straight from Africa via the South and on to us. I wish we could all trace our heritage way back to see what tribes we came from.

But now we've made the music slick; it had to be slick because it was so deep. Take be-bop or avant-garde, or whatever they want to call it; all that came out of a motherfucker bending over all day picking cotton, and somebody slapping him upside his head. That's our heritage. We're playing the same shit 'cause we were slapped upside our heads, only it was more mental than physical. Maybe my great-grandfather was whipped for real, but they whip me, too, man; only they whip me mentally. I'm just as fucked up as he was, so that when I play, the same shit is going to come out of me as came out of him when he had to hum to get some strength in his body to finish picking all that cotton.

What do you think about the mixing of the races?

I'll tell you one thing: All niggers want to fuck white women 'cause that's their way of getting back. White women look pretty, they've got white skin and long hair and they are the princesses of the motherfuckers who run this shit. The white man has told the white woman not to fuck with niggers because we're inferior and all that, and some of them believe it. He also told her that we all had long dicks, that we could play boogie-woogie, tap dance and fuck, and he was damn near right. That's all we had to do: playing boogie-woogie and tap dancing, 'cause we couldn't be presidents and all that.

I guess white women first wanted niggers because of the different skin color and also because it was taboo for white people to be with niggers, which made them want to try, plus lust. Then, after the white women got to know how nice niggers were, how soulful niggers were, how niggers don't go around oppressing people like their husbands, plus they weren't as stupid and silly as white men, they started falling in love with niggers. Then things really got fucked up and they started marrying them. I would say that six out of ten white women are serious about niggers, the other four want some black poodles with long dicks. I fell for it. I used to try and fuck all the white women I could get. I still like white women, but my mental attitude is different. I don't need to conquer white bitches anymore because I found myself. I used to fuck white bitches because I was afraid to slap a white man and that was my way of getting back, by feeling that at least I'd got one of their women. I was sneaking around at night, afraid of the cops; but I've now reached the point where I don't want to sneak anymore, and I'm not afraid of any motherfucking white man. I'm not afraid of dying since I discovered that I've been damn near dead all my life anyway because I haven't had a chance to live. I haven't had any opportunity.

White bitches don't excite the younger niggers like they did before. If a cat had him a fine white bitch when I was young, he was cool. Black guys are going back to the source now; they're getting those sisters with naturals. The sisters are waking up, too, and treating their men more like men. Before everybody's wife was like a mama: "Did you put your coat on? Don't catch no cold, boy, act right around those white folks." Everybody's wife was talking like that, which was why niggers, especially musicians, had a hard time staying married. Now the younger sisters coming up are letting niggers stand up and be themselves, so that they're going to keep their men. Niggers were running to white women because them bitches wanted to be around you so bad that you could do anything and they would go for it, just so long as they could make it with you in bed. Niggers gloried in that, because if a nigger can't sit in the front of the bus or be president, he can get a white woman to glory in him in bed; that's the only thing he's got left. That and getting high. So I can see how niggers got tricked into that shit; I got tricked into it myself. It's just a pattern of life. But the shit is changing, 'cause I like all women now. There ain't no special bitch; I wouldn't care if she was green and had red breath, if she's for real, solid!

*Hamp, you're out of sight! Had red breath, what is that? Okay.
I'm going to turn this tape over . . . You use the word* nigger *quite
often. What is your reason for that?*

To me, a nigger is someone who is definitely black, so that
when we say it to one another, it's out of love. When a white man
says it, it's fighting words. It's like a punctuation mark to let
people know who I'm talking about. That's why I say nigger.

What do you think about the word jazz?

I was brought up to identify the word with what we played. It
was called jazz: a concert, a jazz record. Then they started talking
about this kind of music and that kind of music. Music should just
be music. It shouldn't be classified, and if somebody wants to go
and hear something, they should go and hear it. I think the word
jazz was more or less made up by white businesspeople. Niggers
didn't know what they were playing, anyway; they were just
playing what they felt. I don't know anything about the word *jazz.*
To me, music is music. Jazz music is like classical music or any
other kind of music; it's just sounds. I don't even think about the
word *jazz.* If somebody asks me what I do, I say I play the piano.
When they ask, What kind of music do you play? I say, I just play
music, that's all.

What do you look for in a drummer?

I like a drummer to play what he feels and at the same time
listen to what I'm doing. A lot of cats get messed up playing
drums, because they think the drums should be dominant. One of
the heaviest cats I ever heard on the drums was so subtle you
couldn't really check him out at first. His name was Denzil Best,
and he was the type of drummer that you would listen to for
twenty minutes before you'd say: "Damn! This motherfucker is
playing!" He wouldn't throw it at you, he would ease it to you.

Like in a quintet, volume has a lot to do with it. I don't think
the drums should override the soloist. When a drummer is playing
and we're blowing and he's not playing a solo, he's still playing a
solo because his shit is just as important then as it is when he's
playing a solo.

I look for a drummer who listens, so we can kinda take our trips
together. I don't like an overbearing drummer, but I don't want a

timid one, either. I want a cat to play what he feels, but also to put his shit into mine so we can mix it up together.

Do you prefer to play in trio or do you like to play with horns?

One reason I always play with a trio is because I was self-taught and I didn't play in too many bands. When I played with Bird, I would learn the chords and all that. They have charts in some bands, but I have to hear it. I can't see it on paper, because I never took any lessons. So I always play with my own trio and make up my own shit because it takes me too long to get other people's shit off paper. If they hummed it to me, I could probably play it. What I'm trying to do now is learn how to write. I also want to make a quintet record and to play with a quintet. Mostly, though, I play with a trio, because being a solo pianist, I can get a job quicker that way than with a quintet.

Do you practice a lot?

I used to practice every day when I was younger, but I don't anymore. I think when you start out and while you're developing, the more practice you can get, the better it is. I once practiced five or six hours a day, and I had some exercise books to keep my fingers cool. But now I try to create rather than to just practice. After you get your technique down to a certain point, you have to figure out another way of bringing things out of you that are new. So I try to make up things or to hear new things, so that when I do practice, it's that way, not like I did when I was eighteen. In those days I would be practicing and listening to Bud Powell and seeing how cats would phrase. Now that I'm older, I try to write and to create music.

What's happening in California?

The same shit as ten years ago, as far as what jazz musicians are doing. Ain't nobody making any money, I'll tell you that. They're still working for scale. The cats who are working in the studios are making dough; there are a lot of jazz musicians who gave up jazz and went into the studios only so they could make a living. If I could sightread fast enough, I would probably have been tempted to try and get into it, also. But the only thing I can do is play jazz, so I have to stick with that.

What do you think of Muhammad Ali?

I think he's one of the most beautiful cats . . . I've never met him but I've watched him in his boxing and talking to people. He's a true champion. I would love to meet him. I dig him. He's one of my heroes.

Do you go to sporting events or know any athletes?

I know Archie Moore. I've met John Carlos and Tommie Smith, who are both bad motherfuckers and who burn on the 220. I've always wanted to meet Lee Evans. I like all cats who do their things good. Sports are important. Like music, they've been one of the things that break all this race shit down. Like Jackie Robinson, Willie Mays and Hank Aaron. When I see those cats break records and knock balls out of the park, I'm happy. I feel proud to see black people doing something where they're getting recognition. And if a motherfucker has to hit a baseball over a fence to make some dough, then hit it, I'm for it.

Do you like traveling?

Yeah, but I'd like to travel more slick. I want to travel like rich white folks, to check into the Hilton and have bitches bring me drinks, then to put on my bathrobe and take a steam bath before I go to work. I'd love to do that, but it's not in the cards; so here I am in this hotel, but it's cool. When you travel the way I do now, you catch more of the soul of a country than you would if you were staying out there with all those rich folks. I'd like to have my own airplane and all that. We could fly to Africa or somewhere else for a weekend. I don't think it's square to think that way. I would like to do it, but I'll probably never get the chance. I dig traveling, because in every country you meet somebody who's got soul, and that's hope.

Do you think the younger musicians have as good a chance to develop as we did?

I think they have a better chance, because they have more schooling. I didn't go to a conservatory, I don't have any degree, I came up ignorant from the streets and learned from records. These cats are writing. Herbie [Hancock] came over here and wrote some music for a movie. He can sit down and write because he's got the craftsmanship and knowledge, bookwise. If the younger generation of musicians have any talent, they will go way past the shit we did, which is cool, although we laid the foundation down. I think they can take it and go somewhere else with it.

Well, Hampton, in closing, what do you plan for yourself in the future?

You know how it is, A.T. You came up around the same time I did. Everybody wanted to be cool, to play as hip as they could and to be successful. We wanted to make our parents proud, so that when the cats saw us at home, they would say yeah, man, you're taking care of business, beautiful! Then you reach a point in life where you can only get so much glory. All I want to do now is play the piano, work as much as I can and build up my reputation, so that when I quit, I can do what you're doing and write me a book. I'm going to go into the literary thing. I don't have any goals; the only thing I want is gigs. I know I won't ever sell a million records and be famous or rich. I only want to play the piano and support my family, to try and keep my dignity, and later on to write my memoirs and then get the fuck on out of here. You dig?

—Paris, July 2, 1971

≡ KENNY CLARKE ≡

"Dizzy talked me into playing again."

I became interested in music very early, because my mother was a pianist. As a matter of fact, I began taking piano lessons at the age of four. Unfortunately, my mother died when I was about seven, and I forgot about music until the age of twelve. That's when I started playing the snare drum in a marching band at my school. Then about three years later, I stopped playing music altogether; I never gave it a thought. Some friends of mine from high school played instruments. At that time you were allowed to take your instrument home, and my friends started having rehearsals in small groups. So I picked up where I had left off and started getting back into music. At eighteen I got my first professional job in Pittsburgh, Pennsylvania, which is my hometown. I started playing with George Hornsby's big band; then I played in cabarets. By the time I was twenty, I was playing with Leroy Bradley's band in what they call supper clubs with shows. It was an exceptionally good band for the time, and we did quite a bit of traveling. We went to Cincinnati and became the house band at the Cotton Club, which was sort of a supper-show club. I stayed there for a couple of years; then I came to New York. I guess everybody knows that story.

How did you develop yourself as a musician?

Well, A.T., I'm a Capricorn, and it seems to me that most Capricorns I know have to do everything for themselves. I started studying a little alone, then at a certain point I reached an impasse, so I started going to teachers to really learn the instrument. I went to a drum school during the two or three years I was working in cabarets. I also had a private teacher and started developing myself. At that time there weren't any real drum teachers, just snare-drum, tambour or side-drum teachers. They didn't know much about the bass drum or cymbals in those days, so it was a sort of self-development project. I had a good idea of how to play shows when I got to New York, since I had played at the Plantation in St. Louis, which was a very difficult job. I got into the business because of that experience and because I was able to read music and play a show.

Would you tell me something about Minton's and that period, in regard to the development of our music?

I think that apart from Duke Ellington, the Minton era was the most intelligent era of jazz. There's only one Duke Ellington, and he has always been way ahead of his time. It was the most difficult era of jazz for our generation. It was very difficult to get into jazz because it required a lot of knowledge to play the music of Charlie Parker, Dizzy Gillespie, Tadd Dameron and Thelonious Monk. In those days you really had to know your instruments well and have a good sense of harmony and timing. You needed all your equipment then, but today there's not much equipment required. Rhythmically, music has progressed quite a bit, because the drummer was liberated during the Minton era. Before, drummers were just required to keep a four beat, dig coal in the snare drum and hit the cymbal at introductions and endings. Dizzy Gillespie and Thelonious Monk encouraged me to continue in the style I was playing. This liberated drummers, and from then on they have progressed tremendously.

Do you think people are becoming more sympathetic toward our music than they used to be?

No, not really. Real jazz is classical music now. We're living in a disturbed era, and it's hard for a young musician to get his bearings today.

Have musicians come to terms with the power and value of the medium they're working in?

Some of them have, but not all of them. I suppose most young musicians are playing today to earn money. I don't think they really have the music in mind, and this is a grave mistake which will not be rectified for some time.

How important do you feel technique is for playing the drums?

I think any musician needs just enough technique to express

Europeans are ruling the world. There are only four great races in the world, so it means that the yellow man will rule the world next. Then the cycle will start all over again.

People should think more about getting straight within themselves. To organize you must be organized within yourself first. Because otherwise it turns out like the trade unions—in other words, gangsterism. The Black Panthers, for example, that's all gangsterism, it's not real. Making foolhardy mistakes, lack of organization, lack of individualism. The great Architect of the Universe misleads the people he wants misled, and there's nothing you can do about it: It's destiny. The Indians are on reservations now, and they once ruled the world. I suppose the European will wind up in slavery like everyone else.

Where did the term be-bop come from?

That's some European title. It originally was an old expression of Teddy Hill's. Jerry Newman, who was a student at City College then, began to call it be-bop because of Teddy Hill. Dropping bombs [bass drum accents] and all that. He put the word out to the journalists, and I think that's where it really came from. I was working at Kelly's Stable when Roosevelt declared war, but we had been to Minton's before that time, and we didn't hear the term be-bop. Before the war it was only called that music they're playing up at Minton's. When I came home from the war, I heard it called be-bop, but I didn't understand what they meant by it. I guess it was just a name manufactured by journalists, just like West Coast music and East Coast music and all that poppyrot. It's stupid, but they have to make a living, too; they have to have something to write about, and so they invent things to write about.

The word *jazz* is the same way. Jazz was a derogatory name for the music black people were playing at that time. The word came out of the whorehouses in New Orleans. In those days Louis Armstrong and a lot of musicians used to play in whorehouses. Jazz means "to have intercourse with a woman." Since they were playing music in whorehouses, they gave the music that name; it had nothing to do with the music at all.

himself; I don't think he should go beyond that. It becomes meaningless if it goes beyond his feelings. It's always good to have a little technique to spare, but I don't think you should become wrapped up in technical things as far as music is concerned, because music comes from the heart! It has nothing to do with technique at all as we know it.

Do you miss New York?

Not really. I miss my friends, but the ones I like most come to Europe quite frequently, so I don't see any reason to go to New York. I haven't any desire to, anyway.

Do the drums still satisfy your needs as a musician, or have you ever thought of adding another instrument?

I fool around with the piano, but that's just for amusement. The only instrument I take seriously is the drums. The piano and trombone are just for fun: they are a sort of détente, something I do to relax.

How do you like the Afro hairstyle?

I think it's a whole lot of needless work. The time it takes them to keep their hair in an Afro could be spent reading. It's a waste of time, effort and energy which could be channeled in another direction. It's like a woman going to the beauty parlor and sitting for two hours having her hair done when she could be reading a book, doing some housework or something constructive. Like Dinah Washington said once, "Nobody ever asked me for any hair."

What do you think about the time when a lot of musicians used to conk their hair?

It was a matter of being brainwashed and trying to look like the powers that be. Just being yourself is the best way to be in life, if you can find yourself. That's the hardest job in the world: finding out who you are first before you start adding decorations. If the black man knew who he really was, these things wouldn't be happening. People are searching for identification, that's all. I hope they find it someday.

Do you play for yourself, for the musicians or for the audience?

For the musicians; if they're happy, I'm happy. I don't think about the audience, and I never play for myself. I play for the front line and the rhythm section. Period!

What do you do in your free time for relaxation?

I try to take care of my garden, of my house and of my family. That's quite a job right there.

Do you do any kind of physical exercise?

Yes. I have some special exercises I invented and carried from the army. I go through this bit every day, and it keeps me fit. Too much of anything is no good, so I just do enough to keep myself in shape. I also like to swim a lot.

Would you tell me something about the army?

It was a hectic experience, and I was a very bad soldier. Unhappily I stayed in it for three years, two of them in Europe. I guess that's why I'm in Europe now; I met a lot of wonderful people during my soldiering days. Fortunately, just before coming home in 1945, I started to form groups and play the trombone, which was very nice. I didn't play the drums much because I didn't like having to carry them around with me, so I began by concentrating on the trombone. This was about four or five months before I was discharged, after which I joined Dizzy's band. I hadn't had a pair of drumsticks in my hands for over a year and a half. I had been planning to quit playing music because I was kind of disgusted with everything at that time. I guess a lot of soldiers felt that way on returning home to start a new life. Dizzy talked me into playing again, and so I did.

Would you tell me something about Bud Powell and Charlie Parker?

Bud and Bird both had their thing all set up. I think Bird was a genius. I can't say the same thing for Bud, but he was an exceptional musician. A friend of mine said once, "Genius is a rare thing," and I believe that. It's rare to get a genius on the scene. I guess not more than one will come along every quarter-century in any field you can think of. But Bird had all the

necessary equipment. You could just follow the leader as 1 Charlie Parker was concerned.

Dizzy is different: He's a saint. Dizzy personally taught a trumpet players who were playing at that time, and a l drummers, too. And he was an extraordinary musician, too on the verge of genius, in some ways more than a genius. He a lot more of himself than any musician I know of—much than Bird, because Bird was like a prophet who brings a mes leaves that message and disappears. Those who are able, thereof. The ones who don't get the message are left bel During Bird's time I've seen a lot of musicians quit the bus because of him, because the message he bore was a little strong or more than they could conceive, more than they c absorb.

What do you think about the publicity musicians have gotten to the use of drugs?

It's all a plan to destroy something in people, to destroy t dignity, their moral content. Drugs is a very well plan operation, and like Malcolm X once said, if the author operation, and like Malcolm X once said, if the author wanted to stop the flow of drugs in Harlem, they could d overnight, but I see it's still flowing, so there's your answer.

You mentioned Malcolm X; what did you think of him?

He had a message, a very open, down-to-earth message wl everyone could understand. A lot of people today are living by words. There's a lot of truth in everything he said as far as bl people are concerned, and that's why he's not with us toda because he had too much to say.

What do you think about the term black *as opposed to* Ne *and* colored?

It's all a plan to destroy our people, and the more our peo can see through it, the more they'll unite. Until that day we call ourselves black or Negro—it means the same thing; negative. In the beginning of civilization the red man ruled globe, then it was the black man, the African, now it's European; everyone has a chance. The red men—in other wor the Incas and the Aztec Indians—were very civilized. Then Abyssinian and the Nubian Africans ruled the world; now 1

Do you accept the label jazz *for the music you have been playing all these years?*

You have to accept things you can't change. It's too late to change the word now, so it just has to be accepted. Most people today don't know where the word originated, so it doesn't really make any difference.

Do you think all the music that's called jazz is jazz?

Any music that's danceable is jazz. Any syncopated music is jazz. If it isn't syncopated, it's not jazz. I remember a time when any club could put a sign out: Colored Orchestra Tonight, and draw as many people as they do today for a name person. There were no special stars in those days, just black musicians. Anyone could be a bandleader; it didn't mean that much.

What do you plan for yourself in the future, musicwise?

Not very much. I hope I can stop all this business in five years and just play for the sake of playing. There's very little to be done now, because the music has gotten into the wrong hands. Musicians everywhere are sitting home by the telephone waiting for a white man to call them for a gig, and I don't see any future in that. I've been playing the drums for forty years, and the only future I see in our music is for black people to have their own thing going; otherwise it's no use.

I've heard that musicians had more control over the music in the twenties and thirties. Is that true?

Yes, they did. Then the Jewish people bought them out. When I started out, black people had their own publishing companies, their own dance halls and they did their own booking, because no one wanted to touch jazz. White people thought it was the music of savages and so they didn't want to be bothered with it. The Jews found out it was a gold mine and they took it over, bought the black people out and bought a lot of their souls along with it.

By the late thirties it was all over. That's why fine people like Teddy Hill quit playing music. Teddy quit as a bandleader because Moe Gale, Billy Shaw and all those people wanted to tell him who to have in his band, where he was going to work and why he was going to work. He had nothing more to say, so he quit. I'll probably wind up following in Teddy's footsteps. I hope in another five year's time I can say I don't want to play anymore.

Do you see any way these things can be regained?

No, it's impossible now. You can't backtrack. In the first place, black people haven't got enough money to do it. In the second place, they haven't the leadership they had in those days. To join a band then was like going to a school. Nowadays bands don't exist. As far as the black man is concerned, I don't see any future for him in the United States or in any other white country. There's a future for a black man only with his own. If some intelligent black Americans went back to Nigeria, Kenya or Ethiopia to form their own record companies, then I could see progress. But there is no future in the white man's world because every black musician today is waiting for the white man to call him to give him a job. Even if it's a black musician who gives you a job, it's through another white musician or a white manager who hired him to hire you. It's a vicious cycle.

As fast as you create something, white so-called musicians take it away from you and exploit it, because they have the money and the means of communication to do it. They have radio, television, records, and they pass off everything you create as their own. They know that if they expose it on television, everyone will think a white man created it, because they'll never let the black man expose the music that he created in the different mediums of communication they have invented. In my time we only had the radio, but now with all these long-playing records and with television, they have just taken it right away from us. That's why I don't see any future in music for black musicians in a white world. It's a sad thing to say, but that's the way it is. You create something and you see who has it the next day. Like the Beatles, who are copying Chuck Berry; or Blood, Sweat & Tears, who are copying Ray Charles. You got this chick Julie Driscoll copying Aretha Franklin; Janis Joplin copying Bessie Smith and Peggy Lee copying Billie Holiday.

—Paris, August 24, 1971

≡ FREDDIE HUBBARD ≡

"I usually play off what a drummer plays."

How did you become interested in music and the trumpet?

By coming from a musical family. My mother played the piano, spirituals. My sister played the piano and the trumpet. I had a brother who played bass and tenor saxophone and another who played the piano, so there was music all day, and by the instrument being around the house, I naturally picked it up.

Where was this?

Nap Town, which is Indianapolis. You've been there.

A lot of fine musicians come from Indianapolis, like Wes Montgomery. Were you associated with him?

He was my main inspiration before I really got into music. I was able to play with Wes one day a week, and it was my life while I was in Indianapolis. To me, he was so great, and I loved him so much. I would practice all week just to play that Saturday jam session. This Friday I'm going to do a benefit for Wes's brother, Buddy Montgomery. He's trying to get into the booking field. Along with Joe Williams, McCoy Tyner and Eddie Harris, we're going to do a benefit which will help him get started.

What did you do to develop yourself as a trumpeter?

Listened to other musicians. By hearing what they play, I can judge what I would like to play or not to play. It's kind of weird. Like when I listen to Clifford Brown, I say wow, he does some beautiful things, and I get so many ideas which I can take and formulate into my own. I listen to all kinds of cats, like Eddie Gales, Don Cherry, Miles, Dizzy, Kenny Dorham, Bill Hardman. My whole thing is listening to music. I don't practice as much as I listen. I found out that practicing is not what jazz is all about. I've always been thought of as very technical, and I don't practice. It's just like a natural feeling. Some things come to you like technique, but soul is another thing! Being able to play like Louis Armstrong or Miles is different—it's something you have to feel. I don't want to play like Louis or Miles, but I can learn so much from them.

What do you think of the word jazz?

This is something I encounter all the time when I'm on the road. That's the first thing a white cat will ask me. A disc jockey will say, "What would you like to call the music: jazz or black music?" It has a stigma, but it's just a word to describe music which doesn't bother me at all. It's like classical music—if people really knew what that meant, they wouldn't judge it. Classical music is something that lasts through the years that people dig. They keep it. To me a Charlie Parker composition is a classic, it's a work of art!

Jazz is a label white people gave to the music. How do you know some black cat didn't say it? You know. "Hey, baby, that's jazz." That's usually what happens: White people will take up your phrases, use them and tell you that they're new.

Just like the word *jazz,* so what. Jazz has connotations of barrooms and prostitutes and having to play in those kind of conditions. That's why I'm trying to get into the colleges. If some professor asks me what jazz is, it's a music and it's a word that I heard describing the music and it's beautiful music regardless of what you think about it. It's just a word, just like your name. Somebody says Arthur Taylor, then looks at you as a black person: It's the same thing. It's a white name, it's a slave name. White people would like to create that kind of mystique about it. It's jazzy, it's black and it comes out of the underground, which it does.

Do you play for yourself, for the audience or for the musicians?

The older I get, the more I'm trying to get involved with other people's feelings listening to me, whereas before I used to play whatever I felt I ought to play. But now the whole thing works off vibrations. If I feel the people are cold, I think maybe if I do this, it will warm them up. That's what music is about. You try to connect emotions no matter what you play. Even if there are only one or two people, you want to be able to get to them; otherwise you're just playing for yourself.

How much do you play for the musicians?

If I'm soloing, they're with me, we're playing together. I usually play off what a drummer plays. That's been my thing. Since I'm being the creative force at that moment, solowise, usually I'm trying to lead the drummer, but I will use certain licks I hear him play and play off that. You notice I've always worked with drummers. I used to hear something Max [Roach] or Art [Blakey] would do and I would say wow! And that would help lift me. I got to the point where I didn't try to outplay them. Some cats are just playing for themselves. They don't listen to the drummer.

Are you your own boss as a man?

I think so. No matter what you say about people controlling you, you're still your own boss. Say you're going to work in a club—you don't have to, but you must make a living. Right? Now that's the reason the white man always stays ahead of us. I've been to places in Brooklyn, thinking a black man owns the club, and I would try to talk this man into hiring me, letting me get something started. I told him: "Why should I go to Slug's when I can go right up the street? Your club is hipper, it looks better, plus I'm in the community. So why can't we get something started?" His outlook is so slow that he can't see it, whereas a Jew is able to see it. That's the reason the black man went to the white man. Still, you're your own boss. We've got to create our own thing, but we need the white man now.

I've thought about starting my own record company, but it's a question of having money for promotion and distribution after you get the records pressed. They put clamps on you, but if you've got the right people and some bread, you can do it. That's what I'm going to do, but I'm not in a position to do so until I can hook up some of the right managers. There are people who are in the business who will come over and help, because you've got smart black people out here who know business.

They say jazz isn't a big commodity, that it's not selling now, so why get involved in it. Promoters won't promote jazz because they've been told that it's not going to sell. You can be your own boss in that sense. It's just that I don't think I'm in a position to totally sell myself right now, even to the black man.

What do you think about the strife going on in America with our people?

It's good. The more strife, the more advancement we make. You as a black man living in another country are not confronted with all these problems, since there are not that many black people to cause problems. But the same conditions exist in Europe, too. I've been to Europe about nine or ten times, and I don't see that much more work, I don't see that many more business opportunities. I'm not talking about you as an individual, I'm talking about black people. So in fact the only problem Europe doesn't have is the racial thing; it's not as tense as it is in the States. But they use you in Europe, too, if they can.

It's just as tense in Europe as it is in the States, but a little bit more undercover.

I think revolution is good for the United States. Black people are beginning to wake up and say wow, he's been doing this to me, he's been prostituting me and using me. The strife in America is going to go on until the black man can see his way into this society; otherwise he's going to have to leave. But I am not leaving this country for that reason. My problem is here, and the only way the black man is ever going to get anywhere is by always fighting and bickering. If you went to Africa it would be the same thing. It's fighting for equal rights. We've been slaves and we're still trying to get out from under the hammer. I don't think it's a question of taking up arms and dying, because we're a minority; it wouldn't work. I'm involved just by trying to continue to play this music and make a living. That's strife.

There's always going to be strife in this country, because they're white and we're black. They tried to teach us that they were better, but it doesn't mean anything. I'm glad to see what's happening today. I think this will eventually tune these white people in. If we can burn down a few houses, that's good, because they've got to put up new ones. We as musicians—and black people in general—should learn to trust each other and get out of this petty ego trip thing. Once black people realize they're black and that white men have still got the hammer, it will be better for all of us. I'm not totally blaming whitey. If only you could get musicians to think on a business level . . . but they won't stick together.

We're mixed; we've been slaves. That was the master plan. J. A. Rogers states it in his book, *Black Cargo*. It was a plan for them to mix us up. If we could only get black people to dig themselves! I'm just beginning to dig myself as a human being and to be proud that I can play the trumpet. I'm proud of the fact I can do what I'm doing, and that's the message I want to convey to all my black brothers. Plus my craft and my skill and what God gave me. I appreciate it, and I'm trying to do my best. If I could teach some young brothers how to play the trumpet or leave some music here, that's what should come first. We've got to unite as one people and start digging each other. That's the reason I'm going to stay in America.

I'd like to talk about my knowledge of the history of the black man's plight in this music, which is a plight because it's always been considered subculture since black people created the music when they were slaves. We chanted, we beat the drums and we sang the blues. We sang the blues because it was a way of communicating, an outlet. In Africa the chants meant something else; it was another type of feeling. When we came here, they took our language. They didn't want us to speak our own language amongst each other. The same thing is happening today. They don't want you to speak your own true feeling, which is the blues. They don't even want you to sing the blues in a modified way. You grow up in this society and go to a white-oriented school. You learn chord changes, you learn how to notate music the Western way. So this music is included in jazz. Yet they still tell us it's not beautiful. We're using our chants, our spirituals, our soul, our theories and including their style of music and writing, and they still tell you it's not hip. Improvisation on a theme is the hippest thing that's ever happened in music!

First black people must realize how beautiful the music is; then the white man will realize it, and he won't be able to stop it. Jazz is slick music, it's beautiful music, it's modern, it's creative. I just want black people to start getting down with the music. Then we will be able to make big money. We'll be able to get a lot of people to listen to us and do what we want to do. Wherever I work, I say, "Look, brothers and sisters, you're black and I'm black. You've got no more sense than me and I've got no more sense than you. This is the music that came out of my neighborhood. Don't wait for somebody else to tell you whether it's good or not, come out and dig it."

When I get some money, I'm going to produce my records and hire you as my artist-and-repertoire man. You can do your thing. Let's get black people interested who love the music and would like to invest in it. I figure I'm doing something when I hire a band. I've got four men besides myself making a living. In other words they're one step behind me, although I don't have control of the distribution and the making of the records.

Look at people like James Brown and Berry Gordy. They're promoting blackness. I'm black, and I dig the music, and I'm going to play until I die. If you dig history, the music isn't really based on money, because it's not a commercial thing. It can become commercial if you play for the people, but the jazz musician does not play totally for the people. When you do certain licks that you know will get over night after night, that's not creating. But if you want to get into a commercial bag, you keep repeating something and it will eventually work, which is not the creative thing of a jazz musician.

What do you think of Charlie Parker and Bud Powell's music?

I loved them from the first time I heard them. What amazed me about their music was that it seemed like it was a frantic period. It was a fast-moving-pace thing. It was new, it was fresh and it was happening. I think people were really tuned in at that period. They set a new trend with that music, a new way of living and a new way of talking and acting. When I heard Bud Powell and Dizzy Gillespie, it really made me want to get into the music. To me, they were true geniuses to create something that spontaneous. You have to be a genius to do that. Not everybody can do that—not everybody can even conceive that! The be-bop era is still the strongest era that we've had. I really think so. Because it was a complete switch from the Western music.

What do you think about electronics being used in the music now?

It's beautiful. It's good if you get out of it what you want. I intend to use it as a means of communication, because with the speakers the people can hear better, and electronically there's more you can do with one tone. I notice I don't have to blow as hard. If I go into a club that has a sad sound system, I've got my own I can use, which is good. I'm going to play this record for you that I did on Atlantic called *Sing Me a Song*. I collaborated with a guy from Turkey who teaches electronic music at Columbia University, and we did a record date. It's a collector's item, because it was the first time jazz was included with electronic music, and the Moog synthesizer is used in a musical sense instead of just as a noisy volume.

Randy Weston told me you were a heck of a basketball player.

Kareem Abdul-Jabbar called me tonight.

I was talking about your being a heck of a basketball player.

That's what I'm saying. He knows it because I grew up with Oscar Robertson, and he's the baddest! Sports is a big thing in the Midwest. When I got into music, I got away from it, because it takes a lot of my time. Physically there's no better exercise than being athletic and knowing how to use your body. It's helped me to play the trumpet, because I play very physically. I play hard and I play long. If my body wasn't in a certain physical condition, I couldn't do it. Basketball helps me. I played the other day. I got tired, but I played. Randy's six feet ten, and I got out on him. I like a little bit of everything. That's the reason I wanted you to come over—because I'm really supposed to be in bed, cooling it.

I'm going to New Orleans to eat some oysters and see if we can get these brothers elected. I campaigned for Mayor Lindsay. Why can't I campaign for my own brother-in-law? J. J. Johnson hired me for the Lindsay campaign. When Lindsay came to Brooklyn to campaign for mayor, he brought Sugar Ray Robinson and went to the biggest Baptist church in Brooklyn. That's how they do it— they wire us up. We have to wire each other up! But we're not going to do that, because we're mixed up. My mother told me, "Don't play jazz." I asked her, "What do you know about it? Why don't you want me to play it? Do you know more about it than me?" My mother said, "Go ahead, Freddie, go on to New York." I packed a big trunk and split. Nobody can tell you about this music.

When are you going to Europe next?

I'm not going over there to stay and play with those dudes. There's not enough of you all over there. If you don't have anybody to play with, it's a drag. Let's unite and help our brothers. It's connected.

We once formed a group called the Jazz Communicators: Joe Henderson, Lou Hayes and myself. We worked for a minute, but Joe and I had separate recording contracts and we couldn't get together because we didn't control our contracts. We wanted to do a date under the name of the Jazz Communicators, and the record companies said no. That's why I dig what Tolliver's talking about. Until we get control, it's not going to work. A musician is not a businessman. Any businessman goes to an investor, a man who knows the business. I don't have time to create music and run around and negotiate. It's two different entities: negotiation and music. Until we are able to hook up black people who know the business, it's a lost cause.

What do you do when you have some free time and you're able to relax?

I write music, because I can't think of anything when I'm working. Now I'm in the process of getting a new band. I want to change my music a little bit. I want to broaden it for the people. I want to play a bit of everything. I want to play some symphonic, rock, me—everything.

That's what I like to do. I'm not going to play just one way. It's still going to sound like Freddie Hubbard, no matter what I do, because it's got my sound. I have finally reached the point where I've got a sound and realize it. It took me fifteen years to get it. When you hear it, if you've never heard me before, it's not going to sound like anybody else. I feel better about myself now that I've attained that. Now I've got to get a band and musicians who like what I'm doing.

This music is beautiful. The thing that's hung us up is the rewards. We should have statues of people like Charlie Parker and Miles Davis in every square. I've got a brother who's going to make a sculpture of Charlie Parker for me, and I'm going to have it put in the Museum of Modern Art. I want to be in there when I die. I want all the great jazz artists to be in the Museum of

Modern Art in New York. They have one of Sidney Bechet in France, and he was born in America.

Whitey creates a farce; that's his thing. He doesn't have any contentment, so he has to continue to look for things outside of what's really happening. We've been made to feel as if they are superior, but they aren't, because they're always looking for the untrue instead of the true. Put that in the book! When you mention Charlie Parker, the first thing people think about is dope instead of thinking about the man's music. Instead of saying, Those were some beautiful things he played, the first thing they say is that he was strung out. When I hear Charlie Parker, I just think about how pretty it is. I don't care what he did. What he played was out of this world.

What do you think of the Beatles' music?

I just did one of their tunes. It's creative, for what they do. I'm not going to knock his stuff because he's sending men to the moon. We always knock a white cat instead of trying to figure out why he's doing this stuff and can get away with it. Running in your house and shooting you. Try to figure that out. Try to get over that hump without getting shot down. It's like playing chess. Why do we have to be the losers all the time? Why not figure it out, plan it? I could have a big house now, but so what? I'm not ready to move into any white community. I'll stay right here until I feel like moving. I might go to Jamaica. It's how I feel. I'm not going to move out of the neighborhood because there are black people here. I have a nice pad; it's hip, and I can practice my horn.

Usually when black people get a lot of money, they move out of their community. You see what that does. You're taking money out of the community; you're taking knowledge; you're taking the example you've set for other black people who may not have as much on the ball. What you're doing is leaving the ball to them. Instead of staying in that neighborhood and saying, Let's do it like this. Instead of moving to New Jersey, stay here and try to construct something to help these people get together. Keep this man from raising the rent. Let's buy the building, or tear it down, build a new one or burn it down. You don't dig it until you're in it. I've thought about these things. Why, when you make one hundred thousand dollars, you've got to move out of your neighborhood, instead of investing in the building or trying to keep the rent down, trying to get other people to live better and keep them from sleeping three in a bed, or keep a tree growing. Like in Harlem, if all the black people had stayed on Sugar Hill and set some kind of example, it would be better today. But they had the money and didn't care.

It's hard to get the message across to black people in general, because they have their way they want to live, and that's the way they've been brought up. I told you I had a white grandfather. He was a preacher, and I used to go to his house and just look at him. He looked like a Caucasian; he had blue eyes and straight hair. That amazed me as a kid. But as a cat, he was down, and still is, because he had my grandmother. So maybe he was one of the good guys, like Jesus Christ. I'm going out to lunch now!

I'm going to put this down.

Put it down. I don't care. I don't forget too much of what I say. Dizzy Gillespie is the most beautiful cat that I've met. Here's a cat that convinced me that everything is hip. He'll talk you to death, and he knows. He's beautiful. He's a serious, funny cat. He's globe-trotting and leaving a hell of a message. I'm looking to see how beautiful he is as a man, and the music he's playing. When he opens his mouth to say something, he means and knows it. I'm not looking whether he's on TV every night. I hope he gets there if he wants to be there. I'm trying to look on the brighter side.

Eldridge Cleaver is talking about coming back over here, and he better be ready. I'm going to have to go to the airport. They're going to jack him up, and that's getting into law and order, which is something else. The Black Panthers say he's not with the Panthers now and he's got his old lady over here campaigning, trying to get him back in the country. He says he's coming back here to get this country together. You know what that means. The Panthers are going to be at the airport to greet him, and the police are going to be there, too. They are going to grab him and the Panthers are going to say no, you're not going to grab him. It's going to be some funny stuff. It's going to be law and order.

It's going to be a shootout at the airport.

It's going to be funny. They're going to take him.

Some blacks are going to die, is that what you're saying?

Right! Well, some whites are going to die, too. That's what I
call force. Here's a black man coming into this country who hasn't
done anything but open his mouth, and here's some whiteys
saying we're going to lock you up. That's what we need. Like if
you're standing by when the police bust a cat and you don't know
the reason he's getting busted, that makes you feel funny. So
they'll just put Cleaver in jail, collect some money and later let
him out or shoot him. What do you think is going to happen?

I don't know. Did you see that movie he did?

I didn't see any movie.

It's called Eldridge Cleaver Black Panther, *by William Klein. It
was filmed in Algeria. At the end of the movie, Cleaver asked the
interviewer, "What do you think is going to happen to me?" The
interviewer answered, "The only thing that can happen is you're
going to get shot down here in Algeria or get shot down in America
or you will wind up in prison for the rest of your life."*

What did Cleaver say?

*He said, "The harder it gets, the better I like it." And that was
the end of the film. They just looked at each other.*

That was drama. Jews are funny. They got black Jews, too.
Turn that tape off. Dig this record.

—New York, October 18, 1971

≡ RICHARD DAVIS ≡≡≡

"New York was like a magnet."

How did you become interested in music?

My two elder brothers and I used to have a little trio. A girl cousin would conduct and give us harmony notes to sing. Though I was the youngest, I had the deepest voice, so I sang the lowest part. We often tried to get on amateur shows, and we would sing every day after dinner. I always listened to the bass on records or on the radio. It was the instrument that attracted my attention most. When I went to see the bands in the theaters, I always watched the bass player. My cousin had always wanted to play the bass, and she encouraged me when she saw I was interested. She felt it was a little out of place for a girl to play the bass, so she said, "Why don't you study the bass?" I had never thought about it.

I then became conscious of Jimmy Blanton, because I liked Duke Ellington's band, Oscar Pettiford and cats like that. I decided to study bass at Du Sable High School in Chicago. Johnny Griffin was leaving the school just when I was coming in, and he was like a giant even though he was only about sixteen years old. His name and Gene Ammons were something you had to work up to. Gene was at school at the same time as the cousin I was telling you about. They were like gods, so we always had to hear their names and work up to where they had been. Gus Shapell and Bennie Green were at my school, too. When I started with the high-school band, there was another bass player called Carl Byron, who was a genius on the fiddle. He died when he was about twenty-one years old.

The school had a good environment, because it was musically orientated and had a good jazz band. After our first year they would send us to study with some symphony guys, but the director, Walter Dyett, would still check us out and see how we were coming along. We had to play for him individually every week. I studied harmony with him privately. He would suggest directions to take with the bass. He advised me to join a youth orchestra that had musicians from all over the city. I auditioned and got in. Later Mr. Dyett said, "Why don't you try for the civic orchestra, which is a training orchestra for the Chicago Symphony?" I auditioned and got into that.

I ended up going to Vandercook College, and everything they said I had heard before, because Walter Dyett was a Vandercook man. When I got into college, I didn't have any trouble, because it was all old hat by that time. I then started playing gigs around Chicago. One of the first gigs I had was with Andrew Hill, Harold Ousley and John Neely. Then I started getting gigs playing for dances. I began working with Ahmad Jamal around 1952. Don Shirley was looking for a bass player, and Johnny Pate was working with him at the time. Johnny took the gig I had with Ahmad and I took his gig, because Don was supposed to go to New York and Johnny didn't want to go. Ahmad had a tight trio. I started working with Don, but I didn't feel the classical thing at first, so I told Johnny that I wanted to go back to my own gig. But he said, "You better go to New York, because that's where it's happening."

I went to New York and got off the train at Grand Central Station, nervous as a cat. I looked at New York and hoped I wouldn't run into Percy Heath or Ray Brown walking down the street. I went straight to the Alvin Hotel, because Roy Haynes had told me it was a good hotel. I started working at a club on the East Side with Don Shirley, and we worked around New York for about eight months, between the Embers and Basin Street.

When I first came to Birdland, you were the first cat I saw working there. You were with Bud and Mingus. I said, "Damn, you mean this is right across the street from where I'm living?"

I started feeling comfortable around New York and decided I wanted to stay there. I was traveling between New York and Chicago in 1956, but then I figured this is it, New York is the place. I left Don in about 1956 and worked with Charlie Ventura and the Sauter-Finnigan band, then with Sarah Vaughan for about five years. About twelve years ago I decided to stay in New York. I didn't want to travel anymore. I wanted to do a lot of things, not just play with one group. I had heard about cats playing different kinds of gigs in studios, so I said, I think I want to do that. I can get a symphonic gig on one day and a nightclub gig on the next. I started doing a lot of recording with folksingers. I just dig what's happening in New York. Everything is here.

What was the major factor in your development as a bassist?

I had a good start with a good teacher. Walter Dyett started a lot of cats out. This man had everything to give you. All you had to do was listen. If you saw him on the street for a minute, you left him thinking you had gotten something. He was into mind power and mystical things. He saw way ahead of his time, always growing. As a matter of fact, you never knew how old he was. I saw him about a month before he died, and he gave me something to live with. He would say get this book, get that book, do this or concentrate on that.

I developed by learning how to practice the instrument. I would be practicing before I even saw the bass, because my mind would be on it. I would wipe everything out of my mind except the instrument. I almost felt as if I were playing even when I was walking down the street. Sometimes I used to walk in the street in a daze, thinking about the bass and running a scale or chord. I could visualize it on the instrument. When I got to the instrument, it was just a matter of applying the physical to the mental.

Walter Dyett was a violinist, so he had that string thing down, like shifting and playing in tune. It's very difficult to play the bass in tune, because you've got so much space between notes. You have to hear it and think about measurement before you even play a note. So if you have all that in your head, you've got a better chance of playing in tune. I studied the bass privately ten years and studied four more years before I really played a professional gig. I had a pretty good foundation in the mechanics of the instrument before I played my first gig.

In Chicago they have gangways in between each building. It goes for the whole height of the building, and you can hear everything going on around you. There was a tenor player who always had records on. As I grew up, I could relate back to that time and say that was Ella Fitzgerald I heard on that record, or Louis Jordan or Billy Eckstine. And all because this cat played records so often. I think about that now because there is a baby in the bedroom next to mine. I always have records on, and maybe years from now the baby will relate back to them. He might not realize it now, but someday he'll say, oh yeah, I remember hearing that. I found out later on that this cat was a hell of a tenor player. I think his name was Eddie Davis, not Lockjaw. He was very prominent around Chicago. Hearing cats like that keeps your ears tuned. It was a black neighborhood, so you had your ears tuned up anyway.

I kept studying and playing with orchestras, which involves a different technique than when you do these studio things in New York, without knowing what bag you'll be in until you get there. They might have parts to be bowed that require some kind of technical facility or other parts which are completely left up to you, just some chord symbols. Any experience you get, no matter how dumb it might seem at the time, pays off later. You can reach back and grasp some of it. In New York you play with some of the best musicians in the world, so it's the right place to get inspiration.

How do you feel about bass players raising their strings?

When I first started, the idea was to have the strings very high from the fingerboard because it was said that you could get a bigger sound that way and that it would develop a lot of muscle power. I used to have my strings higher than they are now because the older bass players all had their strings fairly high. When I started studying thumb positions with a teacher, I could see it was very difficult to go high or low on the string and get a fluid feeling on the bass. Crossing strings was ridiculous, and I decided to look for a way of compromising so that you could get a big sound when playing jazz. Whatever kind of music you're playing, when you're playing up in the high positions, you have to have some kind of facility on the bass. It's got to be set up so that the action is easy. I started dropping my strings down just enough to keep them from hitting the fingerboard. You get a much more fluid sound that way. You can play double stops more easily, and you don't tire as quickly. They tell you to keep the strings high and to develop certain muscles, but you don't really need those muscles. Of course, they now have adjustable bridges to quickly change the height of the bridge according to what kind of sound you want to get or what kind of gig you're playing. Mine always stay more or less at the same height, except for seasonal changes, when I have to heighten or lower the bridge. In cold weather the fingerboard has a tendency to go out because it expands, and in the summer weather it comes down.

Do you like traveling?

Right now I find traveling nice because it's by choice. I can take a gig on the road if I want to, but basically I work here in the city all year 'round unless I want a change of pace. Then I get a gig on the road for maybe a weekend or even a week. I can come home from the gig and sleep a full night, get up, practice, do a lot of reading and sort of mingle with different people on a different scene. When I was on the road, it was beautiful, but I always wondered when it was going to end. On the road you're always thinking about getting home to your family or friends. You don't see any way out because you're away from New York all the time. Finally you decide to cut this loose and see what's happening in the city. I haven't traveled much for about ten years, but if somebody wants me to go to Europe or to someplace a little different than just going on a gig, it's beautiful. I've been to Japan and to Europe, but that was mostly by choice.

When did you first hear Charlie Parker?

All the cats at high school had heard Charlie Parker before I did, so I had been digging his sounds from the guys in school. I had noticed that the cats were playing a lot of sounds on the blues. When I finally heard some Charlie Parker records, I thought he was playing like those cats in school, but I was told they were playing like him. I started buying a lot of records, and my brother bought quite a few Bud Powell records. He was crazy about Bud. All this frightened me, because these cats were playing some swift stuff. The records were coming out of New York, so New York was like a magnet. This was the place to record, the headquarters for exposure. I used to think, Wow, there are some mean cats in New York! We would hear Bud, Ray Brown, Max and Roy Haynes and say wow!

By that time I was just beginning to feel comfortable with fast tempos. Being able to play fast was a whole thing. I remember some cats snatching the bass out of my hand because I couldn't keep the tempo. Another bass player would come up and he could make the tempo, so I would say, "I'm going to make that tempo next time!" Gradually you get to know how to relax your muscles and think of the tempo as not being that fast. Then you can feel comfortable. It's a matter of the physical keeping up with the mental. Charlie Parker set the prime example of that. It was good exposure just to hear those records and try to keep up with them. I used to try to keep the tempo on one note just to see if I could play that fast.

What do you think about musicians getting so much publicity due to the use of drugs?

I think writers feel they're in on something. The fact is that musicians are very exposed to the public because they're always onstage. The writers seem to get satisfaction out of being able to point at certain musicians or at the whole scene of musicians and saying something which is relatively true in some cases. It's just that it's more appealing to write about the musician than to write about the everyday cat on the street. I think the percentage of guys on the street who take drugs is much higher than among musicians. But the musician has more drawing power for readers because he's in the headlines, a celebrity, so to speak. An ordinary cat on the street doesn't make the newspapers. In fact, statistics show that three or four categories of people contain a higher proportion of drug takers than musicians, people such as doctors and housewives.

What do you think about electronics?

I dig it, but not to the point where you can't decipher the individual quality of the instruments. Each instrument has a unique color and timbre. I don't like it when that naturalness is lost in electronics. It should only be supplemented.

Bass players always have had a problem being heard and getting through. I don't think any musician can play well unless he can hear himself and everybody around him. With amplifiers a bass player can hear himself pretty readily, and the band can hear him, too, which inspires the whole setup. He doesn't have to depend on house microphones or the acoustics of the room. Electronics change the colors of the instruments, and this is good for a little variety, although too much of anything is bad. As for electronic recordings, some are interesting but others mean nothing to me. They have to have some kind of meaningful direction. I've found that if musicians who have played without electronics get involved in it, it tends to come off more musically than with guys who are into electronics only. They seem to respond to music differently than musicians who are adding electronics only as a supplement.

Have you ever gotten any bad writeups?

Yeah! I take them just like I do the good ones. I think a cat is entitled to his opinions. I don't think about writeups when I play. I just play the way I feel. Sometimes I don't feel good, sometimes I do. Sometimes I feel like I've played well and sometimes I feel like I haven't played well. The way you feel is probably the most important thing.

Do you use the same technique when you're playing in a club as you do when you're recording?

I would be more conscious of the mike in a recording. In a club you can play, move around and do a lot of things, but in a recording you try not to make any unnecessary sounds. When you're playing on a recording, any move you make might come over on the tape as a physical noise. That's why I prefer remote recordings, when you're playing in a club and recording at the same time. When I'm playing a commercial date, I use a different picking technique. I'm conscious of the mike and I know that certain sounds come off better. On the playback in the control room, I can tell the difference between one sound and the other. I do a lot of jingles for commercial advertisements and pick a certain way. If it's a big band I'll pick differently than if it's a small group or a solo, so it's best to develop a lot of picking styles for the sound you want to get. The most natural picking sound is when you don't even think about what you're doing, you just play.

What do you think about the word jazz?

To me the word *jazz* means a certain life-style. I don't know what the term is derived from. They say some guy heard the music and labeled it jazz. I don't like to label nothing! You're stepping on dangerous ground if you put a label on something, because you're open to criticism. I'm just playing music. There is a fine line between some people's definition of what jazz is, but I feel that as long as it's swinging and feels good, it's jazz!

We call it black music now. Black music belongs to a particular environmental culture, and nobody can develop it except black people. Only black people can be innovators of new styles, like Coltrane, who was the last innovator to take a completely different direction. I think our music reflects black society and anything else is a copy. It's a drag that black music hasn't been successful commercially. You hardly ever hear of any real black music being a successful moneymaker. I think black music is a better term to use than jazz, because Marvin Gaye and Curtis Mayfield represent black music, too, and they have been more successful financially than jazz.

Now, of course, they're going through a new kind of struggle for independence. They don't want to sit in a white man's office trying to get some kind of representation. "I give you a certain percentage of what my talent brings so you can survive." I saw the play *Black Terror*. It was about revolution and counterrevolution. One side wanted only guns and destruction, while the other side was philosophically saying, Let's train our people for revolution. Revolution doesn't always mean getting a gun and liquidating the oppressor physically. It can mean not having to depend on the oppressor for survival. A lot of things are involved, economically and politically. You're not just erasing a physical barrier but also the spiritual fetters of dependence.

Let's say I have something I want to give society. Why do I have to share that particular thing with someone who is only in it for commercial reasons? Why can't a black industry benefit from it? Why can't I produce my own thing? Why can't I take my music and sell it? Why can't I take my musical talents and sell them myself instead of having to depend on other people?

A lot of guys who own publishing companies also have recording companies. They know where things start and where they end. They control the whole interest. A few years ago you had to take your wares and play them to an impatient agent who had lines of people waiting to get in. They don't have to do that now. They have their own successes to relate back to. They can go to a black industry and say, Let's collect our wares together and get this thing on the road. They can promote their own concerts without paying a certain percentage of what their talent is going to bring in. If you do a recording through your own production and see it through to the end, you know exactly how many dollars you're making as well as how many you put into it. If you record something you don't take a percentage, you take it all. To me this is what the black revolution is about: not having to go to the white man for things you can control yourself.

Do you do any kind of physical exercise?

I do exercises every day. I was into yoga for about a year, then I decided to go back to calisthenics, because I like to sweat. I put on a sweat suit and exercise for thirty or forty minutes a day. I go riding three or four days a week. That's good exercise for muscle tone. But my thing with horses is also for pleasure and a hobby.

Do you find that exercise helps you with your instrument?

I don't think of it that way. I think of it as a way to remain in good shape. I find it stimulating. It makes me feel light on my feet, and that of course gives me a good mental approach to the bass. But as for physical exercise being related to the bass, I think the only exercise for that is playing the bass.

Do you change your way of playing with different drummers?

I like to feel I'm playing with a drummer. Some drummers play at you. When you play with certain drummers, you get a caressing feeling that everything is going right. Sometimes a drummer's conception is so different from yours that it's like somebody scraping you in the wrong direction. Whereas at other times it's like you're grooving because it feels smooth. When I play with Connie Kay, I call him the security officer, because he gives you a sense of balance and makes you feel secure. Luckily, most of the drummers I play with are security officers.

What do you think we as musicians can do to help our people?

So much attention is being focused on black people today. To be black is almost fashionable, because we are the only people who are really making any moves, making any strife, making headlines. Anything we do is really being watched. I guess the establishment is trying to see how the things we do or want to do are affecting the things they have and which they think we might want to have. I believe the only thing we as musicians can do is to concentrate on our music. Real art lies in doing your thing and expressing yourself through your instrument. Not only musicians but poets and actors are doing this.

What do you think about the concentration camps that are set up for black people in America?

That's true. Look at Angela Davis, Bobby Seale and the Tombs prison. Concentration camps don't start with slamming the cell door, they start with the guy on the street. Concentration camps don't only mean the jailhouse, they mean a particular image you don't fit into, so right away you're concentration-camp material.

I was arrested for loitering once. I had just finished a job at Shoe Alley, and a cop told me I couldn't stand in front of the theater. I was waiting for some friends to come out, and he asked me for identification. A black man walked up and asked, "What's happening?" I said: "This guy says I'm loitering." He told the cop I had just finished working in the theater. Now that was identification enough. But it so happens he's black and has a beard, as I do, and the cop ignored him completely. The people I was waiting for came out of the theater, and he still couldn't back down and say, well, I was wrong and you had every reason to stand here. He couldn't be logical and intelligent. He was on the tactical police force and could only relate to the fact that he was a white officer approaching a black man who didn't fit his image, of maybe a Madison Avenue white fellow. He had to show he was in authority. He had no authority to approach me in the first place. His mind wasn't tuned to the fact that a black man could resist his approach. I said, "I have every right to stand here. I'm not showing you identification because it's not necessary to carry identification in the States." He arrested me and put handcuffs on because I was considered to be a loiterer.

The whole idea of concentration camps is very true, because any black resistance seems to get more prominence in news writeups than white resistance. The Ku Klux Klan has been hanging around for years and you never hear of their members getting shot up like they shot up the Panthers. I believe there are concentration camps, because they use concentration-camp tactics in their approach to black people. Even young white kids are concentration-camp material because they resist the establishment. The kids don't like the idea of wars and have their ideas about how they want to dress. They say clothes don't make the man, the man makes the clothes. But people don't seem to believe in their philosophy about these things.

What do you think about me compiling all these interviews?

I think it's one of the greatest things that's happened, and this is one of the greatest interviews I have been involved with. First of all, I'm being interviewed by a fellow musician, and a brother at that, so we could sit and rap all day about things common to both of us. It's another approach, and you don't ask me stereotyped questions. It's very relaxing and comfortable to sit here and rap. The fact that this book is going to be published is great. I'm sure it's going to express a lot of feelings some people never really get a chance to read about. You see a musician onstage but you don't really get to know or approach him. You see him at a distance, and he stays at a distance. People will get an inside track of how a guy really feels. They might be able to understand why he plays like he does, but they might not dig him after they hear what he's talking about, so it works both ways. I'm sure people will pick up a book like this and try to read it through at the first sitting.

—New York, November 6, 1971

≡ ELVIN JONES ≡

"Learn how to make a perfect roll."

Elvin, would you tell me about Detroit and the early stages of your career?

In 1949 I got out of the army. There was a place in Detroit called the Bluebird Inn, and I was working there with Billy Mitchell. In this particular club single stars would come in—the big names in the business like Bird, Sonny Stitt, Wardell Grey, Miles Davis—and work with us, as we were the house band, for a month at a time. Miles came and stayed for six months or longer. I worked there with him for six months. There was a great interest and an undercurrent of support for the music all over Detroit and that area. Everybody loved the music. They loved to see a young cat develop, to follow his development and to encourage and support him. Consequently, where I lived in Pontiac, which is not far from Detroit, on our off nights at the club, I started asking the cats if they wouldn't like to come out to my house just to jam. My mother made everything comfortable for everybody.

Every Monday the house would be mine, and all the musicians from Detroit would flock out there. We would jam and have a ball. That went on for a couple of years. It was that kind of community support. In the Detroit and Pontiac area there were a lot of budding musicians like Barry Harris, Tommy Flanagan, Pepper Adams, all the McKinneys [Ray, Bernard, and Harold, who was a piano player], Kenny Burrell, his brother Bill, Ernie Farrell [a bass player who died who was Alice McCloud's brother], Pancho Hagood—all the cats. They were too numerous to mention: the Jacksons [Milt Jackson, his brother Alvin], and another Jackson family, Ali Jackson and the drummer, Bop Jr. [Oliver Jackson], Eddie Locke, Boo Boo Turner, Abe Woodly. Some of these guys never got to New York, but they were very popular around Detroit. You know—Yusef Lateef, Frank Gant, Lou Hayes.

I remember Lou Hayes and Roy Brooks when they were little kids. To me, they were little kids because they weren't old enough to get in the club. From the street you could see the bandstand. There was a window with venetian blinds, and since the drums were right at the front, they would ask me to open the blinds so that they could see. And I would do that for Roy and Louis. Along with Frank Gant, they became attached to me. They asked me a lot of questions about drumming and music, and I'd try to give them as much true knowledge as I could, or as much as I had. It's good to see that they took some of the things I said seriously and followed them through and really became serious about music. I'm not saying I had all that much to do with it, but I must have been a partial influence in some of the things they wanted to do. At least I wasn't a bad influence.

That period must have played a great part in your development.

A great deal. It introduced me to modern music. In a nutshell, that was it. I had listened to radio and records and all that, but I hadn't actually been part of a group. Before I met Billy Mitchell and he hired me, I used to go to the club and listen to Wardell Grey and all these cats. Art Mardigan was the drummer, and he was always very friendly and helpful to me. He used to ask me to sit in, but I would never do it. I thought it was presumptuous to sit in with these musicians, because to me, they were the greatest people I knew. I found it an honor even to speak to these cats and to know them socially. I never had the faintest idea that I would actually become a member of the group and be a regular.

My hero worship sort of modulated into an actual, realistic participation, for which I am eternally grateful. There were a lot of things happening around Detroit at that time. The musicians in the band were Billy Mitchell, Thad [Jones] and James Richardson, a bass player. At one time Ted Sheely was playing piano; one time it was Tommy Flanagan and the other time it was Barry Harris. Terry Pollard also played with us. There were so many things happening that it's hard to get them in any kind of chronological order at this moment.

There was an elderly man then who was a jazz patron of the arts, you might say. He was quite wealthy and had retired from business. He used to run one of Ford's plants in Ohio, as the general manager or something like that. He lived in Royal Oak,

Michigan, so he used to come to the Bluebird a lot. He decided that he wanted to sponsor concerts like Norman Granz. He asked Thad and myself to get some musicians together and from there we would see about hiring a hall, get publicity out and put on a concert. So we did it.

Doing these concerts is where I really got acquainted with Kenny Burrell and Barry Harris. I met a lot of these people by asking them to play these gigs. They weren't paid much money, but it wasn't for free—fifty dollars or something like that was a nice little taste for a Sunday afternoon. It was all part of the cultural activity in the Detroit area. That wasn't the only part of the city where these things were going on—it was happening all over Detroit. The people who came to the concerts were just as hip to music and just as informed as the musicians, so there was no question of jiving. If you couldn't play, you would get heckled off the stand. I don't think anybody would have had the nerve to get on the bandstand and try to fake something, because everybody in the audience not only loved the music but also probably played some instrument. It was amazing! I've never seen anything like it before or since: a whole community actively participating in the development of the form. It was really a beautiful thing to see. It made for sort of a camaraderie, an affinity and a sympathy that we had for one another.

When I reflect on these things, I consider myself a very fortunate person to have been involved in it. There was another thing we used to do at a place called the World Stage. This was a theater group which put on plays, like a summer-stock theater. We used the facilities of this theater to give weekly concerts on Tuesday nights. So we would be at my house on Monday and at the World Stage on Tuesday nights. This was supported heavily by the community. It was near Wayne University campus, so a lot of the audience would be college students. The respect that the audience would show, even in that little place. One hundred and fifty people would have been a real large crowd, because the place wasn't big. It was just as if you were in Carnegie Hall. It was the same kind of reverence, the same sort of atmosphere. We tried just as hard to give a good performance as any group of musicians, professional or otherwise, on any stage in the world.

Then there was an after-hours place where everybody would go on weekends. This was in Del Ray, River Rouge. It was quite a drive from Detroit, but everybody would go out there. It was a hotel and dining room. This was one of Kenny Burrell's gigs. He eventually married the owner's daughter. We used the place for jam sessions. The owner would pay four people, and anybody who wanted to come by and sit in was welcome. It was beautiful. It was nothing to go and work your gig from nine till two o'clock in the morning and then afterward go out there and play again until eight or nine in the morning. That was a really nice period, and it contributed a lot to my development in the music business and to my awareness of the need for a great deal of self-discipline. It gave me an exposure to the world of music and to some of the dues you would have to pay as a working musician.

A lot of these things I have since experienced over and over again. I look on that period as a valuable part of my education. I really had the chance to play as much as I wanted, the way I wanted to and with people who had the same thing in mind concerning their instruments. I heard some of the best solos and had some of the most emotional experiences I've ever had in my life during that time. Everybody would come there.

There was a club near there called the Rouge Lounge that brought in topflight musicians from all over the country, and when they were off, they would come out to the place if only to have breakfast, because they had some good food there. A lady cooked homemade bread and biscuits, grits and eggs, chops and steaks and things. It was very nice.

How do you view the business at that period as compared to now? And in conjunction with that, what do you think is the reason we as musicians don't own record or production companies?

Most of the musicians at that time were naive businesswise, me included. I had the mistaken belief that since I gave an honest performance on my instrument, people who were otherwise involved in the business would do the same. The booking agent would do his part; I was thinking of it all as a great harmonious team. I suppose that due to this way of thinking, I didn't feel it was necessary to protect myself. I think it is a form of protection for musicians to band together and combine knowledge. I'm sure there's enough expertise among six or seven musicians to form a publishing company or a record company, and that possibly they have the technical knowhow for recording, engineering and whatever else would be necessary.

Why hasn't it been done?

For one thing, it requires a great deal of money, and mainly you have to want it. Most of the artists I know are just that: They're artists. This is what they want to do. They don't want to work in an office. They don't want to accept the responsibility of being an executive in a publishing or a record company, because it's not something they feel they can do. I'm sure this is the reason we don't have that kind of industry among black musicians. Individually, and taking isolated cases, there is enough expertise and knowledge among black musicians to do all these things. I could name half a dozen men who have all the knowledge in the world, and, as a matter of fact, some of them owned their own companies. As far as doing it as an industry in direct competition with the white record companies, this hasn't occurred. Motown Records was supposed to be a black company—well, I know that it is not. Maybe originally Berry Gordy conceived the idea, but the time has long since passed where he has anything at all to do with that company other than just being a front-office man. I think it probably belongs to the Bank of America. I'm not positive, but I know they have one of their main offices in one of the largest Bank of America buildings in Los Angeles. I'm sure it's not controlled by the finances of Negroes. It's controlled by the established finances who control everything. It's just another company now.

How do you tune your drums?

Well, usually in intervals of fourths or fifths. I use two tom-toms and a snare drum, of course. So there's four drums, tuned in intervals of fourths. Starting from any given pitch would give you enough of a variety of tone to construct unlimited tone combinations. Using the dynamic intensity of stroke and whatnot can give you every variety of sound for solo construction.

Do you play for the audience, for yourself or for the musicians?

I play the music! And I play the music because there's a way I know it should sound. This is what I'm striving to achieve: the interpretation that I know the composition requires.

Do you do any physical exercise aside from playing the drums?

I don't think you need any. Who needs it? Playing the drums is enough physical exercise. I was an athlete when I was in school, so I've never really gotten out of physical condition. Fortunately, I've never been seriously ill or incapacitated physically, and my body is in a reasonably good state of health.

Did you practice a lot?

A great deal. I used to practice anywhere from four to eight hours a day when I first started, from the age of thirteen to when I was about twenty-four.

Did your family influence you to play music in any way?

Actually they had nothing to do with it. I must have been influenced by the fact that my brothers were musicians, but I think I would have been a drummer anyway, because I've always liked the drums. I never really thought seriously about any other instrument. The drums have always been my love.

What do you think about the vast publicity musicians have gotten due to the use of drugs?

I think it's a distorted image that has been given to a vast majority of musicians. It's a stigma that's totally undeserved by the greater number. I imagine that anybody who has any real depth of thought would be able to see that it can't possibly be true of every musician. Just because a man is a musician doesn't mean he has to be a dope fiend. It's like saying that everybody who is a sailor is a drunkard or a homosexual, which is ridiculous. Or that all people with hairlines close to their eyebrows are criminal types. Or that if you've got thick lips you can't play a flute. Ridiculous thinking of this kind creates distortion, and I think no intelligent person would place any credence in it. Most people don't like to think very much, which is why the press should explain a lot of these things in more detail. There should be just as much publicity about musicians who are not dope addicts as about the ones who are. If they deserve that publicity, then they should get it, by all means. But the ones who don't should get what they're due.

You worked with Bud Powell. What were your impressions of him?

I always had the impression that Bud had been hurt so much.

He was like a very delicate piece of china. I think he was an extremely sensitive person, a very beautiful person. He was really nice, and I loved him. I thought he was a genius in what he was doing. His ideas about modern music were revolutionary. There are very few pianists even now who have approached the level of proficiency which Bud Powell attained and consistently maintained. He's one of the masters.

Well, Elvin, you told me you were in the army.

Yeah, for a while . . .

You don't want to talk about that.

No. I did my bit and that's it.

That rhymes. Let's lead into your association with John Coltrane.

It was an unprecedented opportunity to do something I really wanted to do. To me it was the best of all possible worlds. Not only did I admire Coltrane as a person, but as a musician there was no one for whom I had a more profound respect. To share musical experiences night after night with this man and in this group was, like I said, the best of all possible worlds. It was a great experience which taught me a great deal.

What do you think about the word jazz?

It's misleading in a lot of ways, and it's an inadequate expression, but I don't think there's anything degrading about it. I don't feel any reluctance to tell people that I'm a jazz musician: I am. Also I don't ever hesitate to add *musician* after the word *jazz*. When I use the word *jazz*, I always say *jazz music*, because I think it is a complete art form. It's unfortunate that this word was chosen to express it, but nevertheless that's what it is. It's a pure art form developed here in this country by black artists and which is continuing to be developed by everybody who has any musical aspirations at all or who has even thought about becoming a musician, whatever color they are. I think the fact that it's pure transcends all colors and races.

Do you like traveling?

Yeah, I like traveling. I enjoy it immensely.

It never becomes a strain?

Well, I don't say never. I have had some trying experiences in traveling. I have traveled in some directions that I didn't originally intend. But nevertheless . . .

What do you mean by that?

Let's put it this way: I've had some bad experiences with the police in my travels. I've had occasion to run into the law for one reason or another, but that still doesn't dampen my enthusiasm for traveling. It's just an unfortunate incident that occurred which has nothing to do with the reasons for my traveling and it has no bearing on my future plans. I like to travel. I like taking this music all over the world. This is what should be done, what must be done. I'm perfectly willing to be the purveyor of this truth.

What do you think we can do as musicians to further the advancement of our people?

To be as good a person as one can possibly be. Self-examination of character. To really be what one claims to be. To be an artist and a musician and to make certain that this is what one's life is, that this is what it's all about. In that way I think we will help our people, because we're a living example of what this particular race of people can attain in this field.

Are you interested in using electric instruments?

I am. My piano player uses an electric piano, and the bass player uses a Fender bass and an upright bass with a microphone attacher and a speaker. I think that when it's used properly, it adds another dimension to the things you can do. It can also be a crutch for some people, because you can turn it up as loud as you like and get all this volume of sound with very little effort. Say you were a guitarist or a bass player—you'd have a tendency not to develop the muscles which are necessary for you to produce a true, unamplified sound. I think people who are involved in electronics have to be very careful about how they use them in relation to the development of the physical requirements for playing an instrument.

Are you religious?

Yeah, I think so.

Do you adhere to any particular religion?

No, I just believe in God, and I was raised as a Baptist Protestant. I believe in the power of prayer. Mainly I know there is a spiritual contact between people when more than one are concentrating on a thing that is truthful.

Can you relate this to music?

It does relate to music. It relates very strongly to music. I don't like to get into an area where I'm not an authority. I don't think it's explainable. I think it just is and it's a phenomenon. Either it happens or it doesn't happen. I think most people know this.

Have you ever gotten any bad writeups?

I don't know, because I don't think I have read everything that's been written about me. If somebody thinks enough of you to write anything, then whether you consider it good or bad depends on your point of view. A lot of things that seem bad may have the effect of making you reflect on what created such an impression, and perhaps it is something you ought to know. Maybe you need to practice another few hours.

I'm not saying that somebody should inadvertently sit down and write something about you without any knowledge of the subject. This, I think, would be a distortion of facts. It might not be an outright lie, but it would definitely be misleading. I don't think all writers are gifts from heaven or that all musicians are, either, but if someone has to write about music or about a musician, he should have a certain amount of knowledge on the subject so as to intelligently relate what he really thinks or what actually happened. A critic should be something more than a reporter at a football game.

What do you think about musicians putting political aspects in their music?

There's so much politics, and politics can be such a subtle sort of subject. The musicians who do that think there will be some advantage in it for themselves. Either you're going to be a musician or a politician. During some of the marches Reverend King was having down South, a big cavalcade of musicians and artists went along with him: Harry Belafonte; Sammy Davis, Jr.; Peter, Paul and Mary and others. I met some of this Peter, Paul and Mary group and they couldn't care less about what Martin Luther King was doing, but they were very aware of the fact that they were being seen by millions of people. They're in the record business, and being associated with the marches in that way might persuade people who had never even thought of them before to go out and buy one of their albums. I believe that's why they did it. I don't think they had any great sympathy for the black cause. I think it was for personal advantage. I singled them out because they just happened to cross my mind. Maybe I'm wrong. I certainly hope I'm wrong, but I don't think so.

Were you influenced by anyone when you started playing?

Yes. I was influenced by the bandleader at my school. He had all the integrity and dignity of what I really believed in and still do. I listened to Kenny Clarke a lot and Max Roach, Chick Webb, Jo Jones, Baby Dodds, cats like that. I used to listen to all kinds of parade drummers and circus bands, the American Legion Drum Corps. All these things influenced my early development, because it made me aware of the importance of the instrument.

What about freedom music, avant-garde?

The ones I've seen were just fishing around on their instruments and bullshitting the public to a great degree rather than doing anything constructive musically. It sounded just like a kid picking up a horn without knowing how to finger it properly, running up and down the keys, creating some kind of distorted sound without any pattern, at the end of which this is freedom. I don't believe that at all. There's no such thing as freedom without some kind of control, at least self-control or self-discipline. It's impossible. There are such things as free forms, and I think I've heard that done. Coltrane did a lot of experimenting in that direction, and so did a few other people. I was closer to Coltrane than to anyone else, so I can speak with more authority on him than on others. He was perfectly aware of what he was doing and had almost supernatural control over what he was doing. Even though it gave an impression of freedom, it was basically a well thought out and highly disciplined price of work. Sort of a rendition of musical modes.

What would you recommend for a youngster aspiring to be a drummer? What would you suggest he practice or study?

Learn how to roll: Learn how to make a perfect roll, starting from the very basic pattern of "Daddy-Mama." Try to be able to execute a five-minute roll. I think that would keep any young student busy for about two years!

You mentioned control. How important is it in regard to your instrument?

It's extremely important. It's probably the next most important thing after learning the structure of the composition. I think you develop control though practice and mainly through trial and error. Every time you play you're going to get that many more minutes of practical experience on the instrument. I think any true student should feel that whenever he plays, he will have learned something when he gets up. No matter how great or small, he will have found out something else about his instrument. This is how you gradually build up a backlog of control.

Would you use the same approach to the instrument if you were playing in a club or in a studio?

There's no basic change. The instrument doesn't change when it's in a studio or in a club, so why should you change? You should use the same self-discipline and control, no matter where it is.

Not many drummers have been using brushes much in recent years. What do you think of that?

It's part of the standard equipment. I think everything which is part of drumming should be learned and used. It is just as essential to know how to play brushes and to use them properly as any other component of the drum set.

What do you think about my compiling these interviews?

I think it's something you could never really finish. The material that you're gathering is quite interesting. I don't think you could get it any other way, and by your being who you are, you should be able to do a great deal more than a regular writer for a newspaper or magazine. It's a very good, healthy thing that you're doing, and I wish you success with it. It's something that should be done and you're doing it. I'm glad that you are.

Anything you would like to say that I didn't ask?

I want to say that I'd like to see peace on earth eventually!

—*New York, November 11, 1971*

≡ KENNY DORHAM ≡

"Bird really painted Milwaukee red."

Would you tell me how you became interested in music?

Well, my sister heard Louis Armstrong in about 1936, and she mentioned the fact that they called him Gabriel, saying he must be the Gabriel written about in the Bible. I was about eight or nine years old at the time, and when I was playing the piano, my sister used to say to my mother, "See how he jumps around when he plays? Maybe he's going to be a great musician like Louis Armstrong." Then I got a chance to listen to Pops on some records, and it kinda started from there.

In 1936 I moved to Austin, Texas, with my uncle and went to high school there. It was at high school that I really got into the trumpet. I had a friend who lived down the street from me, and he played the trumpet. He used to go to East St. Louis every summer, and he knew Clark Terry and Miles Davis. He would tell me how these guys could really play the trumpet. Texas was pretty well known for having good trumpet players, because they had a lot of football games and competitive band meets.

In 1939 my sister persuaded my father to buy me a fourteen-dollar trumpet. I had it for a week or two, and the bandmaster suggested I ought to have a better trumpet which would at least play in tune, so that I wouldn't get discouraged before I learned something. Well, they got me a silver Conn trumpet. It took me about a half-hour to even get a sound out of it. Then I began going to band practice, where they start you right out in the books. After you learn the fingering you start to play études and concert stuff. After two days in rehearsal I was sent home by the bandmaster, who was very stern about music. He didn't allow you to play jazz or anything until you had learned all the fundamentals of music. I was sitting in the band and I started playing "Dipsy Doodle," which I had heard Larry Clinton's orchestra play. I was stomping my foot, and the guys were behind the curtain urging me on. The bandmaster looked over his glasses, pointed at me and hollered, "Leave the bandstand! Leave the music room and don't come back." I was out of the band for three or four days, and I was really itching to get back. He spoke to my parents, and I got my discipline together for the music room. From then on I was just a student and not trying to do anything special.

Whenever I wanted to do a little extracurricular stuff like jazz, I did it in our barn, which was a great resonator for music. You blew in there and you had all this good wood; it really made a great sound. I sometimes used to practice in that barn for five or six hours a day. After learning all the band music at marches and playing like Louis Armstrong in the barn, I heard Roy Eldrige, and he was a big influence on me. Later I heard some Charlie Parker, because my friend who lived down the street had all the hip records. I first heard Charlie Parker on a Jay McShann record; I think he was playing "Swingin the Blues Away," and it sounded so great that I learned the solo. I started to try and play the trumpet like Bird. After listening to Walter Fuller, who used to play with the Earl Hines band, I started playing like him, too. He played a strong punctuation style. Finally I got to listen to some Dizzy, and that was the most fantastic trumpet I had ever heard. Although Louis Armstrong's music was beautiful and melodious, Dizzy's was something else. So I started to play Dizzy's solos, too. I was playing like all these different trumpet players: Walter Fuller, Louis Armstrong, Roy Eldridge and Dizzy Gillespie.

When I started going to college, I was too late to get into the band, so I worked in the kitchen, washing dishes and helping prepare food for the students. I got to know a lot of guys there like Russell Jacquet and Wild Bill Davis. Davis wrote music for the college band, and they played in the style of Jimmy Lunceford and Milt Larkin.

Would you tell me about the period in your career when you were playing with Bird and Dizzy?

When I first came to New York, I was working in the house band at the Savoy Ballroom. I would always go in and out of the bands with another trumpet player from Texas called Henry Boozier, because they needed a first trumpet player and a soloist. At that time I played a lot of first trumpet and I also soloed, but

Boozier was mostly a first man with a big, pretty sound like Freddie Webster.

By the fall of 1944 I had started going to Minton's, and Lockjaw Davis invited us to play there one night. He liked our playing, and he gave us an open invitation to come and play anytime we wanted. I met Dizzy, Fats Navarro and Miles at Minton's. I had met Miles before on Fifty-second Street. I had also met Dizzy before, because when I first came to New York, I really came looking for him. He was going to start a big band, and he invited us to audition for it. The next day we went to the big-band rehearsal at Minton's Playhouse, and we got the gig.

We stayed with Dizzy during the whole time he had his first big band, and I learned a lot playing with him. I sang a couple of tunes in the band, but later I got him a singer from Fort Worth called Dexter Armstrong. When we were on tour, I learned a lot of things Dizzy did that I could kind of duplicate, and from that point on I really started to grow musically. I was writing Basie arrangements. I would try to get the sound of Ellington arrangements without much success, but I knew what I was doing.

Bird used to come to Minton's, and he was so great that everybody would leave the bandstand when he played. All the bad saxophone players showed him respect and let him have the bandstand. They would sit down and listen. Dizzy would usually play with him, or sometimes Miles or Fats. Dizzy, Lorraine, Gillespie, Sarah Vaughan and I used to hang out at Minton's and play a lot at that time.

After being in Dizzy's band I took Fats Navarro's place in Billy Eckstine's band. Later I played in about twenty other big bands in New York, for anywhere from one day to three weeks or a month. I was living up on Sugar Hill at 157th Street, and Harry Belafonte, who was working at the Royal Roost with Bird, came by one day to let me know that Bird wanted to speak to me. So I went down to see Bird, and he told me that Miles was leaving to form his own band and that I could have the job if I wanted. I went there the following night; that was on Christmas Eve, 1948. I played with Bird from then on at the Royal Roost through the spring of 1949, when we went to Paris for a French festival. I was with him for about a year after that. Then he started doing things with strings where he didn't use a trumpet, so I started to play with various people again.

In the fifties I started to do things on my own. I made my first
record date as a leader in 1954 for Charles Mingus. I was writing a
lot of songs; in fact, I wrote some for your record date and for
Freddie Hubbard. I have between seventy-six and eighty songs
registered as a BMI publisher. But I had a family, and it was hard
to do a lot of different things, so I got an advance on the
publishing company and later sold it.

Would you tell me more about Bird?

Well, Bird was a real happy person, and it never seemed like he
had any acute traumatic grievances. He knew our society wasn't
right, and he would talk about it sometimes. His thing was like
he'd just get high and blank that other part out. I guess he saw it
wasn't going to get together in his lifetime.

We made a lot of nice trips together. Just before going to Paris
we worked in Milwaukee, and Bird had to go back to New York
one day for something. He returned to the job at twelve o'clock
that night. The job started at nine or nine-thirty and we played
until two A.M. The place was jammed. Bird came in, perspiring.
He had on that black pinstripe suit . . . he was famous for that
suit! He was happy, and he came up on the bandstand. Although
we had missed him, we had been having a lot of fun, and we had
everything rolling. This was in the early spring, and it was a little
warm that night.

He called a tune I had never heard before called "Painting the
Town Red." He played that for about half an hour, and each
chorus was more fantastic than the one that had preceded it.
After he had been playing for about ten minutes, I said to myself,
what is he going to do next! Because everything was flawless; it
was perfect. I sat down in a corner of the bandstand, crossed my
legs and just listened to him play. Max Roach, Al Haig and
Tommy Potter were in the rhythm section, and it was beautiful.
Bird really painted Milwaukee red that night!

When it was over, Bird asked me what I wanted to play, and I
said, "Do you know 'Circus'?" And he started singing it. I said,
"Yeah, that's it." He said, "Okay, let's play some 'Circus.'" He
let me play the melody and the first solo on it. This kind of
triggered my feeling for the song. Although I had never played it
with Bird, I knew that Al Haig was familiar with it. Bird just
played his can off on that.

Between times I never saw Bird. He was very mysterious. The only time I would see him was on the job. I had only one rehearsal during the whole time I was in the group, because I knew all the tunes Bird played and just how he played them, which I guess is one reason I got the gig. I could play the ensembles so that if on some nights he didn't feel too well and might falter a little, I could hold the group together. When we did a record date, he would come to the date with some of the music written down; then he would write the rest of it at the date. We would run it down once or twice, look at it and play it off the sheet. Then we would record. It was really nice playing with Bird!

Do you think musicians should use their music for political ends?

I'm not sure, because music is one thing and politics is another. Sometimes people manage to blend them, but most musicians look upon it as a gimmick. People from the world of politics look upon it as some kind of rabble-rousing weapon, especially in this country. The politics are used just to obtain some kind of recognition, to get some credit for what one is doing. They don't really want to give you too much credit here for what you do, so they're quick to holler on anything that sounds political, whether it's a song or a poem.

I've always had a feeling that it may not be a good thing to only want to be in the music, but that was the thinking of musicians who came up in the Louis Armstrong era. Pops wasn't political; he was all music. Maybe one can't afford to be all musical today, because politics have a lot to do with the economic situation musicians find themselves in. Maybe putting politics into music is okay if it's advantageous to the musician. Musicians usually never benefit from anything. They can't borrow money or get any kind of economic satisfaction. Recently there have been some endowment grants and humanities, and a few musicians have gotten a little money. The amount of money you get is kind of insulting. Musicians like myself and a few others I know get such meager amounts. You figure, well, what was it all for? Maybe I should just have made bombs and have belonged to the destructive side of society. That may be why people mess with drugs; they feel it's a way out, at least for as long as they're high.

Politics could be useful in music. The music business itself is a political machine. If you're not managed by someone who is on the inside, you can float around out here for a lifetime and nothing ever happens. You see people come up who are less qualified, and everything is all rosy for them. Musicians will probably have to be more political in the future. They will certainly have to be businessmen, because they mustn't leave it up to the guy in the booking agency. He's their real enemy. Originally the booking agent was working for the musicians. He was like a secretary, who would keep their appointments and set things up. But somehow it got turned around. Instead of the booking agent working for the musician, the musician works for the booking agent. That's all wrong! The musician now has to call the booking agent to find out when he can work. In the meantime the booking agent is double-dealing, taking money under the table and on top of the table and looking out for his own interest, not the musicians'. That's political!

What do you think about electronics?

I think electronics is a part of automation, and it's removing the human aspect of the work. It's eliminating the effort of the man who owns the hand. It's not a natural thing and it can never be as good as the human element. It's the kind of thing which defeats itself. That's political, too, because they try to eliminate people from different walks of life. Then the people are controlled by just a few elements. You get ready for music, you go to the machine. You get ready for milk, you go to the machine. Everything is going to the machine, and it's losing that natural thing. It will probably affect the physiology of man. It's got to change his chemistry, and we may develop into monsters or freaks.

Do you do any kind of physical exercise?

I haven't done much recently, but I used to do a lot. When I was in the army, I did boxing. I started in high school because I was playing the trumpet and I was getting roughed up a bit. When I was living in Oakland, I used to box at John Henry Lewis's gym with some of the pros who fought out of Oakland. I don't know if you remember John Henry Lewis, but he fought Joe Louis and got knocked out. He had two brothers who would box at the gym. In Oakland I used to do a lot of exercising, and I would run halfway around Lake Merritt. My trainer's name was Al Moore. He had a fighter named Lenny Morrow from Tulsa, Oklahoma, who was the light heavyweight champion of California at one time. He knocked out Oakland Billy Smith, who later became known as Boardwalk Billy Smith. He also knocked out Archie Moore, though he was later knocked out by Archie. Al Moore had a lot of good fighters who used to fight in Nevada and California back in the fifties.

I also worked for the United States naval ammunition depot. I helped make rocket shells with yellow powder. That's the powder which goes into those 54-pound rocketheads for ships. They had black powder and yellow powder. I worked in the rooms where all those powders were. We put the powder in the shells with compressors. We didn't put the detonators on. We just inserted a fuse, and the rest was added on when it got to where it was going or when they were ready to use it. I also did a lot of boxing in New York, where I used to go to the Uptown Gym on 116th Street with John Lednam, Skippy. Do you remember Skippy?

Yeah, I remember Skippy.

I used to go to the gym with Skippy and keep time for him. Artie Towns was at Sugar Ray Robinson's stable, and I used to keep time for him, too. Miles also used to come and work out. I never did go into the ring. I used to just work on the bags. The guys would always be pushing you up to box because they liked to dust you if they got the chance. I stayed out of that because I was trying to lay with the music. So I've done a lot of exercise over a long period of time, but for the last year or two I haven't done much except for riding a bike and things like that.

Are you religious?

That's quite a question to try and answer. When I was growing up, I used to ask my father about religion, and he would tell me about God. He was not very educated, but he knew about the Bible and he had some sense about it. I wondered why we were so poor if God had all these powers. We were supposed to be good people, so why were we poor? And there were people who were bad and were very rich. So I sort of lost my faith in religion then. Religion is also political. It's used to keep world order. If people didn't have something to believe in, it would be impossible to keep order on this earth. It would be suicidal. But believing in something that you can't see, believing that there is a hereafter, believing all these things can make life on earth tolerable, if not worthwhile.

Do you think our music stems from Africa?

Maybe instinctively. A lot of it is instinctive. We learned our tools here, but it probably came from Africa, because we inherited something that goes from tribe to tribe. It has to do with how we are put together. Although we are similar to everyone else on earth, we are still different. We have something that's unique, just as every other race has something that's unique. So our African roots underlay the historical evolution of our music, but the rest was developed from our trials and tribulations on the plantation. And we're still on the plantation!

Do you change your technique in any way when you're playing in a studio, as compared to when you're working in a club?

In a studio I try to concentrate more on finesse, to play flawlessly. I might not be as inventive as I would be in a club, because there I can try to straighten it out while I'm doing it. It takes a lot of nerve to do that when you know you're going to hear it played back. It's not as loose when you're playing in a studio as it is when you're playing in a club. In a recording you really want to turn it on. You lean in wherever your position is from the microphone and try to take care of it from there. Whereas in a club anything goes!

What do you think about the stigma that's been put on musicians regarding their use of drugs?

Usually it's upper-middle-class people who put a stigma on musicians. Unfortunately a few of them happen to be black. This stigma has a political angle. When you have a stigma on you, it affects your earning power—you can't make money. Drugs have always been on the scene, and musicians are noticed because they are always in the public eye. Whereas other people who are not in the spotlight can slip and slide around for their whole lifetime. Whatever a musician does is known, because people like to talk about musicians.

To wrap it up, would you tell me what you plan for the future?

Musically, I will probably end up working for the Board of

Education. That's what I've been working toward. I have been going to school to get my degree. A degree is your ticket to something that's fairly stable. It's much more stable than being a musician. I always knew this, so I always went to school; but I never took music before I got to New York, because I was a science major. I plan to teach at the University of Connecticut or else I might go to the New England Conservatory in Boston. I'm going there as a resident for two weeks. Richard Davis will be there, too. I plan to lead a quiet life while still playing and writing music, doing the things I want to do and just trying to live like people. I might occasionally make some concert tours to Japan, South America or Europe, but my main goal is to be in education. I can teach a lot of subjects, like English, music or chemistry.

—New York, November 12, 1971

≡ ART BLAKEY

"Our music has nothing to do with Africa."

Would you tell me about Pittsburgh and its relationship to your development as a musician?

Ain't that a bitch? Pittsburgh ain't shit, man!

Tell me about it. You grew up there.

But where you were born doesn't have anything to do with your development as a musician!

Didn't you develop yourself as a musician there?

No. I started playing music there. I developed as a musician by playing on the road. That's where you develop yourself. I really developed as a drummer in New York, not in Pittsburgh. That city never contributed anything to me but chaos.

Tell me about yourself as a kid coming up and going to school in Pittsburgh.

I didn't go to school that long. I didn't have much time.

Well, tell me anything about Pittsburgh!

It's a dirty, greasy town and that's where I was born. I worked at the Carnegie Steel Mill, and that's one of the things I would like to forget in my life. I started playing music to get out of the coal mine and the steel mill. I just had to do it, because I didn't dig working in the coal mine or the steel mill and I had to do something to get out, like playing music. I would leave music at six in the morning and be at the steel mill by eight. I would work all day, then go to the club at eleven in the evening and work. Finally I left Pittsburgh. I never really had a childhood because at fifteen I was a married man and a father, so I missed out on everything a kid has. I was a grown man at fifteen, and I was glad to get out of Pittsburgh as soon as I could with Fletcher Henderson and Mary Lou Williams.

Was that the first time you left Pittsburgh?

Oh, no! I left Pittsburgh with my own band around 1937–38, went west and got stranded. So I came back to Pittsburgh and joined Mary Lou Williams. I went to New York with Mary Lou Williams, Marion Hazel, the trumpet player, and Orlando Wright. Harold Baker was with the Mary Lou Williams band, too. Later we left Mary Lou and joined "Smack" Fletcher Henderson. I left the band and went gigging in upstate New York with a girl called Dorothy Matthews. We took whatever gigs we could get.

I was in Potsdam when Hitler marched into Russia during the summer of 1941, the year before we went into the big war. I went back to Pittsburgh, rejoined Fletcher Henderson and did a lot of traveling. I left Smack in Boston after my episode with the police in Georgia. I had a big fight down there. I went there to join Smack with a white boy. This was before the ride in the back of the bus and all that.

The musicians, entertainers and athletes are the ones who break down the race barriers. We got beaten up because I didn't understand the white police down there. I ended up with a steel plate in my head, and I was told it would shorten my life, but it didn't work out that way. I was arrested for being black, for being a nigger; that's what I was charged with. So I joined Smack in Boston and later left him to form my own band, which played at the Tic Toc Club. That's where I met Roy Haynes, who was a kid at the time. I stayed in Boston for a few years; then I went to St. Louis and joined Billy Eckstine. That's where I met Bird, Sarah Vaughan and all those star musicians. I didn't know anything about them being stars at the time, but they were something else! I stayed with "B" [Eckstine] until he broke up, then I came to New York.

I got most of my experience playing the drums from Fletcher Henderson, the Billy Eckstine band and New York. I came to 117th Street and Lenox Avenue, and that's where I really got myself together.

What stands out in your mind about the period you spent with Billy Eckstine?

That was a fantastic era! Nobody got to hear it. They didn't get recorded, and the records they did make were sadder than

McKinley's funeral. Even the horses cried. Because it wasn't recorded right; they recorded a big band on two mikes, which was very unfair. They weren't interested in the band. They were interested in Billy Eckstine. Later on they wished they had recorded the band right, because the biggest stars in jazz were playing in it. Billy Eckstine had got them all together at that time, and it was a fantastic band! It was like a school for me, and that's when I realized that we had to have bands for young black musicians—big bands, little bands, a whole lot of bands—because this music is an experience. It's a school, and they can train to become musicians and learn how to act like musicians.

When this era ended, it was very bad. After Billy Eckstine, we built the 17 Messengers. I wanted more black musicians to get the schooling they needed to become leaders. That's what we needed in jazz, but it began to fade away because the guys didn't have anywhere to work and didn't have anybody to look up to. Nobody to tell them you don't do this, you don't do that; you do this, you do that. Because in the days of the 17 Messengers, the Billy Eckstine and the Fletcher Henderson bands, the guys would tell you if you were wrong even if it hurt your feelings. But when we didn't have any big bands, it was hard to talk to young musicians.

When I was playing with Fletcher Henderson, one night I had a bottle of whiskey in my coat pocket and I was drinking through a straw from the bottle during the show. I thought I was hip. The chorus girls were out on the stage, and I did the show pretty well. When I came off the stage, Sid Catlett grabbed me, hugged me and picked me up. But when he felt the bottle, he put me down, hit me and knocked me to the floor. He told me, "Next time learn how to master your instrument before you learn how to drink. Next time I catch you, I'll break your neck." So this stopped me from drinking. It helped me, and I never got angry with him. If you did that now you would have a lawsuit on your hands.

This is how the business began to deteriorate, and anyway we didn't have enough stars around to keep the clubs open. Sure you had Birdland and Bop City, but you didn't have enough black musicians who were stars, who could draw people and keep these places open. We did have about ten winners, but they were traveling all over the country. So what happened to the other clubs? They were running fifty-two weeks a year. If there had been enough names to even half-fill these places, we could have kept the business going; but we didn't have the time to produce star names. One thing led to another. I saw the whole thing deteriorate and it's down to where it is now, to nothing, which is a shame.

What do you think of the word jazz?

There's nothing wrong with it. It's only a word. What's in a name? Nothing! Cats say, "Call me Muhammad so-and-so." But what's the difference? A name doesn't make the music. It's just called that to differentiate it from other types of music. Jazz is known all over the world as an American musical art form and that's it. No America, no jazz. I've seen people try to connect it to other countries, for instance to Africa, but it doesn't have a damn thing to do with Africa. We're a multiracial society here. There are no black people in America who can say they are of pure African descent. Our parents were slaves, so you don't know whose grandmother was bending over picking cotton when the slaveowner walked up behind her! There was nothing we could do about it. Otherwise we wouldn't be all the different colors of the rainbow.

If you go to southern Algeria you'll see the blue people. All those people are so black that they're blue. If you go to the Congo, you'll see that the people are all a certain color and they can relate to each other colorwise. But we American blacks can't because we are the product of a multiracial society. So what difference does it make? We are here, we are the most advanced blacks, and jazz comes from us. When we heard the Caucasians playing their instruments, we took the instruments and went somewhere else. If you hear them sing "The Star-Spangled Banner" and then you hear a soul sister sing the same song in church, she's going to sing it different. This is our contribution to the world, though they want to ignore it and are always trying to connect it to someone else. It couldn't come from anyone but us. It couldn't come from the Africans. We made this music, whatever they want to call it . . . they'll call it the lowest thing they can, because it came out of the whorehouses. That's where we were; we couldn't get any further because they ignored us. The only places where we could play our music were in the churches and the whorehouses. They kept ignoring us, yet this is what we created! Our music has nothing to do with Africa. African music is entirely different, and the Africans are much more advanced than we are rhythmically, though we're more advanced harmonically.

Well, where did the term be-bop come from, Bu?

The term be-bop came from Dizzy Gillespie. You can hear it on his records: "Ooh-Bop-Sh-Bam" and all that.

What do you think about electronics being used in music?

Some of it is interesting. I would rather hear the musicians play their instruments without it, but it's going that way. Sometimes if you can't lick them, you join them. I had to pay over five thousand dollars for my equipment. What can you do? This is what they are going in for today, and you have to compete with them. The cats just have to come on in and use it, but with some discretion. They don't have to go way out.

What do you think about the publicity musicians have gotten over the use of drugs?

It's because of the society we live in. I don't think it's the musicians' fault. It's become old-fashioned among musicians, outmoded. It's so corny now that cats don't dig it anymore, which is a good thing. At one time it was the easy way out. I did it because I wanted to have the experience; I thought I was strong enough to do anything I wanted to, but I was lucky. I'm telling you, magilla is something else! We call it magilla gorilla!

So you think there's no reason for us to be stigmatized?

We have to live it down. A drug user goes to a hospital, where they give him methadone and all these synthetics. I think that's bullshit and that you don't need it. If you're determined to straighten your life out, you do it in front of everybody and where all the drugs are at; then you say you're straight. But if you have to go away somewhere to get off drugs you haven't proved anything.

Do you ever get bad writeups?

All the time.

How does it affect you?

It doesn't affect me at all. I'm happy when they mention my

name. Just so long as they spell it right, I don't care what they say. Once people stop talking about you, you've had it. They can say Art Blakey is lousy and I dig it. As long as I can keep them talking, I don't mind what they say. Once they stop talking, out of sight out of mind.

Do you play differently in a studio than in live performance?

I don't think so. I'm always experimenting. I never have anything set to play, and I may repeat a lot of things I have listened to and liked, which is one reason I never listen to records. I'm on the same level most of the time.

I'll tell you the way I like to record: Take the band, we've got arrangements and we go out on the road to play for two or three months at a time. When a musician brings an arrangement into the band, that's one tune; but when you hear it two months later, it's a completely different tune, and that's the one I like to record. After the tunes get down and everybody has the feel of them, I begin to place things where I want to place them. I've done a lot of recording which was rushed, and I'm not the type of musician who can rush and play things like I want. I have regretted most of the recordings I made when I heard them. I like the band to be so together that we can go into the studio and record for an hour and a half, do six, eight or ten tunes and feel relaxed. Most of my recordings were just hurry, hurry.

In those days we had to do it because we were uptight. The cats needed money, and I needed money, so we would just do it and get out of there. A Caucasian jazz musician would be allowed to take up to two weeks recording one album, but we were always made to hurry. You know what happens in those cases: You go to the studio and you haven't done anything. You're not relaxed, the tempos are up and down, they cut it here or there or they edit it without your consent. Then they put the record out, and sometimes it's really sad. Some people say, "Man, that's a good record!" Or they say, "That was your best record." But I have that to make yet.

I don't think most of the things we've done on record were right. I don't feel they were nearly the best I could do. Usually on a record I'm so uptight and trying to listen to the other cats that I can't play properly. I find myself repeating and repeating, because I'm listening and hoping the band will come together, thinking, don't do this, let's hold it together. I can't go off here, I can't go off there because it's too uptight. This is why we have produced some sad records. As time goes on, you can tell. You listen to a record of yours and say that could have been better. On the other hand, some of them come out and they're classics. But how much luck can you have?

How do you tune your drums?

I don't tune them. If I'm in a joint which is damp, I try to tune them up to a certain pitch where I can hear the sound I want. I don't tune them to any notes. The Africans don't tune their drums, and they beat the shit out of them. They sound good. An African uses whatever sounds good to his ear at that time. I see percussionists tune their drums because that's their thing. They know more about it than I do. All I want is to get that feeling and that sound. If I hit the drum and the people in the audience say *woo,* I got them. Going through all that tuning doesn't mean anything to me.

I feel that if you hit the drum and you reach the human soul, they know what you're talking about if it's the truth. I don't think you need all that technical stuff, because people couldn't care less if you're playing ratamacues or paradiddles. But if you get their attention, then you go into your thing. This is the way it works; the human being doesn't care how technical you are. You see guys going to learn all that technical stuff, but what does it mean? Somebody playing a solo for an hour doesn't mean a thing. You come along and make a tissue-paper roll, and you've washed out all he did in the last hour, because people will come up out of their seats if you do it right.

This is where I'm at. I play for effect, not for the technical part of it. Sid Catlett taught me that. He said, "When you're in trouble son, roll!" Nobody can surpass a roll. Chick Webb and Sid Catlett were the most fantastic drummers I have ever heard. I sat up under them, and they were something else! They really were the two most fantastic people I've ever heard in my life. Sid was the cream, right off Chick Webb. He could do anything with a drum. He could play just as soft with a pair of sticks as you can play with a pair of brushes, and he could take the brushes and play with them like sticks. Sid was so big that when he sat down at a 28-inch bass drum it looked like a toy. He was a master. I tried to pattern myself on him. He said, "Just roll."

At the time I was trying to learn how to read music. I was all wrapped up in some books when Sid came to a rehearsal of Billy Eckstine's band. He said, "Don't worry about that. Don't try to read everything, take some and leave some. And when you get in trouble, roll." So the next time we played an arrangement done by Jerry Valentine, there was nothing on the drum sheet. Nobody can write a drum part for an arrangement, anyway. You can only write a skeleton, the stops and the goes which you can hear for yourself.

The drummer is the one who interprets everything and puts it together. After the drummer puts it together, the arranger can't write what the drummer's got on his mind. He would have a lot of trouble trying to write that down! I've seen Chick Webb get a drummer to rehearse. The drummer would play the arrangement while Chick would sit there and listen. Then Chick would say, "Let's run it down and record it." When Chick got to the drums, something else happened. The whole arrangement turned around, because he was thinking along other lines. The drummers are the ones who change everything. Just like today in rock, the rock musicians are coming more over to the side where we are, getting more educated harmonically, but the drummer is the one who changed that whole thing around. They call it the Louisiana beat. Nothing has come out of rock-'n'-roll but the drummers.

How did you develop your press roll?

I didn't think it was developed yet. Teachers say that the way I do it is technically wrong, but it's the way I feel. That's the reason I stopped playing piano. Whatever you do, nobody ought to tell you how to do it, because you have physical handicaps you know about that nobody else knows about. Nobody knows them but you! Nobody teaches you how to eat. You know how to eat when you come here. So if you're going to play the drums, nobody should teach you how because you know your own physical aptitudes, what you can do and how to do it your way.

If we get into something and it's time to roll, I pick up the sticks, and if they're backward, I just roll with it. They say don't do it that way because it's timpani style. What style? Cats in Africa just pick the sticks up and they've got it. We have a technical advantage over here where we hold the stick between the thumb and the index finger of the left hand, which is good for what we're doing. But you don't have to play with a certain end of the stick. If you grab it you can just do whatever happens! If you have to, use your elbows or your whole body to get the effect you want. I made a thing with Stravinsky on timpani. Buddy De Franco had said, "I know a drummer who rolls like crazy." Stravinsky said, "Get him!" I didn't know about any music. All I did was watch the man's downbeat, bash and make the roll.

One of the finest directors I played under was Lucky Millinder. If a note jumped up from the floor and slapped him, he wouldn't know what hit him, but the man was so fantastic, so talented! Ask anybody who worked with him. Ask Dizzy Gillespie; he'll tell you. The music would be going and he'd be bringing them in eight bars before the brass was supposed to come in. And when he'd throw his hands down, you could bet your life that would be one! You didn't have to count. All you had to do was watch him, and he wouldn't make near a mistake at no time on any of the arrangements. This was a talented man.

I think that's within a person. He develops that himself. A lot of times I feel that if a person like that had technical training, he might not be as good a director. Like Erroll Garner, if he had technical training, he probably couldn't play piano like he does; he would have taken another direction. That's why you have to be careful. If a child starts out in music and gets technical training, it's different. But if he starts doing it by himself, then he'll have so-called bad habits.

Philly Joe Jones told me that you and Max Roach encouraged him to come to New York to play.

He's a great artist, and I admire his talent. When I first met Philly, he was driving a streetcar in Philadelphia. Philly is much more than a drummer; he's a natural actor. It's such a shame that this country, this society, lets a talent like his go to waste. It just kills me inside. This man has so much more to offer than just playing the drums; he can do anything. This society may kill him, like Bird, who wasn't strong enough to hold up there.

Everyone is different. The more pressure ofays put on me, the stronger I get. I'm going to live. I'm going to pat them in the face with a shovel. They're not going to kill me. I have something to tell them before I leave. This society we live in has goofed so much. Some of the greatest men the world has ever known passed through our ranks, right here in the jazz field. And society just and killed them. I don't think it's fair, and it hurts. These guys had not hurt anybody. What happened was that they were put in a position where they could destroy themselves.

What was your impression of Bud Powell and Charlie Parker?

Fantastic! Charlie Parker came out with an idea. And the only way you can beat an idea is with a better idea. I think there was a time when Bud Powell was playing more than Charlie Parker. Charlie Parker was playing, but Bud Powell was playing, too. That was another great who left us. Society destroyed him, just like Bird. Do you remember the Christmas before Bird died, when we were in somebody's loft in the Village with Bird and Hank Mobley? Bird said, "Hear with your eyes and see with your ears." I never forgot that. The knowledge Bird had about other things in the world beside music! He was a brilliant man. I watched the way he was put down, how they destroyed him and Bud and the way they're destroying Thelonious Monk now. Thelonious today is not the same as he was when we started out. He has opted out, just like Bud, and it's a drag.

What did you feel when you were playing with Bird?

It was one of the greatest uplifts in my life. Men like that just lift you up. It wouldn't matter if they were playing with a washboard. They would still sound good. Clifford Brown, Fats Navarro, Bird, Bud, Thelonious—when you're on the bandstand with them, they just lift the bandstand up. They have this power. Years ago I was talking with Thelonious and he said, "When you hit the bandstand, the bandstand is supposed to lift from the floor and the people are supposed to be lifted up too." When he said this, some people laughed, but it was not funny to me because I could feel that when he played. You know how Bird would start playing in the dressing room on his way to the bandstand. Even if the people were eating, they would stop and listen until he was finished. Cats like Bird and Bud were out of sight!

How do you feel about avant-garde or freedom music?

I don't understand it. When I hear free jazz, or whatever it is, I feel it's time for me to make my exit. Freedom is wonderful, but freedom without some discipline is chaos. It's got to have a point, to be reaching for something. Where are you going? It can't just be all chaos. You've got to have a direction. If people can't decipher your message, what you're trying to get across to them, it's no good.

The average man doesn't want to have to use his brain when he listens to music. Music should wash away the dust of his everyday life. He doesn't want to figure out what the musicians are doing. He's been figuring things out all day. He wants to get away from that and be taken out of this world. Music is entertainment.

The thing some of those freedom musicians are trying to do—I heard Lenny Tristano do that sort of thing years ago, but it had a direction. It made more sense to me than what they're doing now, with just everybody going. That's one of the easiest cop-outs. I hear those cats put down rock-'n'-roll. I hear them put down jazz. I hear kids put down Charlie Parker when they've never seen him or heard one of his records. But it's only a cop-out. You can't start at the top of the ladder; you've got to work up. You've got to have some foundation.

The music goes on. Charlie Parker wasn't the end of it. The sun goes down and we go through a period of darkness, then all of a sudden somebody rises up, the sun comes up and there's a great leader in music, here he is! People don't dig it, they still miss Bird, but a new leader will come up again. All you have to do is listen and watch out for him. Music is like a religion. There's always a musician who is going to come along and play more, have more on the ball and more to say than anybody else. But nothing can come out of chaos. There's got to be some direction or else the music is finished.

I don't see how the avant-garde musicians can figure that they are discovering anything new. There is nothing which is being played today that hasn't been played before. Maybe they use a different attack, but it's still been played before. I don't think a person should be given credit for knowing it's daytime when he looks out of the window and sees the sun is up. This is a foregone conclusion. You should be given credit if the sun comes up and something happens and you're discovering something. Cats like Beethoven and Bach went through that. They really knew what they were doing. This was their field. The black musician has nothing to do with that. His thing is to swing. Well, the only way the Caucasian musician can swing is from a rope. Swinging is our field, and we should stay in it. The Latin people have never left their thing. The Africans have never left their thing. So why the hell should we give up our thing when we've got the greatest thing in the world? We're going out there messing with something else which has no beat, which just goes yang, yang, yang . . . I can put some records on by Beethoven and Bach that would turn you completely around. They're the masters of that. But it's not for us. Our thing is to swing, and it's nothing to be ashamed of. It's something to be proud of.

We have so many bags we can go in. We can go into a Latin bag, we can go into a calypso. There isn't a greater bag in the world than calypso. We've got the bossa nova, which is in our own thing. We must keep our identity, because once we lose that we've had it, which is what they want us to do. We're not turning out the musicians we should be turning out, because the cats get buried in that freedom thing and they study it or else they say, "What's the use of studying? I'll just go out there and play free." Pretty soon they're going to separate the men from the boys. Those kids are going to be left out, and a lot of good talent will be lost because they didn't get with it, they didn't study. It's really going to happen. Caucasian kids play, but they have been trained and they just take over. All the cats who had groups put some ofays in them and then got completely taken over. We relate more to swing. This is our identity. Once the blacks in this country lose that, they have had it. I hope to God they don't. Drummers have now gone somewhere else and are putting down rock-'n'-roll. But I say those cats are swinging. If you could do what they do and at the same time do like we do, then you could talk!

Bird said he hoped young musicians would come along and learn how to play the blues, because he had only just scratched the surface. The cats haven't really learned how to play the blues yet, and they think it's all been done! There's so much to be done that hasn't been done, so many different approaches. What's happening is very sad. But I know it's going to change. Something is going to happen. Somebody will come and bring it around and say, hey, wait a minute! It's going this way. It's about time we had some new leadership, and I think it will happen. But it's time, because what's happening now is really sick.

The black musicians in this nation haven't reached a stage of working together. Those ofay musicians work together. If you want them to, they'll do the same thing every night, year in and year out. They'll work together, they won't be late, there's no ego thing going on, and when they come out with something, they make it not because they're great but just because of their togetherness.

I feel this way, Art: God told King Solomon that he could have anything in the world he wanted. Solomon thought for a long time and said he just wanted knowledge and wisdom, because if you ask for knowledge and wisdom all doors shall be open to you. What we need is the knowledge and wisdom to work together; then all the doors will open for us. The world beats a path to your door if you've got something to offer. We haven't been able to get together for social reasons. People discourage black boys and teach them the wrong things. One guy always wanted to be above the other financially, and it ended up with all of us not having anything, because we didn't work together. As the years pass, you realize this when it's too late. It's too late for the other cats that are coming. We have to sit down and try to open the doors so they can learn to avoid the mistakes we made.

As you know, I have made recordings with drummers. You yourself made some recordings with me on the drums. Now how many drummers have got together and taken other drummers on a record date? I was trying to think in another way. This drum thing can work, because the world is now drum conscious. We can open up plenty of doors with this thing. Everybody used to be so self-centered. The cats would say, "You're making a record with Bu? . . . Jesus Christ!" They didn't understand it. We weren't there to see who could outplay who; we were there to see if we could get something going.

What do you think of the Black Power movement?

Oh, boy, that sure was jive. A lot of lives were lost. You know, we used to sit around and talk about that. A lot of precious time and a lot of precious lives were wasted only because our people went at the thing so stupidly, and without thinking. I'm telling you, if black people would only sit down and think a little bit, it would be a hell of an experience for them! If you're going to punch a man in the mouth and you tell him, "I'm going to punch you in the mouth," he's going to get prepared for you. He might knock you down first. We never had the right kind of unity, because we don't think alike and we therefore don't act alike.

I remember when the Jews used to walk up and down the street selling razor blades and shoe strings out of cigar boxes and pushcarts. They had a togetherness. They ate alike, more or less, and if you can get people to eat alike, you can get them to think alike. There was really no black leadership. The people rallied around the guy who could holler the loudest, but he was still in darkness; he didn't even think. Where are Stokeley Carmichael and Rap Brown now? And where is all that fat-mouthing they were doing?

We took a giant step backward. You go to Harlem today and it's just like in 1936; there's no improvement. In fact it's worse. You can't even walk up there now. I remember a time when we used to run all over Harlem at any hour of the night. Maybe there were isolated incidents, but it wasn't like today. I never thought I would be afraid to walk in Harlem or anywhere in New York. And it's spread everywhere. If you go to Jersey or to Vermont, it's the same thing. This thing has hit everyone everywhere, but we're hit the worst. It's genocide. First they bring the dope into the country. How come they can't clean up the dope here? They get some of the addicts off dope and put them on methadone instead, but methadone is death. Did you read what they wrote about it in Europe? It takes all the marrow out of a man's bones, and when he's cut off from it, he'll die. This is genocide, and it's all part of a plan that was laid down fifty years ago. They knew where it was going and what to do, because they always plan ahead. While we're fat-mouthing about what we're going to do, the white man isn't saying nothing but he's going in his laboratory, coming out with a whole bag of stuff and placating us while we're still in the same place. I don't see any improvement. I think it's gotten worse.

In the meantime, while the white man is trying to run his genocide on us, it's turning around on him, too. This is the greatest country in the world, but now it's deteriorating faster than any country in the world. It's like the Roman Empire. It's a damn shame to see it fall, because it could have been so beautiful, and it's coming down faster than it went up. The Caucasian people in this country don't want to live together with mankind. They talk that and preach it. They shake hands with you and then run to the bathroom to wash their hands real quick or to brush their teeth for all those lies they have told. It's a shame.

What we need is black management. We have to have black

agents. How can a white man relate to a black man and make him a big star, turn him into something he has to look up to? He's not going to do that because he can't relate to him, but a black manager or a black agency can. If you take a white boy and put him in your band, the white people will be tickled to death, because they're relating to that white boy. I don't care how well you can play. They'll say yeah, you're great, but they still relate to the white boy. This has nothing to do with prejudice; it's just the way it is. We need black management; then we can build. I see a lot of young white agents who have good minds and are good hustlers, but how many of them are going to come along and stick with a black artist? If you don't have a rock-'n'-roll hit record, he's not interested. We need black agents to do it so that there won't be any good musicians left by the wayside.

White people have controlled the business long enough. We've built empires for them. Decca Records, Capitol Records, Columbia Records were all built on black talent. We've done enough for them, and we've got to do it for ourselves now. We needn't run them out of business. Let them stay in business, but let us have a little slice of the cake. Let us have a record company; let us see what happens. I bet you they'll put out better records and we'll put out better records. I don't think the companies should be all black, either. There should be whites working in there, too, but they should be black controlled.

—New York, December 29, 1971

≡ HAZEL SCOTT ≡

"Yoruba is the tribe of the drum."

When I was two years old, I had a potty chair. My mother taught piano, and when her little students came for lessons, I would get off my chair and use it as a piano! This was in Trinidad, before we came to the States. One day my grandmother and I were alone in the house. She was singing a tune, and I kept asking her to sing it again. Finally I knew I could play it. I remember the instant when I realized I could play. I was two and a half. My grandmother finally got tired and fell asleep. I managed to climb onto the piano bench and started picking out the tune with one hand. I kept on doing it until it came more easily. Then my grandmother woke up and asked, "Who's there?" She thought it was one of the students who had come. I said, "It's me," and she said, "Yes, but who?" I said, "Me, Hazel." She jumped up and called in all the neighbors to hear the prodigy! After that I just played everything I heard until I was four. Then, after we came to the States, my mother realized I was going too fast and too far in the wrong direction without any guidance. So she started teaching me when I was four. By then I had been playing in public for a year.

You mean you've been playing in public since you were three years old?

That's right. All by ear, though. Anything I heard I could play. I auditioned at Juilliard when I was eight. My mother had prepared for a concert career, but her wrists were very small and not strong enough. She didn't know this until she actually started concertizing, which is kind of a tragedy. Can you imagine that happening to you? After all the effort and work that went into preparing a concert career. I asked her once, "Didn't you know until the first night that you weren't able to sustain a performance?" She said, "No, because you're not giving a full performance no matter how much you practice. At a concert you have four or five big pieces together, and that really puts a strain on your arms."

What was the main thing you did to develop yourself?

I always listened. Rather than practice; I would practice in performance. The more often I worked, the better I got, which is true of everyone, I should think. I kept studying, of course. I auditioned at Juilliard for Oscar Wagner. Walter Damrosch, who was still alive then, said, "Wait a minute! Who told you to do that?" And he showed me what I was doing. I had auditioned with Rachmaninoff's "Prelude in C-Sharp Minor." Instead of playing octaves which I couldn't reach, I played a sixth, which is the closest harmonically. I explained that I was only reaching the closest thing that sounded like it, not even knowing what a sixth was at that age. He said, "Wow!"

What age were you?

Eight. You had to be sixteen to get into Juilliard then. They've lowered the age now and small children can go, but I was the youngest there at the time. My mother had taught herself how to play alto and tenor saxophone, and she went on the road with Valaida Snow and then with Lil Armstrong. You know, Louis's wife. Lil had an all-girl band. Then she got an all-male band—kept mama on tenor. I was always fascinated by the music business, and when the band played at the Apollo Theater, I was a big shot in New York.

As for my development as a singer, I worshipped Billie Holiday and still do. Nobody ever approached her style. Dinah Washington was a close friend of mine, but I wasn't influenced by her as much as by Lady Day. Around the time I started at Juilliard, I got to know Art Tatum. We became very close; he sort of adopted me. I had a nickname for him: Papa-daddy. Our house was always like a mecca for musicians. My mother had an excellent piano and a set of drums. Lester Young would come by with his mouthpiece and take mama's horn and play.

When you're onstage, are you playing for yourself?

I have to play for myself first. When I was a kid, it was a lot of flash and please the audience, but not now. I have learned that if I can please myself, the audience will go along, because they're getting a better performance.

Are you still as enthusiastic about performing as you were when you started out?

I certainly am! I guess some people get jaded after a while, but I never have. I get more enjoyment today out of working than I used to. Maybe it's because I like what I'm doing now better than what I used to do. I think I've developed and improved, so that when I listen to a playback of something I've done recently, I can hear things I like. Whereas it was always painful to me before. I would say, "What's happening to the tempo? What is she doing?" That kind of thing.

In actual performance I have a ball; I really enjoy myself, particularly when I have my musicians, Fangs [Martin Rivera] and Bill English, who are fantastic. The three of us manage to get a big-band sound. We're very compatible. We sort of feel each other and do a lot of head things. We've developed arrangements just out of things that would fall into place and which have now become part of the book.

I was at the St. Regis Hotel for seven weeks last summer with the guys, and we recorded the last two shows. When people say Hazel Scott, they haven't got a clue as to what I do, because there are no records for them to listen to. The few records I've made were usually songs from a picture. But for the most part, there have been no recorded performances of my work. So the fellow who came down to record me that night said, "If I had seen that you were listed to appear at the Waldorf Astoria, I wouldn't have gone, because people don't know how you sound." He was right. I was tired of wondering what was happening with the record companies, and I recorded the last two shows myself. We wound up with twelve excellent sides, and I formed my own production company, which is the only way to do it.

What is the reason you haven't done much recording? I don't understand that.

I don't understand it either, and that's why I formed my own production company. The record business is very strange, as you know, and for some reason my career in records has been gravely neglected. I've never been able to figure out why.

Would you tell me about your production company?

We have only produced one album so far: *Hazel Scott Live at the St. Regis.* We may change the title, although I think it's all right as it tells you exactly what it is. For the first time I'm satisfied with how I sound on a record. When I heard it, I said, "That's my voice, and that's the way I sound on the piano." I've heard the tapes twice so far, and they still don't sound horrible, though maybe they will after about three or four times. You know how it is. We hear ourselves, then we begin to hear the things we could have done. But it's still the best thing I've done on records, because I was very relaxed and there was no pressure. Another thing—whenever I've been with a company they've always said, "This is what we want you to do." They never let me do what I want. This time there was nobody looking over my shoulder. I was my own artist-and-repertoire man. I picked my material and I chose the repertoire.

It was very relaxed, and the ambience was great. We thought we would have to sweeten it. You know, the way they do now, by adding some strings or some horns on a ballad. But we didn't have to. It's come out right just with the trio. It's cookin'.

We have to make a deal with a record company now, because we have no method of distribution and it's too much of a hassle to go into that. We're dealing with three companies, but when it comes to mixing, I'm going to sit right there with the guy, because it would be a shame to lose any of the quality we have. You know, I had a strange feeling during the past few years that it would be horrible if I died before I had ever been recorded the way I really sound. So now that it's down, I'm really relaxed about it!

I see you're wearing a cross.

I have two crosses on this chain. One is a gift from a friend of mine in Brazil and the other is a gift from a friend in Puerto Rico. This ring has the Baha'i symbol on it, and it's a gift from Vic Damone. I'm a Baha'i, like Vic and Dizzy Gillespie. All my life people have said to me, "The way you talk, you sound like a Baha'i," and I never knew what a Baha'i was. I also heard them say it to my mother. I've known Vic Damone since he was about fourteen. At the Paramount Theater he was too young to run the elevator out front, so they let him run the elevator backstage, where he could kill only the artists. I had a long talk with him one day about the Baha'i faith, and I saw that the change in him as an individual was incredible.

Well, Baha'is don't drink. That's a waste of time. I read your interview with Miles, and he said he had stopped drinking. I've noticed that when guys stop drinking, they become different people altogether. Beyond a certain point, when a person drinks he turns into a completely different person. This is what happens with me. I'm strictly Jekyll and Hyde. It's terrible the person I become after drinking alcohol. It's a wonder it hasn't gotten me killed by now. I have always respected everyone's religion. As I say, there is only one God, and a lot of confused people.

That's what is great about Baha'i; we believe in progressive revelation. We believe that whenever man has been ready to absorb more knowledge, God has revealed it. Beginning with Abraham right up to now.

How do you view the music business now as compared to the fifties?

It's a completely different thing. In the fifties they had just coined the term rock-'n'-roll. They had the older ones like Bo Diddley and Chuck Berry. When I was a kid, we used to have what were called race records. Then we went into rhythm and blues, and from rhythm and blues we went into rock-'n'-roll; now it's just rock with a capital *R*, but it still is twelve-bar blues.

One of the things they tell me in the music business is that if they can find a fourteen-year-old with mediocre talent and make a million dollars off him, why do they need to put up with me? That's where it is! The music business is just like every other business: You're exploited or you're the exploiter. People who are sufficiently independent to be able to negotiate and to manage their own destinies are few and far between. Too many of us just need to pay the rent and to survive. We can't really pick and choose the place where we would like to appear, which is unfortunate.

Even in countries where the arts have subsidies, like in Great Britain, they still have a rough time. Actors and musicians have to moonlight and do all kinds of things. My cousin chucked it all and went down to the Virgin Islands. He was the first black man to be hired by CBS. You know Specks Powell, the drummer? For years he was like a little squirrel in the winter, piling up nuts and doing all that studio work. Then suddenly he said well, later for this, and went down to St. Croix. He wants to open a club for me down there, but the thing is that I've spent so much time in Europe already. I find that Americans resent anybody who goes away from this country for any length of time. As a matter of fact, provincial as this may sound, most Americans will resent you even for going to Europe on a vacation. They think you're putting on an act. It's an inbred, narrow-minded kind of thing, and I don't understand it. Every time I speak to somebody about what's happening in music, they say, well, you've been away. I answer, so what? I'm back. I've had people asking me, "How could you stay away that long?" I replied, "Easily!"

It gets hostile sometimes.

They must resent you for being away from the pressure cooker, as I call this country. When I first came back in 1966–67, people would say to me, "You went away from the fight," and I'd say, "Come on, you're looking for a fat lip! When you were sitting very comfortable either in your Jim Crow quarters or your all-white quarters or in the North snug in Harlem or on the south side of Chicago, I was down South desegregating audiences in town after town and getting out one jump ahead of the sheriff. So don't be telling me I ran away from the fight; I don't want to hear that."

What was your reason for living in Europe so long?

I had a talk with my then-husband before I left. I told him, "Our orbits are about to collide." We were living our own lives pretty much. Everywhere I went, people said, "Look at Hazel Scott, look at what she's doing." Nobody has a right to know what our private lives are. It's not our duty to inform people about what we're doing, so I said, "It's more comfortable for me in Europe. I think I'll stay for a while." I went there for three weeks, but I stayed for ten years. I came back twice during that period, once for three weeks and another time for eleven months.

So now you're settled in the pressure cooker?

Yeah, because I don't believe they can win.

They?

Well, the enemy. Every time Dr. King would come to Europe, he stopped to see me. He or Andy Young would call me from the

States and say, "Come on home, Hazel, because there is a whole generation of people growing up who are not being told of your contribution."

Was that your reason for returning to the States?

No. Actually I got mononucleosis, which is a dumb kind of student disease. It comes from doing too much. It made me very weak, and I couldn't work. Somehow, back in the States, they heard that I was sick. My son, who was at school, picked up the newspaper and read about it, so he called me and asked, "How do you feel?" He was worried. It was too far away for him, so he sent his godmother to get me. When she arrived, she said, "You've got thirty days to put your business in order," and I came on back.

As a pianist, what is your impression of Bud Powell?

Bud is my baby, my child. I remember when Bud was working in Birdland and when he came to work at Café Society. He was very close with Mary Lou Williams, too. He and I were very close. Musically he was unique. He used to like me to play classics for him. He would ask me to play Bach all the time. He would say, "Hazel, play me some Bach." There was a certain kind of otherworldly quality about him that nobody else had. Charlie Parker had it, but it was different. Bud was childlike. He had the simplicity of a child, yet he was shrewd, too! He had a kind of simple, gentle quality. Once he looked at me because he was hurt by something I had said to someone else. He didn't like to hear people raise their voices in anger. I love his music, I love everything he did.

Have you been doing much traveling lately?

Not a lot. I was on the West Coast for about three years, and I did some TV plays that I was satisfied with. I did shots on *The Bold Ones* and *The Doctors*. I played a woman who was dying of cancer. I also did two shots on *Julia*, Diahann Carroll's show, playing a neighbor who had moved in. I did the *CBS Playhouse 90*. I was playing Barry Sullivan's executive secretary, who was a sort of token black and who kept everything in order in this huge industrial complex. Not enough was happening, though. I didn't have a proper actor's agent, only the same old show business musical agent. He didn't have a clue as to how to handle me. I am very proud of the way I am taking myself and my career in hand, because I've never been properly handled. It may be because I never had quite enough drive. I've always known I was gifted, which is not the easiest thing in the world for a person to know, because you're not responsible for your gift, only for what you do with it.

If you're gifted and don't develop it, it's a tragic waste. I've often been guilty of lack of discipline. I can be very disciplined when I want to be. I can sometimes stay at the piano for twelve or fourteen hours. But I have to want to. When I want to, I go on a diet and take off forty pounds without turning a hair. I can do anything I want to do, but I have to really want to do it. And by the same token, nobody can make me do anything I don't want to. I see this stubbornness in my son and in my grandson. I look at it and say, oh boy! I can't complain.

Well, Hazel, what do you think of the stigma that's been attached to musicians regarding the use of drugs?

I think it's stupid. Now that we're into the seventies, people are realizing that it's not just musicians. We were like the Pied Piper. We not only attracted the children, we attracted the rats. Everybody likes to pat their feet and listen to music, to pop their fingers and look intelligent, to sit there and look as if they know what we're doing, to carry on dissertations about what is meant by this form and that form, by cool jazz and hot jazz. I object to the term jazz, because it's a euphemism for something else. We musicians have a tough row to hoe, because the only places which would employ us in the beginning were the houses of ill repute in New Orleans. At one point the church people decided to get rid of some of those dreary spirituals to pull the young people in and have what is now known as gospel. If it weren't for that, the only places where we would have been heard would have been those houses of ill repute and the riverboats. Then on to Chicago and to New York. Jazz-me blues. What does that sound like? So-and-some blues. The expression isn't dignified enough. It's not historically accurate.

Our form of music is erotic; there's no way of getting around it. But it can also be cerebral and very cold when it's played by whites such as Dave Brubeck, for instance. But you take Miles when he's playing a beautiful thing like *Sketches of Spain* or "My Ship." Isn't that fantastic?

Take Dizzy! The musicians know what a fantastic musician he is. His wife Lorraine is my buddy. When I'm in Dizzy's house, the phone never stops ringing. Some musician is always asking Dizzy something, and he's never too busy. They have two lines for that purpose, just so Dizzy can discuss music. One day somebody called for the changes to a tune, and Dizzy went and pulled out his old charts and gave the correct changes over the phone. Diz has that love of musicians and that willingness to help out fellow musicians which my mother had, more than anybody I see around now. Most people are too busy and involved with themselves to really care about you. Lady Day was like Diz, too. God help you if you sang out of tune, but if you had something going, she was very interested and willing to help you.

You were very close with her, right?

Boy, was I ever! I first saw Billie Holiday when I was fourteen years old. As usual, I was playing hooky from school on Friday morning to catch the first show at the Apollo, because Shifman would cancel most of the acts by the second show. All the Harlem school kids used to try and get there for the first show. Ralph Cooper announced: "Here's a lady with a very unique singing style—Miss Billie Holiday." I'll never forget. They used green lights on the stage and an amber light on her face. Her hair was tinted red then, and she wore a white gardenia. She sang "If the Moon Turns Green," and I flipped. I couldn't believe the way she sounded. I had never heard anything like it in my life. I stayed through three shows just to hear her again. She only sang that one tune with Ralph Cooper's band.

Shortly after that she and my mother became friends, and she used to come to our house. I was going to Wadley High School, and when I came out of school, I'd go next door to the candy store and put my money in the jukebox to listen to Lady Day singing "Easy Living," "Miss Brown To You" and "Ghost of Yesterdays," all the great tunes. Then when I'd go home, she would be sitting in the kitchen talking to mama, and they would chase me away. She was closer to my age than she was to my mother's, but she was a woman already and I was still a kid. She always protected me. She had a very fierce protectiveness where I was concerned.

Around that time I was playing in the band with my mother, and she decided I should do a solo. My first single engagement was in the Roseland Ballroom, opposite a band which had just come East from Kansas City. The Basie band! Sixteen men. When they walked off the stand, I went on.

That must have been traumatic.

You bet it was traumatic! When people ask me, "You don't mind following so-and-so?" I say, "No. I've had it all blasted out of me."

Have you changed your style or your repertoire at all in recent years?

Oh, yeah, a lot. My style of playing is much more funky than it used to be, maybe because I'm less self-conscious about it. Max [Roach] and Mingus used to say I was a lady when I played the blues. So maybe I have reached a point where I can relax enough not to be a lady when I play. I do a lot of originals and foreign-language songs. I did some French, Italian and German songs on the album I was telling you about.

What do you see in the future for us as black people?

Well, I don't intend to stop trying to help us get ourselves together. Every time I see one of us doing something separative which will hurt us, I have to open my mouth. I have made a lot of enemies as a result, but I just can't help it. If I see somebody who is wrong, I have to tell them about it. Take this whole sick scene of calling black women emasculators: Now what is that? You're falling into the trap that's been set for you if you turn on your own women.

I wish I had the key. Love, mostly. As Baraka says, "Check yourself. When you find you're acting like Steve McQueen, take a look at yourself. Is that what you want to be?" Well, solid! Our heritage is so great. When you think of the great black men . . . We need to love one another much more than we do. To help one another, to look out for each other. To see that what has gone before us is known to those who are coming along now. To give the children a sense of pride which, thank God, black people have today. What did Malcolm X say? "It's one thing to teach a man to hate another man; that's bad enough. But when you teach a man to hate himself, then that's really a sin." We have to love each other and love ourselves.

I think we musicians are emissaries. Every time we go before the public, we're there to make converts. We can either be ugly and contemptuous in our behavior, which will turn people off, or else we can carry ourselves with dignity and pride. We can't expect anyone else to respect us if we don't respect ourselves. Why should they do more for us than we do for ourselves?

Have you ever gotten any bad writeups, and if so, how does it affect you?

First I read through it without getting angry. If the critic is grossly unfair and it's only a personal attack, I just discard it. Lennie Hayton used to say a beautiful thing: "What do you want to read reviews for? Don't you know if you were good? If you don't, you're in big trouble." But still a lot of critics can be destructive in both ways. They can be destructive if they praise you too highly and you haven't been that good. A lot of people can't cope any better with praise than with criticism. If a critic understands what I was trying to do, then it's beautiful. But if I'm emotionally torn up after a performance and a critic says I skimmed the surface of my material, I want to hit him in the mouth! How deeply involved are you supposed to get? Sometimes they know what they're talking about and at other times they don't. You have to take them with a grain of salt. They're only human. A lot of critics have no right to discuss music. Somebody once said, "I can't lay an egg, but I can tell you if it's fresh or not." He meant that you don't have to be a musician to be a music critic, but I disagree! You may not produce what the artist is producing, but you should know a lot about his art form, otherwise what gives you the right to become a critic?

Do you think our music stems from Africa?

Definitely! My tribe is Yoruba. People are very conscious now of Africa and of their roots in Africa, but when I was a child, I remember that although my people knew my tribe, it was the kind of thing you didn't talk about very loudly, just as you didn't say black. It was Negro with a capital *N* or colored, but never black. Now we say black and feel proud of the fact, which is beautiful. The middle-class black person didn't discuss his African heritage. My father was a Garveyite; he was very hung up on Marcus Garvey and the Black Nationalist Movement, so that I was exposed to it from when I was about four years old. Our music stems directly from Africa, because it's got a definite driving beat behind it and it uses the drum.

The tribe of Yoruba is the tribe of the drum. People talk with the drums. We use little rhythms in our everyday life that black people have been hearing all along, not always knowing what they mean but knowing they are saying something. Take gospel, the up-tempo things they do in church—there's your rhythm again. Of course, there's a lot of music where they try to get away from rhythm, but I can't hear that. I play classical music. I've played it all my life; but I think that when you're going to play black music, it's got to have a beat. It varies, but the beat is always there.

"Some stop by the way," as Jon Hendricks said in one of his songs. Coming from Africa, the ships would stop off on the way to the colonies. They had to get some more salt pork and fresh water, and they had nothing to trade but us. So that's how some of our people were dropped off in Surinam, in Mexico, in Brazil, in Cuba and in all the islands. You get your samba, your Afro-Cuban . . . It's not just in the United States but all through the Western Hemisphere that you get the black man's art form, which is the beat of Africa.

Would you tell me something about the time you spent in Hollywood when you were making films?

It was a never-never land, and I loved it, because I've always been a big movie fan. When I first went there, there was no smog, and it was beautiful. That was in the summer of 1942. I was making a film for Columbia: *Something to Shout About.* Then I went back East and started to work again. The following spring I returned to the West Coast to work at Metro-Goldwyn-Mayer: I did two pictures there with Lena Horne, then I took some time off. Later I did another picture at Columbia, which is when I went on strike.

On strike?

Yeah, I went on strike and held up production for three days. Today I would do it differently. As you mature, you learn things, but I can't get angry when kids start screaming, because I've done my share of screaming. You see, there were eight black girls dancing in a musical production number, and I was dressed as a WAC. There were eight black guys who were wearing summer tans, and we were doing this routine where the eight girls were supposed to see them off. We finished rehearsing, and it was time for costuming. My costume was all fitted, and the guys' were all fitted, too; then they started bringing the costumes for the girls. They were wearing aprons, and David Lesheen said they looked too new. He told the makeup man to spray them with oil and dirt, and I blew sky-high. I honestly did. I said, "I don't understand you. How can you think that young women are going to see their sweethearts off to war wearing dirty aprons?"

If the director, Gregory Rattoff, had been on the set, there would have been no problem. He would have said, "What's the matter with the baby? Let the baby tell me what she wants," and I would have had everything. But he was ill in bed, and Lesheen couldn't understand. He said to me, "What are you worried about? You're well dressed." I finally got them paid as dress extras, and they wore their own clothes. It held up production for three days, and every hour those cameras were lying idle cost thousands of dollars. So I had hit the man where it hurt most—in his pocketbook.

They told me I would never make another picture. I was under contract for one more, *Rhapsody in Blue,* and when that was finished, I never did make another picture in Hollywood. Harry Cohn was the boss of Columbia Pictures and he adored me, but when he heard that I was holding up production, he said, "She'll never make another picture as long as I live."

Later, when I was in Paris waiting to do a stage show, I ran into this movie they were making with Jean Gabin. I'll never forget my first day on the set. I was walking around, it had been so long since I had been on a movie set. I said, "Well, they smell the same all over the world." You know, the paint they use and the glue, the back of the sets. The front looks like a finished building and the back is an empty shell. Instead of saying *cut,* they say *coupé,* but it's all the same.

That night I came home from the studio and picked up the *Herald Tribune* from my doormat. When I looked at the paper, I started shaking all over. I had just finished my first day of shooting, and Harry Cohn had said I'd never make another picture as long as he lived. Well, I read in the paper that he had dropped dead the previous night. Isn't that strange? You see why I don't fool with God.

What are your plans for the future, Hazel?

Melvin van Peebles wants to write a play for me. I want to act now, because I'm a good actress. I know that I could become a great one if I had the right part. I have written down quite a few ideas that could be developed, but I'm not a dramatist. Writing a screenplay, a television play or a stage play is a definite craft.

Acting is what I want to do. I did a scene with the actress Josephine Hutcherson, and when we had finished, she told a friend of mine that I was a superb actress. I would like to play, sing and move; you know the way I move because I have dancer's training. I just love to perform. I'm at my best when the conditions are fine, the piano is good, the mike is good and I don't have to worry about the mechanics of the performance. I enjoy hard work. I have all my life. I want to work and put away some money and leave it to my grandchildren.

I want to finish my autobiography, which is already contracted for. I'm writing it in longhand on those yellow legal pads with lines. Sometimes I go so fast that my hand can hardly keep up. I find it fascinating. I love it when it's coming. But if the inspiration is not there, forget it! I just put a jumble of words together, it means nothing, it's garbage. But when it's right, it writes itself. I wrote an article that wrote itself in about twenty minutes. It was in *Cosmopolitan*. It was called "It Would Be Nice to Be Cherished." It was about black women being unappreciated. It's a tough article. I go into the whole thing, how from the very beginning black women have been entrusted with keeping the home together.

What do you think about integration?

Integration is greatly overrated. I don't think there is any such thing as integration, because you can't integrate a person's mind. Every human being is entitled to have a decent job, a decent place to live in, medical care, education and the comfort of knowing he's giving his best to his children. So when the whites in this country ask us, What do you want? We must answer, We want some of what you've got; that's what we want, and we deserve a chance to have it. It's that simple.

If you mean integration on that basis, yeah, fine. We have always had to prove that we were not only as good as whites, but twice as good in order to hold the same job. Some may say that it's unfair, but I think it's amusing when you're being told that you're inferior and you're coming up with better quality work and a better performance than the person in the same job who just happens to be white. I think it's a little late to worry about mixing the races when not one of us is jet-black. The main thing they're worried about is intermarriage, but it's too late to worry about that.

Is there anything I didn't cover that you would like to talk about?

I write a lot of poetry. I wrote a set of poems on a flight from Panama City to Los Angeles, and there again they wrote themselves. I read the chapter in my book on Malcolm X to a young Puerto Rican poet, and he said it was some of the best prose he'd ever heard, which was very encouraging. I tried to write with a tape recorder, talking into it, but it was no good. I talk one way and I write another. My writing is much more picturesque and I can express myself much more beautifully when I write. So I shall be sitting and writing and working whenever I can. And if I have a record that takes off, I'll be able to work in some of the more rarified rooms reserved for the superstars.

I don't especially want status anymore. I've had status, and I don't care about that. But I would like it to be recognized that I have been underestimated and unappreciated for a long time, because I didn't keep my nose to the grindstone and I was away for ten years. They used to ask me, are you going to stay here now or are you going to go back? They would say, well, how did you like Europe? I found Europeans in their own country much more relaxed than the transplanted Europeans you meet in the United States.

But Europe is getting more like the States.

Do you know why? It's the American military bases all over the world. SHAPE! Just give us a little while and we'll shape your thinking. The black guys in the service call them hillbillies. Everywhere the hillbillies go, they poison the minds of the people in that country. I remember when I first started going overseas in 1951, it was beautiful. I went every year from then on, but it's changing. There are bars in Germany where they don't want blacks to come in and all that nonsense. France started getting weird, too, in 1965–66.

You noticed it then?

Yeah. You know the little drummer Jacky Bamboo? He said to me, "Hazel, when you say you love France and everything, you're in one economic bracket, but you don't hear *sale nègre* till you're down in the poor people's section."

When you're on a certain level, there are a lot of things you don't know about. I guess a lot of people don't consider that. They just consider their own thing.

Right! But we don't live in the world alone. I'm always conscious of the economic circumstance of the person who isn't quite as fortunate as I am. Just as I am conscious of the guy who's got so much more than I have. I look at him and check him out, and I wonder what it will take to make him happy. What will he require, for heaven's sake?

—New York, December 4, 1972

≡ BETTY CARTER ≡

"You've got to find yourself."

When you talk about a singer, you usually think about a pretty voice with a clear tone. Billie Holiday was a stylist with a particular and unique sound of her own. She was untrained, unabashed and uninhibited. This is what I call jazz in a sense, because it's raw. Jazz is a natural way of approaching something, which is what Billie Holiday had with no sweat. Her thing just came out a natural way. You felt that there was no question about whether she was a jazz singer or not; there could be no doubt about it; she was. What she could do with tempos . . . no matter what tempo it was, she could just lilt along with her sound. Her tone was unique, and what she did with her words was unique, too. This is my impression of Billie.

Take Sarah Vaughan: She's a singer and she's got a beautiful voice. She and Carmen McRae never have any problem with their throats because they sing right. They breathe correctly when they sing those notes. But Billie Holiday had a sound and a way of approaching a song that was definitely hers. I mentioned those two singers because their voices are so different. I don't think Sarah had a lot of training. It's just a natural way she has of doing her thing. With training she could have gone as far as Leontyne Price. She probably could have covered that territory, because she had that quality and depth. But I'm glad she didn't, because otherwise we would have lost what she is now. Ella Fitzgerald can swing like nobody else. I mean she can really romp and romp. This is what Ella is good at. Like the other night, I heard her on television. She has perfect pitch. She came out of a phrase on "Body and Soul," and when she ended up, she was right.

I notice you have a piano. Do you play?

Yeah, a little bit. I also write. I learned how to write orchestrations when I was with Lionel Hampton. I could scat, and

I guess he wanted to be in the be-bop world. I knew all the musicians, I could scat and I had a good ear, so he used me for that. He couldn't have Charlie Parker or Dizzy, so he got me! I was the be-bopper in the band, and I was in charge of all the modern stuff. He'd look at me and ask me dumb questions like, "Whose band do you like best, mine or Dizzy's?" I'd say Dizzy's, and he would fire me and Gladys Hampton would rehire me. We went through that for two and a half years.

When he got angry with me, he wouldn't let me sing, so I figured I would take advantage of what was going on while I was out there. I asked Bobby Plater to teach me how to write for the instruments. My first big-band arrangement was on "Good Night Irene." I just wanted to see if I could voice. I used the old Glenn Miller sound, with the clarinet playing top. We played it at the Clique in Philadelphia just to see how it sounded, because I had written it on the band bus. I wrote my score out traveling back and forth, then I wrote the parts, and at rehearsal we passed the parts out and I heard it for the first time. Boy, was I proud!

I then decided to do something else, so I did an arrangement on "Orange Colored Sky" for myself, which I never got to perform. We were going into the Apollo, but Lionel Hampton wanted me to do another tune which I had been singing for years, every time I came to the Apollo. It was a song where the band plays a real hip arrangement he's got in his book and I come out to do four or five choruses of scat on it. Well, I was ready to sing a few words, to let people know that I not only could scat but that I also could sing a ballad. So I wanted to jump out there and he wouldn't let me do it. That was it! It didn't make any kind of sense for me to continue. I had been on the road for two and a half years, and I had been exposed. It was time for me to step out there on my own.

How has your knowledge of piano helped you as a singer?

When you're scatting, you can almost see the notes. You can see your half-tones and you know how they're supposed to sound because you see the keyboard in your head. I couldn't play the same thing with my fingers. I'm not that kind of piano player. I can scat better than I can play on the piano. In learning the piano and writing arrangements for myself, I'm able to know where I'm at. For example, I can tell a musician, "Let's go back to letter A or to the coda." I can explain the music. 1 look at a chord and I know what it's supposed to sound like. I can explain it to the musician if he is uptight about the music. I think it's an advantage to know about the piano.

Most of the time singers know something about the piano.

Right, because that's how you can find your own key. If you find a tune in the shower and you ask yourself what key to sing this tune in, you can go to the piano and pick it out. So that when you get on the bandstand, you can say, "I want to sing such and such a tune," and when the piano player asks you what key you want to sing it in, you can tell him. You don't have to scratch your head and say, "Well, I don't know. Let's find out. Find me a key." You know what key you're singing in. It saves a little time, and you don't put the musician uptight; he doesn't have to be pecking at the piano, trying to find your key.

Can we go to the subject of how you came into music?

I got into music like Sarah did, at the Apollo. I did an amateur show at the Paradise Theater and I won. I sang "The Man I Love," which I have never sung in public since. After that I thought I could sing. I was the a cappella choir student director in my school. I knew how to wave my arms and was involved in the assemblies and things like that. After the amateur show contest I thought I could strike out and become a singer.

At that time be-bop was the thing. You know how everybody in Detroit really latched into the new music. Sonny Stitt, Charles Greenlee, Tommy Flanagan, Barry Harris and Yusef Lateef . . . you know how many giants came out of Detroit during that era. I came into contact with all these musicians, and I hung up under them because I saw this was where it was for me.

Dizzy Gillespie's first engagement in Detroit was at the El Cino club. He had a big band then with choice musicians: Milt Jackson, John Lewis, James Moody and Ray Brown. To have an opportunity to work with these musicians was fantastic. I was in another kind of world. Dizzy discovered I could sing, so every time I came out to catch him at the club, he would ask me to sing with the band. He didn't have to, so he must have dug something I was doing at that particular time. I ended up getting a job in the club, which really helped me.

The next stint was when Charlie Parker came into the club. At that time he had Max Roach, Tommy Potter, Duke Jordan and Miles. We were supposed to rehearse on a Friday afternoon at about one o'clock, and we waited until five o'clock for Charlie Parker to show up. It looked like he would never show. All the be-bop fans were saying oh my goodness, when is he ever going to show up? Finally he made it. The bar was closed, but I had no business sitting there because I was underage. The first person Bird saw when he came in was me, and he grabbed me and said, "Do you know where I can find something to eat?" I was speechless! I said, "There's a restaurant across the street." He grabbed my hand, and we went across the street. He had never seen me before, and he never really looked at me. I sat there and watched him eat. When we went back to the El Cino, I had my chest out. I was on cloud nine, I was really something! It was only later that he discovered I sang.

Larry Steele had a chorus line at the club which included Jeri Grey and Charlie Parker's ex-wife. I forget her name, but she had been married to him a long time before. She was a very beautiful girl. You can imagine what it was like to be in Larry Steele's chorus line . . . all these beautiful dolls wearing long dresses, and then, later on, when they do their masterpiece, they have short skirts on and everybody is kicking high. Charlie Parker was rehearsing them with "Hot House," "Confirmation" and all his fast things. Those poor girls were kickin', and it was really something to see. How those girls managed the week I don't know! Tempos at that time were lightning fast. Once in a while they played a ballad, but everything was brisk. Everybody came to hear Charlie Parker rather than to see Larry Steele's chorus, so the line had to suffer. It was one beautiful experience!

After Bird discovered I could sing, it became a thing: "Come on up and sing!" I would get on up there and do my thing. That's how I really got started. It's the chief reason I feel the way I do about jazz. Because I came up during that era and I know about it. When I hear it being abused by anybody, it hurts! Nowadays I don't care who knows it hurts me; I'll let them know. Whereas before I would keep quiet and not say anything. I'll never forget that era.

After that it was Lionel Hampton, and he got me with the band because I was modern. I had that be-bop feeling he was trying to get at that particular time. He figured my influence would help. I didn't sing enough to really develop a voice. I had the ear, the knack, the personality and everything else, but I didn't have the voice. The voice had to become mature. It takes time to develop a sound. But I had that other ability, and that's what he used.

What do you think about the publicity musicians have gotten due to the use of drugs?

It's not like it used to be. But you have to face it, Art, we were on drugs. I wasn't, but I say *we* because I'm a musician. A lot of them were really involved with drugs. It was a fact, and because of it we got the stigma; but it's quite different now; the whole world is using drugs and not just musicians. I don't think we have to worry about that stigma anymore. Still, when you look back, you have to face reality: We did use a lot of drugs.

You don't think it's as prevalent now?

No! It's another thing now, because the whole world is doing it. Greed is what has taken control of everything. There's so much money involved in drugs, and it's quick, easy money. People want to make a lot of money, and they don't care about individuals. The more people use drugs, the more money they make. Greed!

In the music business they're so greedy that they're turning over records like in a factory. A hit record lasts about a week, maybe two weeks. If you stay on the charts for a month, you really are taking care of business. You get a record going, it arrives at the top fast and it goes off the charts just as fast as it went up. The artists who have a hit get a few jobs, but if they don't get another hit right after that, you can forget they even exist, because the audience and the people forget they exist. All they care about is that one hit record. Ninety-nine percent of the new performers coming up today think about one thing: getting a hit record. Getting the money. That goes for everybody now.

A lot of musicians today feel that the only way they can make money is by becoming electronic. The acoustical instruments are almost obsolete. You find young bass players today who play the Fender and know nothing about the master bass fiddle. They don't want to know anything about the master bass fiddle. When I get ready to go to work someplace, they have to get a piano. They can get an electric piano, but they have a problem getting an acoustical piano. This is what's happening today. Everybody is on the bandwagon, and I mean everybody! For instance, they've now got the synthesizer. If one person starts with the synthesizer, everybody's going to get it. I heard Herbie Hancock had a synthesizer. I said, "Well, if Miles got one, I guess Herbie had to get one, too." There's no individuality, no creativeness. They're just doing what everybody else is doing so they can make some money. Before, you could tell the difference between Ben Webster and Lester Young, or between Coltrane and James Moody or Sonny Rollins. Today you can't tell the difference between the trumpet players or tenor players; you can't say that is so-and-so unless you've looked at the record and seen who's playing.

It's the same way with singers. After me there are no more jazz singers. What I mean is that there's nobody scaring me to death. No young woman is giving me any trouble when it comes to singing jazz. I'm not even worried about it, and that's a shame. It's sad that there's nobody stepping on my heels so I can look back and say, I better get myself together because this little girl is singing her thing off! They're all doing what everybody else is doing, and as I'm not doing what everybody else is doing, I'm not even worried. It's a crime that no little singer is back there sockin' it to me in my field. To keep it going, to keep it alive, because I'm not going to live forever. I'm going to die eventually, and I don't want it to die with me, I want it to keep on.

When I go to sing in colleges, I hope that I can encourage some young woman to take a shot and eventually to come out on top. To pay some dues and really do something creative instead of just trying to make a hit record or getting on television without ever knowing the feeling of being on a stage and having an audience appreciate what you have created. To have them stand up and applaud your ideas, your imagination, your thing. That feeling is so great! Having money can't be greater than that feeling. Like coming off the stage at the Copacabana with the audience applauding what you have done with everybody else's songs. You can't get any greater feeling than the one I get when I come off the stage and the audience feels what I have done. I've turned them around. They expected maybe this and I've given them that, and they dug it. This feeling keeps you alive, it keeps you going, it keeps you on your toes, because you killed them once so you want to kill them again the next time you appear. You say, well, I've got to go back to this club, but you can't go back there with the same thing. You have to add something so they will know that you've been thinking since you've been away. But now artists have people planning their acts, telling them how to stand, how to walk, how to talk, how to put their tunes in the right place so that they will get the audience, and they pay a price for this.

Betty, I am very impressed with your sons. They are very respectful.

Thank you. A lot of people don't know I have kids. They're nice boys, and I'm proud of them. They're not musically inclined. Maybe they'll get it later. We expose them to all kinds of music, because we listen to everything. Let me get this across: I'm not knocking the media, but all I want is for young kids to be exposed to other music so they can make a choice. I make my kids hear all kinds of music, even the classics. We rehearse here, and they get a chance to hear the stops and goes and accidents. If they don't go into music, it's not because they weren't exposed to it but because it was just something they weren't ready to do.

I'm doing a children's album right now. It's going to have a jazz feeling. I read somewhere that music has to have a folk feeling to get across to kids, but I don't believe it. I don't believe it has to be played on a guitar and sound like folk. If kids hear jazz young enough, they'll understand what it's supposed to feel like. Why should they wait until they're in high school or college before they're exposed to it? Kids often come up to me and ask, "Where have you been? I haven't heard of you before; how long have you been singing?" I ask them how old they are, and they say maybe twenty-two. Why have you got to be twenty-two before you know anything about Miles Davis? Right now there are some black kids in high school and college who know nothing at all about him. When it comes to picking out something on one of those records that have been released lately, you can't find anything to talk about because there's so much sound going on. It's just sound. It hasn't got anything to do with music. New gimmicks coming up, the wa-wa this and the wa-wa that, the synthesizer this and the Fender that. And CBS needs more money? They don't need more money! They're making plenty of money out of us.

We can do things the white man could never do when it comes

to swinging consistently. We were steady. You remember in the fifties, when we had it sewed up? We made our marks then. We had plenty of giants during those years. What has happened in the last ten years?

Everybody wants a sound, even Miles Davis. I'll use his case as an example: As long as Miles has been with Columbia Records, he's been one of the most consistent record sellers in the jazz field. It wasn't until he did *Bitches Brew* and came up with the sound that they decided to put his picture on the trade magazine *Record World*. He'd made money for Columbia for years. How come they didn't respect him enough then to put his picture on the trade magazine? But he had to join them and do what they wanted him to do before they put his picture on *Record World*. And he stands up there with the biggest smile on his face! He has disappointed me, because I want to hear something, not just sound. If you're going to make some sound, let's do something musical with it at least. Let's not just have sound for the sake of sound.

This is what's happening today. We're sticking it right into our own thing by playing sound and not music. Our young musicians are going to pay dues behind sound, because sound is all over the place, and we should learn our instruments. For instance, they don't know any songs or melodies. Forget the melodies, forget the roots, they don't even want to play ordinary blues. You hardly hear Charlie Parker's name mentioned anymore.

It's old-fashioned!

Right! So they do a play called *The Musical Tragedy of Billie Holiday,* and Archie Shepp writes the music. To me, and I don't care if you put it in print, it was an insult to Billie Holiday, because he wrote rock music. I know she wouldn't have dug it, because that wasn't what she was all about. But they were influenced by the white media. They put up the money and hoped it would be another *Jesus Christ Superstar* or another *Hair,* with the story of Billie Holiday involved. No, no! What do you think this play could have done for the young individual who went to see it if only they had told the story the way it really was musically? It could have educated a lot of young kids. But they don't want to do that, they just want to make some money and distort the issue at the same time. I wouldn't even insult myself by going to see it. I heard the music and I know that Archie Shepp wasn't the man who should have written that music. Maybe the white people thought he could do it, but you can go uptown and ask ten people on the street who Archie Shepp is and they won't be able to tell you. Ninety percent of his audience is white.

I feel that if you're playing something black, black people should know about it. You shouldn't avoid them. You ought to go to them to get the stamp. Unless they give you the stamp, you're not doing anything worthwhile, because it's their culture. Charlie Parker didn't run away from us, he came to us. Do you remember The Paradise at 110th Street and 8th Avenue, when he used to come on the scene all the time? One day I was on the stage singing, and he came in and sat down in front of me and said, "Can I play with you?" I almost fell off the bandstand!

We were involved at that particular time, but today most of our musicians, like Ornette Coleman, avoid black people. When you go to their concerts, you don't see any black people there. This is our culture, and I don't care who the musician is, if he avoids black people, then he is scared of something. He doesn't have confidence in himself or else he doesn't believe in what he's doing. I would rather be told I'm not playing it right so I'll know what's happening.

One thing that black people know about is music. They may not be able to play it, but they respect your skill. They might say, "He doesn't kill me, but he sure can play," or, "He may not knock me out, but he knows his instrument." They know and respect that. I don't want anyone badgering me into liking their music. You don't have to play a song for an hour to make sure I'll like it. I heard a singer on television saying that if she hasn't got the audience after the first eight bars, she just cancels. Doesn't she know she's got twenty-four more bars to go? When you feel after eight bars that you've lost the audience, then you had better do something quickly to get them back, because you can't just stop singing. It's true, you can feel when you lose an audience; your whole body can tell. When the audience is tight, you can feel it, and if you get tight they get tighter. But if you feel it you should say, "I've got to straighten up. I've got twenty-four more bars to go, so I'd better get myself together." You fight for it, you don't give up.

I hate to go to a club and hear somebody who is going to play a song for an hour. Life isn't that way. You eat, you sleep, you walk, you run, you dance and it's quiet sometimes. It's not all badgering. I know the racial thing is uptight, but you still sleep and eat. You're not always out there talking about how you hate whitey. You may say you can't dig the scene, but you still talk to your wife and kids, you still do other things. I refuse to let a musician badger me into liking him.

There is another group I want to mention: Sun Ra. They play Europe a lot. He's got his metallic clothes on, his lights flashing back and forth, and he's got the nerve to spell orchestra a-r-k-e-s-t-r-a. It's supposed to have something to do with the stars and Mars, but it's nothing but bullshit. Sun Ra has got whitey going for it. He couldn't go uptown and do that to blackie. He would be chased off the stage in Harlem or in Bedford-Stuyvesant.

We've lost a lot of our women with that music. Because women have another kind of thing going for them. At first it was mostly men who dug jazz. Seventy-nine percent of our audiences were men. You've got to make love to women. This is what they're all about; they're soft. They don't want to be badgered into digging anything. They want to go and enjoy themselves with their old man. They go out with him and here's this music. The old man may dig it, but they're sayin' what is it? Or I can't stand it. They might want to say something to their old man quietly, like I love you, but how can they say it with the tempo of things going on like that. So we've lost a lot of females, and we didn't have to lose anybody.

Like I told you, I feel deeply about the music because I lived it. I haven't prostituted myself, and I'm really proud of it. I feel very deeply about it, and I hate to see it having the kind of trouble it's having now. I hate to see clubs close up, but they have to close when you're not cooperating with them. Because it's a three-way thing between the artist, the audience and the club owner. The club owner has to make money to keep you working, and you have to please the audience to keep the club owner happy so you can go on working. You can't just cancel the audience. You can't say that just because they don't like you, there's nothing wrong. There's got to be something wrong, and you must find out what it is, why it is that you cannot get to the audience. If you're going to stay on the stand for two hours, the club owner can't make a turnover. He can't make enough money to keep himself in business so that he can keep you and other people working. If you don't want clubs to close, you've got to think about the club owner, the audience and yourself. That's the art of being an artist. Then if you want to be an individual, you've still got to be unique on top of that. It takes time. It doesn't happen overnight. You have to really inquire into yourself; what you may be doing wrong or what you should do.

A lot of musicians out there should be bookkeepers; they shouldn't be playing at all. But they don't know it because they don't get enough work to know it. In order for you to know what you're all about, you've got to keep working. Some musicians really ought to be composers or arrangers; others should be just sitting in a section, because not everybody can be the one out front. Geniuses don't come in bunches, they come every now and then.

You've got to find yourself, where you're at. Some musicians write better than they can play, but they want to play, they want to be the one individual on the stage, too. Maybe you want to be out front, but you're not qualified. You should know this about yourself and do what you do best. If it's writing or if it's going and getting a job! You know what I mean. Let's face it, if you get enough work you can find this out. But we can't get enough work if the musicians are going to completely ignore the club owner and the audience and think only of themselves. The audience is going to suffer, the club owner is going to suffer, and that's the reason we've lost a lot of clubs. The women were the ones who could really get that club thing going, and you just can't get them out anymore. They're not going to sit there without knowing what's going on.

Would you tell me about the Ella Fitzgerald Foundation you're planning to form?

I'm in the process of forming a foundation that will present scholarships in Ella Fitzgerald's name. I have put all the wheels in motion that will make it successful, and I hope I won't have too much of a problem. I want to do two shows a day in Harlem for a week, with individual singers at each show. For instance, Lena Horne, Sarah Vaughan, Carmen McRae, Aretha Franklin, Barbra Streisand, Morgana King, Vikki Carr, Nancy Wilson, Totie Fields and Moms Mabley—all women, in other words. We black people have never paid tribute to Ella Fitzgerald, and I don't think we should wait until it's too late. I don't think we should wait until it's too late with anyone who has contributed as much to the business as Dizzy Gillespie or Art Blakey. Or Kenny Dorham, who is not with us anymore. We shouldn't wait until it's all over before we do something to say thank you. We want them to participate and to feel proud.

Are you religious?

I'm not religious like those people who get up in the morning and go to church, but I believe there is a Supreme Being. I believe that somebody has to control this thing, somebody has to keep you believing in something. For instance, when things are bad you say oh God, how in the world am I going to get out of this? And all of a sudden something happens and you're out of it.

With me being a woman in the music business, I could easily have become a prostitute. The pimps encouraged me not to become a prostitute, would you believe that? They often used to come to the clubs to catch me at work, and for some reason they liked what I was doing and felt that it would just go down the drain if I went any other kind of way. So they never tried to do anything but encourage my work. I know four real top pimps from Detroit and New York who said to me "Betty, whatever you do don't become a prostitute." When you have cats shooting at you all the time, it's easy to get carried away with yourself. I don't think I would have done it anyway, but I felt it was a feather in my cap that they even wasted the time to speak to me in this way when their business was getting girls to do anything they wanted them to do. I was proud of the fact that they thought enough of me to tell me this, because their game was big.

I believe there is somebody who puts things in your way for you to get yourself together. Either you stumble over the obstacles or you learn from them. One of the tunes on the children's album I'm putting together says *"Don't be afraid to make a mistake! A mistake is all that it is."*

When you're performing in a club, as compared to making a recording, do you change anything?

It's hard to record me because I don't change anything. It's difficult to record me anyway because my voice is not piercing.

They can record a steady, piercing sound more easily. The dials work better, or whatever it is. But I have a sound that does strange things, and in a studio I tighten up because I want to record right and something just doesn't jell too well. I have decided that if I ever record again it will be live, because then I'm natural and less tight. I can just do it and hope it comes out right and that the sound man can get himself together. I don't have that natural thing where you can go to the studio, set the dial and bang . . . Nancy Wilson and Aretha Franklin have that kind of crisp, clear sound.

My sound is heavy. They don't know what I'm going to do when I get upstairs because I don't know, either. I don't have that sort of training. I can do it, but it just isn't a natural flow. I'm not that good for recording, so I give engineers a headache. They don't know what to do with these pipes.

I have my own company. Nobody else was recording me so I recorded myself, and it actually did quite well. In other words, I know exactly how many records I sold and I got the money, so it was to my advantage. It's out there, and people are buying it. It's not overwhelming, but it's mine. It belongs to me, and this makes me feel good.

Is there anything I didn't cover that you would like to talk about?

I hope my life will have done something to stimulate the individualism in our youth, because that's almost obsolete now. To become an individual is like being an idealist, and I don't think there's anything wrong with that. The youth of today is lacking in individualism, and I don't mean just black youths; I mean white youth, too. They're all caught up in a trap, paying their dues, trying to imitate everybody out there, and they're frustrated. If I live and am able to do anything about it, I want to stimulate individualism again.

In other words I want to be able to tell the difference between one tenor player and another tenor player, or between one trumpet player and another trumpet player. I want young people to respect the wood of an acoustical instrument, to respect the ivory on the keyboard, to respect the strings on a giant bass fiddle. I want them to know what that feeling is. When it says boom, it says boom! This is the message I want to spread. Making money doesn't really have to be the only thing for them. Other things might be better for them, anyway. I want them to realize that if they keep on trying for other things, they can win. They don't have to lose.

Right now there's a sort of down trend, as they say. There are not enough clubs and not enough work for the guys. We were talking about Johnny Griffin and Benny Bailey earlier. These are two giants that we've got to see back here for a stint, so that young musicians can get an education just by listening to them.

When I was with Lionel Hampton, we did a gig at the Strand Theater. Charlie Parker came in one day and he needed a fix, so he asked Hamp if he would give him some money. Hamp said, "Charlie, if you sit in my reed section, I'll give you fifty dollars." Charlie Parker said, "Crazy." So he sat in the section. There were five or six reeds in the band at that time. When Charlie Parker sat in the section, the whole band's attitude changed. Everybody started to think. This is what I call really exerting an influence. You only have to appear, and everybody starts thinking. Hamp started to stretch out. With this tune he was going to take a thinking solo. This is when Benny Bailey came down from the trumpet section, and you have never heard such trumpet playing in your life! Charlie Parker and Benny Bailey together at the Strand Theater in 1949. The influence that Charlie Parker's presence had on Hamp and on everybody in the band was unbelievable. Hamp was really trying to breathe, pause and think: I'm not going that way. I'm going this way today, because Charlie Parker is in the section. That's what you call genius. Charlie Parker had that kind of influence on musicians.

—New York, December 12, 1972

(Page numbers in italics indicate interviews)